Excellence in NLP and Life Coaching

How to Structure Success and Create Influence at the Expert Level

Dr. Richard K. Nongard

SUBLIMINAL
SCIENCEPRESS

www.SubliminalScience.com

Excellence in NLP and Life Coaching: How to Structure Success and Create Influence at the Expert Level

ISBN: 978-1-7344678-5-7

Dr. Richard K. Nongard

Cover design by Pankaj Singh Renu

Edited by Tamelyda Lux

https://TamelyndaLux.com/

First Printing: June 2021

This book is not intended as a substitute for therapeutic advice of a Licensed Professional. The reader should consult a mental health professional in matters relating to his/her individual mental health needs.

About Dr. Richard K. Nongard

Dr. Richard K. Nongard is a popular conference and keynote speaker known for his relaxed and engaging style. His focus is on real-world solutions based on the science of leadership, NLP, life coaching, and counseling psychology. His presentations focus on leadership, engagement, and actionable strategies for business success. He works as a professional hypnotist and life coach, helping people make rapid change in their health, wealth, and habits. He holds a Doctorate in Transformational Leadership (Cultural Transformation) from Bakke Graduate University.

Richard is a business expert who started his career in 1983 as a cold-calling salesperson in the auto industry. He has engaged in both medical and educational sales, administration, and product development positions. Richard is a serial entrepreneur who has owned successful business ventures over the years.

Richard is the author of numerous books, publications, and training videos. His book on leadership, *Viral Leadership: How to Seize the Power of Now to Create Lasting Transformation in Business*, has already become a popular resource for leadership development. He has written many other books as well, including psychology textbooks that have been adapted as textbooks at the university level, and his 5-star reviews are a testament to the value Richard provides in both written and spoken media.

Dr. Richard K. Nongard is a coach, consultant, and lecturer, offering services to business groups, sales groups, and healthcare organizations. You can bring him to your organization to train your executives or front-line employees in Leadership, Appreciative Inquiry and/or Emotional Intelligence.

To bring Dr. Richard K. Nongard to your organization or conference as a keynote speaker, contact him at SubliminalScience.com or (702) 418-3332.

You may download free resources for this book and the actual forms I use with clients at:

SubliminalScience.com/NLPbook

To earn your certification as a Profession NLP Practitioner and as a Professional Life Coach, visit:

SubliminalScience.com

Table of Contents

Foreword by Dr. David Snyder

As one of the foremost recognized experts in neuro-linguistic programming (NLP) and hypnotherapy, I have worked tirelessly to help my clients create rapid and lasting change. I have made it my life's work to share with as many people as possible how this human technology can change lives.

I am a Doctor of Acupuncture and Chinese Medicine, an ICBCH Certified Professional Hypnotist, and a well-known advanced practitioner trainer of neuro-linguistic programming.

My expertise is and has always been finding solutions that are fast, effective, and permanent in many fields of application ranging from influence and persuasion and in healing, using these combined technologies for helping, teaching, and training people to create profound and lasting change and transformation both on an individual level and a community level. Although I have been doing this work for decades, it seems as if it was only yesterday that I first met Dr. Richard Nongard through our mutual acquaintances in Southern California many years ago.

In addition to our professional interests, we share some personal commonalities and a deep understanding and love for ancient wisdom, especially the influences on our current understanding of mind-body connection from the Far East. Both of us are married to women originally from China, and both of us have Chinese-American children. Although Richard speaks more Chinese than I do, we have enjoyed both our professional time and personal time together.

When I received my advance copy of this book to review, I offered to write the Foreword because I was so impressed by how Dr. Nongard was able to see that although the ideas of NLP have only recently been articulated, the principles of NLP have been at work in Eastern culture for thousands of years. Before Dr. Nongard, never once have I heard a speaker or read the words of a writer who was able to equate the NLP presuppositions and the processes of NLP with the ancient teachings of the Guiguzi or Taoist thinking and then describe the relevance to modern practice that this ancient wisdom gives us to create change in our office with a client.

This book is a practical guide to NLP skills and life coaching practice, yet it is predicated on the principles of change work with a long and rich history in Eastern and Western thought. In these pages, you will learn practical NLP patterns, many coming from the foundational work of Bandler and Grinder and other well-known developers of NLP. You will also be able to see beyond what is typically taught as NLP or life coaching and gain from the insights he brings that extend our learnings back thousands of years, as well as Nongard's engagement of new understanding of neuroscience, influence, and communication that were not discussed in the early days of NLP.

Of value to the practitioner are the insights from both business and therapeutic applications that the author brings to us. Nongard has an extensive career as an NLP and life coaching practitioner and a business consultant and sales trainer. He also has spent years working to create community change, and he understands that the context of effective NLP is not reserved for one profession or a certain type of individual but has broad applications for anyone who wants to transform their own life and then powerfully influence others in positive ways.

This book shares the timeless ideas of classic NLP and new ideas in a way that will allow any practitioner of influence or change work to apply the ideas with real clients who come to see them to create success. It also shares ideas that speak to the health and wellness of both mind and body. The examples that are given throughout these pages and the processes taught are true to the spirit of the original ideas of NLP.

I can recommend this book to anyone who is a new practitioner of NLP and life coaching to ensure a solid introduction. I can also recommend this book to seasoned professionals who want to create a deeper and richer understanding of new ways to impact others.

Dr. David Snyder

Orange County, California 2021

Foreword by Chase Hughes
Author of *The Ellipsis Manual*

D r. Ignaz Semmelweis lived in 1846. After serious problems began to occur in his practice, he suggested to other doctors that washing their hands would keep patients from getting sick and might even stop the spread of disease. Even doctors were dying of similar things their patients were.

When he suggested that doctors wash their hands, he was laughed at, fired, and eventually beaten. He died soon thereafter. The other doctors in the medical community refused to believe they had contributed to patients' illnesses. They denounced his ideas as "hysterical" and pronounced that 'the way things had always been done' was the only right way to proceed.

Hypnosis has been through a very similar journey. In the hands of a practitioner, it can drastically alter the course of someone's life. The medical community continues to look with cautious skepticism upon hypnosis as a practice that might reduce the credibility of the provider.

Time seems to be the great justifier.

Not only therapists, but patients as well, tend to see their issues as requiring lots of time to correct. Hypnosis works so effectively for so many issues that it continues to be criticized, despite a mountain of evidence showing us that it is largely more effective than most of the traditional approaches to correcting patient's issues.

In all the academic research on the subject of hypnosis, regardless of where you look, there is one single thing that is completely ignored; the skill level of the practitioner. Somehow, the techniques are prescribed as if there were some universal protocols to a group of study participants. Researchers read boring, dry scripts from a clipboard and measure whether or not patients' conditions improve. Those numbers, good or bad, are then published as a "finding" in a journal, never once taking into account the quality of the process, the skill of the provider, or even the social connection to the patient.

In this book, Dr. Nongard pulls back the curtain and shows you the most ignored, and what I would argue is the most impactful aspect of the practice—human skill in hypnotherapy, NLP, and Life Coaching.

This book delivers powerful lessons in NLP and Life Coaching, with applications to hypnotherapy practice that were hard-won and time-tested. Your ability to produce change in others will always come down to the factors that the academic community ignores: Your skill level. You're holding this book because you understand that, and Dr. Nongard is about to deliver on a massive scale.

Whether you are just beginning or entering your second decade as a practitioner, this book will bring powerful methods that will surely provide tremendous leverage and power when it comes to what matters to you most - client results.

Chase Hughes
Author of *The Ellipsis Manual*

SECTION ONE

Ancient NLP, Traditional NLP, and New Ideas in NLP

Chapter 1
Introduction

In this book, I will share some useful ideas with you on current trends in neuro-linguistic programming (NLP) and life coaching. Why do I connect the two?

Neuro-linguistic programming is a set of strategies that are effective tools for helping people communicate, helping people to connect, and helping people to live life at their highest level of peak performance. These are skills that come from replicating the success of others that have gone before us, and one of the central ideas in NLP is the idea of the exemplar—who can we model so that we can follow the patterns of this person and replicate the success?

I speak about NLP in the context of life coaching often, and the reason why is that once we learn NLP, it almost always must be within the context of some other service or at least some other profession. Neuro-linguistic programming is widely used in the context of politics, in the construct of leadership development. Those in authority positions certainly use NLP, whether they are teachers, trainers, mentors in the corporate structure, and NLP is often used by hypnotherapists as a strategy within the context of their change work. These strategies often replicate earlier successful hypnotherapists—Milton Erickson being the primary name.

Psychotherapists often use the concepts or the ideas of NLP to create a practical strategy for their clients to practice stepping into success and to be able to overcome the problems that brought them to the office in the first place. As an approach to psychotherapy, NLP is experiential, allowing the client to accept change, practice strategies, and act on new ideas.

In the last forty to fifty years, not only has NLP exploded in both its acceptance and its use but so has life coaching. Life coaching is far different than counseling. Life coaches traditionally are not helping people who are in crisis return to an adequate level of functioning, but rather they are individuals who are working with people at an adequate level of functioning and helping them arise to their highest level of peak performance in their families, within themselves, within their communities, within their jobs, and in a number of different settings as well. Life coaching becomes a great context for NLP.

It provides a structure to the life coach, so the life coach knows what to do in the sessions when they are working with clients. It also provides a set of resources and strategies for the individual who wants to make a change in their business, in their family, in their community, and within themself. The good thing about NLP is that its practitioners first transform themselves using the strategies and techniques outlined by John Grinder and Richard Bandler back in the very early days of NLP and apply those in a way that can help themselves and others to rise to their highest level of potential.

The good news here is that, in this book, you are not only looking to learn how to help other people rise to their level of peak performance, but you are also learning some strategies that are going to be particularly useful to *you*.

I am talking about *new* NLP. And the reason why I am talking about new NLP is in the last five to twenty years, a lot of exemplars have come along whose ideas we can pattern, whose ideas we can emulate, whose success we can step into when we know how to do that.

A lot of people have the idea when I talk about new NLP that I mean out with the old and in with the new— it is not that.

We are going to retain the classic ideas of NLP in this book, but we are going to look at new research, new information, new ideas, and new exemplars and ask how can we apply the models of NLP to solving the problems in the current era, using the strategies with new exemplars that we know work based on our earliest experiences with NLP?

We will retain the relevant old ideas, but we are going to add to them a cadre of new ideas so that we can transform ourselves and create transformation in others. This is actually very exciting. I call this *dynamic NLP*. It is NLP for the current era that we are living in so that we can solve the modern problems that we have and be able to do that in a way that is most effective. A lot of people have made a significant adjustment to the way they learn. They are now learning at home because of our experience with COVID-19. A lot of educators are learning how to teach online, and teaching online is entirely different than teaching in a classroom. This trend, accelerated by COVID-19, is not going away. It is the new normal for our future in many situations.

How can we take the principles of learning, and how can we take the principles of educating within the context of NLP skills and apply them to our current problem?

That is really what this book is all about.

The field of coaching has changed how it is that we deliver services. State legislative bodies and regulatory agencies have looked at the division of psychotherapy and life coaching and began to ask questions about whether life coaches are duplicating the work of psychotherapists. We want to make sure that when we are offering services to people who want to move to their highest level of peak performance that we are doing it in the context of the current regulatory environment and in the context of what we now know about life coaching, which is its own unique and distinct profession different from that of psychotherapy.

There have been a lot of new ideas in the last forty years. In this book, I will talk about Chase Hughes' work in body language, and I will look at an old figure historically in public relations, Edward Bernays.

We will be looking at some of the old ideas in persuasion and public relations from the new perspective of NLP and cover Robert Cialdini's work on influence. Robert Cialdini is a professor at Arizona State University. His ideas were not looked at by NLP in the early days because his books were written later, but NLP practitioners are interested in influencing people in positive ways. Cialdini's work gives us a set of patterns that we can replicate to influence people in positive ways.

We will look at a couple of different ideas that are really the modern embodiment of applying NLP and how we can bring those ideas into coaching people—whether that coaching is life coaching, individual coaching, coaching teams, coaching in corporate environments, or even in the family. One of my favorite things has been to use the principles of NLP and coaching within my family so that my family can do well together.

We can use the same principles and techniques in our community as well. We will also look at cognitive neuroscience. This is one of those ideas that was not addressed in early NLP. There were assumptions made about how the mind works. But we have a body of knowledge now that we did not have before with new exemplars like Cialdini, Chase Hughes, and others. We are also going to take a look at the documentation that we need in the current era of life coaching in order to really make clear the type of services we are providing.

I have been practicing NLP, life coaching, professional hypnotherapy, and family therapy, as a mental health professional, for almost thirty years now. I will share with you my experience and how I have applied these principles to real-world clients.

I will share the structure of success, the patterns of progress, assessment of appropriateness, and a metatheoretical approach that can take the body of knowledge that we have developed in NLP and apply it to today's context.

There is the idea that there is nothing new under the sun. What Bandler and Grinder started in the 1970s was actually a continuum of previous knowledge. When I first posted about ancient NLP on social media, somebody asked me, "What? You're going to go all the way back to 1969?" In this book, we go back 5,000 years. Some people ask, how is that possible? After all, Richard Bandler and John Grinder articulated the ideas of NLP in the late 1960s and the early 1970s. But King Solomon said something amazing. And that is, "There is nothing new under the sun." And we can see that even though it was not described as NLP in early or ancient literature, the techniques, the methods, the ideas behind NLP are ideas that have endured the test of time. Certainly, Bandler and Grinder's fantastic contribution of systemizing this and helping us to really understand the mechanisms of NLP is important.

The thing about not limiting ourselves to a modern era approach to NLP is that we can create new patterns from a wide range of different resources, both Eastern and Western.

I hope you are enthused by the endless possibilities to look both in the current era and in years gone by to find methods that can genuinely help produce change.

When you finish this book, you will have a new set of ideas, a new set of strategies that are going to help you in the work that you do, whether you're working in business or sales, or whether you're working in therapy or counseling, or whether you're working with individuals in your community, helping the community to become a better place and applying these principles in your own life as well.

Chapter 2
Neuro-linguistic Programming

What is neuro-linguistic programming (NLP)? The reality is if you ask this to just about anybody, you will find a similar but different set of answers. I like to describe NLP as praxiological (meaning encompassing many different disciplines and ideas). I have used NLP as a strategy to help my clients achieve their highest level of potential and recover from their deepest lows. As a certified professional hypnotist, I have incorporated NLP techniques into the professional hypnosis that I offer to help people create faster responses, more predictable outcomes, and to help them achieve success at really, a faster level than maybe they even expected themselves. I view NLP as an applied method of helping people make change wherever they are and wherever they are going in life.

NLP deals with our emotions. It deals with our resource states. It deals with all the aspects of how we go about thinking and how we can go about changing the automatic or the subconscious thought patterns. Neuro-linguistic programming is also a guide to interpersonal relationships. Would you like to be a more effective communicator? Would you like to be able to communicate more persuasively or with greater levels of influence? That is important if you have children. It is also important if you supervise employees. These communication and interpersonal guide skills that come from NLP have applications across relationships, personal as well as professional. I am very lucky that I was exposed to NLP when I was just eighteen years old. I have used the techniques and the strategies to build effective friendships and business relationships, and to navigate the difficulties of life in many different ways with the many different people I've encountered by being confident in my ability to use effective communication patterns to persuade, influence, bring people together, and create a sense of community.

Neuro-linguistic programming is the systemizing of success. What Richard Bandler and John Grinder did in the late 1960s and early 1970s was to look at some therapists who are known for being highly effective at helping people make change. They picked three people to look at initially. There have been many other exemplars in NLP over the years, but initially, they looked at Fritz Perls, the creator of gestalt therapy. They assessed what it was about his language, the way he worked with individuals, the techniques that he used to produce such profound change. They also looked at Virginia Satir, a renowned family therapist from the Family Therapy Institute of California. In any family therapy training program today, they still teach and talk about the methods of Virginia Satir. Bandler and Grinder worked with her to distill the techniques that she used in her therapy to help families come together and function at their greatest potential.

They went to Phoenix, Arizona, in the early 1970s and spent time with Milton Erickson. Milton Erickson was a medical doctor who was a renowned medical hypnotist. He was a psychiatrist, and he treated individuals in his medical approach with hypnotherapy. He is really considered the father of modern medical hypnotherapy. They evaluated what separates Erickson from others, the language he used, and the techniques and methods. And they asked whether they could distill the techniques, the methods, the language of these highly successful change workers and then teach these to other people so that they could be repeated. And the answer, of course, was yes! They replicated the success of others. Bandler and Grinder really systemized the idea of creating success. They provided models and patterns, and strategies so that each one of us could step into our greatest potential version of ourselves and help other people— whether they are family, colleagues and coworkers, or clients in therapy or coaching or hypnosis to experience success as well.

Neuro-linguistic programming is also about creating an understanding between the yin and the yang, between the dual nature of people, between the mind/body, between the thoughts and the actions that people take, and between the patterns and the people of the planet Earth. All these ideas related to NLP are, of course, simple definitions. The great thing about NLP is that it is really a big tent idea. There are many different strategies underneath it, a lot of different teachers of NLP, and each one of them has brought their wisdom and unique ways to this profession. Robert Dilts was an early pioneer in NLP training, as were Steve and Connirae Andreas. The ideas and contributions that they have made have expanded our understanding and definitions of NLP and helped us create replicable patterns to truly help people experience success.

The N in NLP stands for *neuro*. That is the idea of our brain. Much of modern psychotherapy now concerns itself with the idea of brain science and neurons. We understand how the brain synapses work and the chemical codes, program our previous experiences and produce responses with our subconscious mind. Bandler and Grinder, by paying attention to the neurological or the physical component of how NLP functioned, offered an important way to differentiate between doing the same thing this person did to have the same outcomes, bringing it to a deeper level.

The L in NLP is *linguistic*. John Grinder was a linguist. He taught at the University of California as a language professor. And he understood that language represents and symbolizes ideas, experiences, emotions and that when we use language, we elicit behaviors, responses, and change. By combining the mind with the tongue, we can teach people to program themselves for success.

What would you like to accomplish with your life? To what level of success would you like to rise? Neuro-linguistic programming gives you a system for understanding these ideas, for accessing that success, for creating important relationships in the world around you, and changing the *stinking thinking*, the psychological potholes along the way that keep us from rising to our greatest level of performance. Underneath all of this, though, is a foundation for the idea of modeling success. What Bandler and Grinder did was amazing. They went to highly successful people, and they asked to observe them, work with them, and study them. They wanted to understand how it was that they had created their success so that they could then create ways of teaching other people to rise to the same level of success. This is the P in NLP, the *programming*.

In many NLP training programs, those early ideas of Bandler and Grinder and the modeling and the patterns that they established are still consistently taught. But rarely do most teaching look beyond the golden era of NLP development.

In this book, we will be looking at not just that period of the sixties, seventies, and eighties, but the current era. Are there new exemplars that we can model? Can we find people whose successes we can replicate in different and important areas of life? Can we apply these to our coaching? Can we apply these to our hypnotherapy? Can we apply these to our psychotherapy, our leadership, our business acumen and use the strategies to help build a business? Can we apply these new exemplars and these new models to our own personal development and rise to our greatest level? Can we make this the best year yet using these strategies? The answer is yes.

We are going to go back 5,000 years ago. We are going to ask what systems have been written about and talked about that can help lead us into success using the ideas of NLP to create a new understanding of old ideas. There was no NLP 5,000 years ago, but there was Guiguzi, the Sage of Ghost Valley. There was Sun Tzu and *The Art of War*. Many other strategy teachers taught us not just about war but about business, community, relationships, and success. Those are the things that we are going to be exploring in the rest of this book.

Chapter 3
Hallmarks of Neuro-Linguistic Programming

NLP Presuppositions

This book will describe each of these hallmarks in detail during appropriate chapters. This section provides some key concepts that are hallmarks of NLP. When we think of the foundations of NLP, the classics of NLP, we are also talking about the presuppositions. You see, NLP is not built on a bunch of theories. It is based on what works in the real world. Bandler and Grinder were famous for saying, "If it works, it's NLP." What we are doing here is we are looking for people who have the desired outcomes, and then we are figuring out if what they did to reach that outcome worked.

This is one of the things that makes it difficult to put to the academic test with peer-reviewed journals. Peer-reviewed studies look at the theories and test the hypothesis, but in NLP, we really do not have any hypothesis. What we have is the experiences of people who have gone before us—it is very practical.

Replicating Patterns of Success

In the earliest days of NLP, the creators were so excited to be able to replicate the successes of Virginia Satir, medical hypnotherapist Milton Erickson, psychologist and psychotherapist

Fritz Perls, as well as others who they studied. And they were excited to share those outcomes without giving much attention to the philosophical basis. What has happened in the last forty or fifty years, which we really do not spend too much time focusing on in teaching NLP, is that we have learned the psychobiology of behavioral responses and emotional responses.

We now understand the mind/body connection from the work of Bruce Lipton and other people who have written on this subject, both in academia and popular psychology. And we now understand the importance of our brain, the literal brain, in creating the ability to access and replicate the patterns of success, which NLP has shared and discovered.

I love writing about NLP within the context of acceptance and commitment therapy, within the context of mindfulness-based stress reduction. We know that the mind is not primed to stay in the present moment. Because of evolutionary biology, our mind looks at the past and tries to predict the future. And it is always scanning the past to make a decision about the future. This is how the mind works, but we can create, practice, and utilize techniques like mindfulness-based stress reduction that can teach a person to do what the brain is not naturally inclined to do, and that is to live fully in the present moment.

The result of this is that people handle stress better. They handle decision-making better, handle relationships better, and it is more likely that they will be able to step into their intentions and dreams.

Primary Representational Systems

Classic NLP really focused on the primary representational systems. You can think of this in the context of the five senses— olfactory, taste, gustatory, smell, etc. Most people are not olfactory or gustatory learners. They are usually auditory, visual, or kinesthetic learners. Kinesthetic is tactile, feeling, touching. These five senses are how we experience the world around us. And the earliest writers in NLP recognized the value of determining a person's primary representational system. Are they functioning as an auditory learner and experiencer? Are they functioning as a visual learner and experiencer? Do they experience the world around them from a kinesthetic perspective?

How do you know if you are auditory, visual, or kinesthetic or if somebody you are working with is auditory, visual, or kinesthetic? I put it in the context of the modern era and IKEA furniture.

How can building IKEA furniture help us determine what representational system we have?

- The auditory learner experiences the world by hearing things, by saying things. They read the directions because the directions are literally "heard" in their mind.

- The visual experiencer takes the picture that is on the box, looks at all the pieces, and tries to build what they see.

- The kinesthetic experiencer takes the pieces, touches them, feels the painted side and the unfinished side. They align those together. They see which pieces are heavier, bigger, and smaller. And they build it by feeling it.

The way you build IKEA furniture can reveal what your primary representational system is. Our primary representational system is essential. Our clients are experiencing their problems from an auditory perspective, whether it is self-talk or the messages imposed by others. They are experiencing it visually, seeing their future either negatively or positively. Or they are feeling their emotions weighing them down or a lightness and a power of success. The early NLP practitioners focused on being able to assess the client's primary representational system and then encouraged us to be congruent so that we were able to work within the skill sets they had to help them achieve their greatest level of potential.

The problem with that idea is that it is rather limiting. It is limiting because our clients are going to go back into the real world. And the real world is auditory. It is kinesthetic. It is visual. It is olfactory. It is gustatory. There are multiple sensorial experiences. When I have a client whose visual acuity is high but kinesthetic acuity is low, I work with them to help increase their kinesthetic acuity. When my clients have a low level of auditory acuity and a high level of kinesthetic acuity, rather than simply trying to master kinesthetic awareness, I help them learn how to increase their auditory acuity to operate holistically in the world around them.

Rapport

The idea of rapport is central to helping other people, whether you are a hypnotist, a psychotherapist, a business leader, a boss, a parent, or a good community member. To influence other people, we have to engage them, and the easiest way to engage people is to create rapport with them. And NLP training is always focused on skills and rapport.

Proxemics

Proxemics simply means to attend or to be with somebody and the impact that has on them. We respond psychophysiologically to the presence of other people. This tells me how I can increase my rapport-building skills by understanding proxemics and my relationship to other people's relationships. These ideas worked around forty or fifty years ago, but they are ideas we can put to use today.

In the office, how do we position ourselves with clients? I often deliver my pre-talk as a hypnotherapist and as a life coach at my front table. My client feels safe because there is some space between them and me. When comfort and rapport are built, we move to the hypnotic furniture, my client to the recliner, and I to my chair—near them, closer to them, sharing trance experiences with them.

I do not view myself as doing hypnosis *to* anybody, or doing therapy *to* anybody, or doing coaching *to* anybody. I view myself as sharing trance with them, sharing expertise with them, or sharing the resources that have helped me transform and help the clients I work with transform to get the benefits that others who have gone before them have.

Patterns of Success

In classic NLP, we talk about patterns replicating success.

This is at the heart of life coaching, helping people to reach what they believe their greatest level of potential is. Patterns are replicable. Patterns of success can help in overcoming difficult emotions, becoming motivated, and building a set of resource states that are of value to me. All these things are the ideas of NLP patterns. Some of the classic patterns you may have heard of are the Swish Pattern or the Six-Step Reframe. They are all classic NLP patterns, but the question is, what new patterns can we develop? And can we develop them in multiple professions?

In the context of sales, we can look at exemplars who are exceptional salespeople, such as Zig Ziglar. We can create a pattern from these folks because these were not looked at in early NLP. But if one wants to be a successful salesperson, we need to look at the modern exemplars in this industry or any other industry and ask can these steps to success be distilled down into a formula or a pattern, taught to other people, and then replicated? The answer to that is almost always yes.

Neurological Levels

Neurological levels deal with the who, what, when, and how. These are classic concepts in NLP, as are language patterns. But language changes. The same language that we use today was not available forty or fifty years ago. It is said that in fifty years, twenty percent of the common language, the everyday language that people use, will have changed from what it was in previous years. How do we know this is true? Read an old book. The language is archaic. And the language patterns that were studied in early NLP and are still taught in many classes are not necessarily the language patterns that people are using today.

Chapter 4
New NLP and Coaching

I want to share some specific ideas from some exemplars that I think can give us a modern approach and a modern understanding of neuro-linguistic in the context of life coaching. These are some exceptional ideas.

Many of you have read Chase Hughes' book titled *The Ellipsis Manual*. How do I know that? Because it is the best-selling book in hypnotherapy and the best-selling book on body language and is one of the best-selling books in law enforcement. It is a fantastic book written by a military intelligence specialist, Chase Hughes, who shares his twenty-plus years of experience in studying body language and interrogations, and leadership, and a range of diverse yet related topics. Chase shares some ideas that can help us to develop rapport back to the classic NLP idea. The ideas have influenced the language patterns that create success, and NLP is largely dependent on language. John Grinder, the co-creator of NLP, was a linguistics professor. So, it makes sense that we focused in early NLP on the spoken word.

Chase Hughes is an expert in body language. What it is that people are saying through gestures, motions, placing of their body, their eyes, their conscious, as well as their subconscious gesturing and movement, can help us become a more effective communicator, parent, teacher, politician, friend, life coach, and clinician.

Let us take a look at some of the ideas that Chase Hughes has developed in the last twenty years of studying this and published in his recent book, *The Ellipsis Manual*. The ideas can help you to help other individuals reach their highest level of performance as you also reach your highest level of performance. We can call this the five suppositions or five pillars of nonverbal communication and body language from Chase Hughes.

- There are three types of body language. A lot of people are interested in body language but are afraid they have to learn a whole new body language vocabulary. Chase assures us that in his many years of nonverbal communication studies, that there are only three types of body language. There is either opening, closing, or aggressive communication.

I had an interesting discussion with Chase about the idea of the scrolls of Guiguzi, the Tao, and the ancient idea that whether a door is open or closed, there is opportunity in both. Chase teaches that when we understand that all body language comes down to either opening or closing or aggression, we can then find ourselves on the right side of the door to interact in a way that builds rapport, builds alliances, can help us to problem solve and to influence other people, and to put ourselves in a position of authority in situations where before this, we might not have had that. Does that sound like it would be useful in parenting? Teaching? Absolutely.

- Most of our observation is on accident. Deliberate observation puts you light years ahead of other people—practicing the art of observation.

The art of observation begins by observing yourself. We can go back to an ancient practice of yoga. We can learn body scan meditation. It will teach us to begin to observe other people. We can go to Milton Erickson's method of self-hypnosis, which was to sit before a mirror for twenty minutes in silence, simply reflecting on your observation of the self in that mirror. If you have never utilized that as a self-hypnosis technique, let me encourage you to do that. It is remarkable what the results of that twenty-minute session can be. And, if you do this multiple times, you will discover that there is something really deep about observing the self. When we practice observing the self, we can then begin to observe other people. Neuro-linguistic programming has always talked about the observer self. Meditation talks about the observer self. Chase Hughes ties it all together for us in the context of body language. If I want to be good at understanding other people, I must be good at understanding myself.

- Fear makes us move faster. He gives a solution to the natural inclination to move faster when we have fear. And that is that if you want to build trust with an individual, make the decision that you are never going to move faster in your conversation or your presentation than you can if you are underwater. In other words, if you never move faster than you can move underwater, you will not be broadcasting the nonverbal message of fear or a lack of confidence. And the result is other people will be drawn into you. And trust will be created.

- We can physically position ourselves and other people to make decisions. We ask people to make decisions in parenting, and sales, and psychotherapy, leadership, and life coaching. Chase points something out that is really important. Never ask a person to take an action or make a decision while their back is against the chair. Rather, we should have them on the edge of their chair when we ask for commitment, when we ask for change, when we ask for action.

If I were sitting across from somebody who was leaning into the chair and I was about ready to ask them to make a decision, I might simply say to them, "Go ahead and take this pen and write on this paper." They must lean forward and away from the back of their chair. I am asking them to get into the position nonverbally with their body language of acceptance, commitment, follow-through, and making a decision. This is a simple strategy, but the profound nature of these strategies from Chase Hughes, a modern exemplar that we can look at in the context of NLP in life coaching, is truly useful.

- Create the body language that you need from somebody *before* you ask any questions. Again, we can hand somebody a pen to have openness, or we can ask people by giving them assignments or tasks. In life coaching, I give all my clients a lot of homework and a lot of tasks to complete. They put themselves in the body language of openness and acceptance. They put themselves in the body language of congruence and partnership to achieve the goals that are important to me.

You can see that even though Chase Hughes might not have even been born when NLP was first discussed, now in his adult life, he has revealed for us a tremendous amount of information on body language that we can now use in our sessions and with our clients to create success at the highest levels.

These simple strategies that Chase has articulated in his research and his book *The Ellipsis Manual* are useful tools that can help us to become more effective NLP practitioners and more effective life coaches guiding other people.

Chapter 5
New Ideas Since the
Beginning of NLP

Robert Cialdini

Robert Cialdini is a research professor at Arizona State University, and he wrote a book on influence aptly titled *Influence*. This book did not come out until about 1985. He has written numerous books since then. Because he is a university professor, the ideas behind what he has written about are based on theoretical foundations, unlike NLP, the philosophy being if it works, it's NLP. This is important because we need to move NLP into a more research-based approach. At the heart of NLP classes and discussions on the internet is often the question of how to influence people. Robert Cialdini gives us the answer. In his books, he talks about the six elements of truly influencing other people. This can be influencing a community, a large group, or another individual one-on-one. His ideas are particularly useful in a coaching model. Let us take a look at the six ideas that are the heart of his six rules for influence.

The six rules for influence are reciprocity, scarcity, authority, consistency, liking or likeability, and consensus. Let's explore each one of these in the context of NLP and how we can use these as part of a modern approach to NLP patterns.

- The idea behind reciprocity is that I do something for you, and you do something for me. This is often used in sales, and sales professionals are interested in the idea of NLP. And we can borrow the concept of reciprocity. If I am a car salesman at a Honda dealership, I can get some Honda key chains, and I can give them to people that go on a demo ride. I might say, "Imagine what it would be like to have your key hanging on this? Here you go. Here is a key chain for you." I gave them something small, a gift.

What are they going to give me? They are going to give me a sale. The idea of reciprocity can be used to motivate people. It can be used to encourage people in a certain direction. It can be used to influence people and achieve the outcomes that we want. We can also use reciprocity linguistically. I can say, "Thank you." I can say, "Please." I can use kind language, expecting to get kind language in return. I can use assertive communication like, "I feel . . ." or "I want . . ." or "I need . . ." expecting a return. This is important in coaching couples—to receive assertive communication back. The principle of reciprocity can be used in several different ways in the context of coaching and NLP.

- The second idea, the concept of scarcity, is very important. In NLP, we talk about motivating people—either toward motivation or away from motivation. Toward motivation is going *to* something. Often though, it is the *away from* motivation that is most powerful. People want to flee from scarcity. A coach can use scarcity as a tool for helping people move toward something.

Let me give you an example of how that might work. I might be coaching a business client who is trying to make a big decision about moving forward in their career and considering whether to say yes to a big project. I can remind my client of what scarcity is like. "Remember twenty years ago when you didn't take advantage of the opportunity that was in front of you? What was the result of that experience? Now that you face the same choice, making a decisive decision, do you see the choice that is obvious that will have the long-term results that you desire?" I have just used scarcity as a tool for influencing in a positive direction.

- The third idea is authority. In my office is my wall of authority. Hanging there are my diplomas and a doctorate in transformational leadership from Bakke Graduate University. My degree is in cross-cultural engagement. Right below it is a certificate from the former governor of Texas, Ann Richards. In 1994, she said I was a "ray of light" to other Texans. When people walk into my office, they see that wall of authority, the certificates, the diplomas, certification as a professional hypnotist, and as a life coach. They think Richard knows what he is talking about. Now I hope that my experience, my many books, and the results that I have had also speak to my authority, but when clients do not know me, that is the first thing they see. That wall of authority is one way to establish authority, but you do not need a lot of certificates, certifications, diplomas, degrees to establish authority.

You can speak with authority. This goes to both the nonverbal communication that Chase Hughes teaches us and the language patterns that NLP has distilled from Milton Erickson. We can speak to people, and we can establish our authority. I always stress to my clients that the techniques we are using come from my own application of the material and my own self-transformation. I teach my clients the tools that I am using in my own life. Authority also comes from seeing the results with the many clients I have worked with. My clients know they are not the first ones. The methods that I use are based on the research that we know works. In other words, Richard, who is also a professor, understands research, and he uses empirically validated ideas. That does not mean we will not use experimental or experiential or other ideas in the work that we do, but that some of the ideas are coming from a basis of authority in the research.

- The fourth idea here is consistency. Consistency was important when I was growing up, and it continues to be important to me to this day. You can set a clock by me because I am usually doing the same thing at the same time on the same days. This has helped me, I think, be an effective parent. If we want to use strategies for influencing our children, consistency is one of them. A lot of people come to me for business coaching, but really, it is the family issues, especially in family-run businesses or in the current era where people are working from home.

- The next idea is likability. Likability creates influence. People really do not vote for the person—for president—they agree with most. They vote for the person they want to go to eat lunch with. Likability counts. Likability is important. Is your hair cut? Do you dress okay? Is your shirt ironed? Do you have a Swiss chronometer? Are you a likable person? Do you use kind language? Do you communicate assertively rather than passive-aggressively? All of these, again, are ideas related to likability. Do you ask other people during your rapport-building phase about them? Or are you using self-disclosure in coaching as a primary strategy and not asking about them, instead talking about yourself. That is less likable. There is a place for self-disclosure, but it is a balance.

- The sixth principle is the idea of consensus and consensus-building. In our political climate now, half the people are red, and half the people are blue. The blue people hate the red ones, and the red ones hate the blue. It seems that there is no consensus, but at many times in our political history, we have come to a point of conflict.

But it has always been consensus-building that has led the way to compromise. It has always been listening and attending to others. Neuro-linguistic programming gives us a whole host of listening skills that we can implement, that we conduct ourselves now verbally and leaning in. I was taught years ago S.O.L.E.R. — **s**it down, have **o**pen body posture, **l**ean forward, make **e**ye contact, and **r**elax. This establishes rapport and helps us to influence people.

These ideas by Cialdini are rarely ever talked about in NLP training programs. But every one of these ideas is a useful strategy we can implement in the work that we are doing as we move NLP toward a modern approach that helps people with the current era issues they are facing.

Chapter 6
Modeling Excellence

The ideas of NLP were really based on John Grinder and Richard Bandler's observation of three primary characters: Virginia Satir, a family therapist in Southern California, Fritz Perls, a psychologist at the University of California Santa Cruz, and Milton Erickson, a psychiatrist who practiced medical hypnotherapy in Phoenix, Arizona. These are three excellent exemplars, and, as one who is also a licensed therapist, I have really been able to use the ideas derived from those therapists who were successful with their clients to help the individuals with whom I have worked. I have appreciated the history of NLP that was founded essentially on these three exemplars, as well as some others. But the reality is there are multiple exemplars in multiple professionals. There are people in sales, community development, parenting, politics, and leadership whose work we can model to create success. A modern approach to NLP asks the question who else could be an exemplar? And what patterns of NLP from these individuals can we create or utilize?

It is interesting that, while Milton Erickson, Virginia Satire, and Fritz Perls were fantastic exemplars, one of the focuses of NLP early on was influence. And yet, I have never seen anything written in any of the early NLP books that was based on Edward Bernays' work.

Edward Bernays

You may have heard Edward Bernays' name before if you are in the public relations field. Edward Bernays, who was Sigmund Freud's nephew, was an interesting character whose work changed the fabric of American society. He worked on numerous public relations campaigns.

One of his campaigns was to help cigarette manufacturers make female smoking acceptable. He tied it to the idea of suffrage, women's leadership, and the right to vote. Edward Bernays' ideas were both controversial and interesting but powerful.

The luggage industry went to Edward Bernays early on and said they were worried that they weren't selling enough luggage and wondered how he could help them sell more luggage. Edward Bernays was the person who could do that. Bernays developed a way to help the luggage industry sell more luggage. He sent articles to magazines with titles like "What the well-dressed woman needs to wear on the weekend." The strategies in these articles that were then published in national magazines included having multiple wardrobes, which would have to be packed in protective luggage. He gave free luggage to cinemas for movie displays and to theaters for plays, and that luggage could be used as props and seen by audiences in the newly developed Hollywood movie industry. In his public relations campaigns to health departments, he suggested that they stress the importance of each person having their own luggage, not sharing luggage with other people for hygiene reasons. He encouraged stores to put luggage in their window displays. A fresh relationship was created between new styles of clothing and new luggage styles. He wrote to colleges and universities to send to their new students lists of what they would need, clothing, etcetera, and the luggage that they would need to move onto campuses.

He created an industry trade group called Luggage Information Service (L.I.S.). This then could be an easy way for any journalist or salesperson who wanted to know more about luggage to make a phone call and get answers about luggage.

Bernays urged architects to build homes with closets big enough to store luggage. He wrote to sixty-six railway companies and ten steamship companies, and he urged them to make sure the designers left plenty of room for the luggage people would need.

He lobbied foreign embassies to increase the free weight allowances for those traveling abroad.

And he gave luggage to movie stars to pose with and be seen with. Edward Bernays' technique is still used today in the fashion industry, giving Instagram stars t-shirts, purses, jewelry, etcetera. We have a whole new industry called influencers. This is really based on the ideas of Edward Bernays, who was also a controversial figure politically. He was a fascinating figure, this nephew of Sigmund Freud. Nonetheless, in the history of public relations, Edward Bernays is one of the most influential people.

Edward Bernays helped the luggage industry to increase their sales and popularize the individual ownership of luggage early in our country's history. I do not think we would have rappers shilling Louis Vuitton bags without him. And I do not believe that we would have Gucci suitcases and laptop cases if, in part, it was not for Edward Bernays. We can see that here is a person who systemically created patterns of success for persuading large groups of people, societies as a whole to take actions.

How do we put that in the context of the coaching work that we do? Our clients come to us because they want to transform themselves, and they want to transform others, but they also want to leave a legacy of success. I like to quote Randy Dobbs, the author of a book titled *Transformational Leadership: A Blueprint for Real Organizational Change*, who said that "Good leaders leave behind a cadre of other leaders." This is often done through public relations, through influence on a community scale, or even, in the case of Edward Bernays, on a nationwide scale.

We can replicate the success of others in other industries by creating NLP patterns in the current era that help us help other people and help ourselves as well. We can look beyond just psychotherapy for solutions to change work to all the exemplars that have genuinely helped us to create success in our world.

Chapter 7
Anchoring

If you have taken hypnotherapy certification or are familiar with NLP, you know about the idea of anchoring. Bandler and Grinder described anchoring as the tendency of one element of an experience to revivify the whole experience.

Anchoring Example

An example of an anchor is this scenario: You are walking through the mall, and you hear a song on the speakers, a song that was played at your wedding. Suddenly, although you are walking through the mall, you are walking down the wedding aisle one more time or, in your mind, walking onto the dance floor to have that dance one more time. Anchoring is the idea that when we have an emotion, a thought, an experience, when we have a cue in our environment—a sound, feeling, sight, sense, taste, touch— a simple element can bring us back to a different time or place. Sometimes it can bring us back to distressing events. Anchors are set naturally. They do not require a therapist.

We all experience anchors every single day in our life. Whether we have a therapist or whether we have a hypnotist or a coach or not, many times, we have set anchors to bring us back to anxiety, to depression, to distress.

Part of the NLP or life coach's job is to help an individual to be able to break these anchors that have been set that revivify negative experiences and to set new anchors so the individual can step into positive experiences.

Anchoring Technique

In the world of hypnosis, one well-known anchoring technique is to touch the thumb and index finger together, pressing them tightly. A hypnotist will often have a person in hypnosis create a resource state, such as a state of joy, confidence, happiness, or whatever it is they would like to feel. They have them touch her thumb and index finger together. Then they give the post-hypnotic suggestion that anytime in the next day or two or week or two, the individual needs to access this state of comfort, calm, or confidence, they will touch their thumb and index finger together, and it will bring them right back to where they were at the time the anchor was established.

This is a simple anchoring technique that is used very often in hypnotherapy. It was one of the first techniques in NLP or hypnosis taught. But the idea behind NLP goes far beyond the conscious decision to engage in an action that brings us back to previous experiences and helps us to deal with the subconscious reservoir that we have all created between our experiences and our outcomes, experiences, and expectations. It helps us to break the old patterns and step into new patterns. Would you like to know how to do this in your own life so that you can reach your highest level of peak performance or help clients to be able to break these patterns and to step into a pattern of success? Robert Dilts, one of the early pioneers in NLP education, referred to anchoring as stimuli that will constantly recreate. What is important here is the idea that when an anchor is fired, whether it is conscious or unconscious, it does predictably and consistently revivify that resource state that is going to be of value.

Chapter 8
Ancient NLP

I want to give you a couple of examples before I talk about the Sage of Ghost Valley and the wisdom that he gave us that changed the history of a nation and perhaps, even the history of the world. The Nine Hand Seals, or 九字印 in the Chinese language, is both a Chinese and a Japanese strategy that is based on the Dao (the yin and yang). It is the idea that everything coexists together and that when we are experiencing, for example, a lack of confidence, we have the ability to access confidence.

The Nine Hand Seals

The idea in the Nine Hand Seals as applied to martial arts is that certain seals, certain things that are done with the hand, and certain signals are tied to a mantra. That mantra can produce a resource state of value to the fighter, the warrior, the father, the leader, or the business executive.

The significant thing about the art of warfare is that it does not just deal with warfare but deals with the ability to create internal resources. There are Nine Hand Seals taught in martial arts and, in this book, I will cover two of them.

- Rin: This was tied to a mantra of the thunderbolt and power, and it is done by placing the hands together, fingers interlocked, and the index (or sometimes middle) fingers are raised and pressed together. When martial artists create this hand seal, they access the resource state that is going to be a value to them— one of power.

- Tō is known as the "outer lion." It is a hand seal where you put your hands together, cross the index fingers over to touch the opposite ring fingers, then cross the middle finger over. The ring and pinkie fingers are kept straight and separated. The tips of the ring and pinkie fingers are pressed together to form a V shape. You have likely seen martial artists strike a pose and create something with their hands. This is a symbol to them, an anchor that they have created to then access a resource state that is going to help them in the challenging situation that they are facing. This is an example of anchoring from our ancient wisdom and our ancient understanding.

Religion

We do not have to go to the East. We can go to the Hebrew Bible. We can look at scripture verses. It does not matter if you are a believer or a non-believer; you are probably familiar with these verses if you grew up in America:

- Psalm 23, which is read at almost every funeral. "Even though I walk through the valley of death." Why? Because this passage has been anchored to creating comfort in difficult times.

- Matthew 6:28 comes from the Beatitudes. It is a calming verse Jesus taught when he said, "Consider the lilies of the field, they toil not, neither do they spin." This passage is interpreted as meaning they do not worry about what clothes they are going to wear. They do not spin and toil as you do.

- Psalm 139 is a verse many people are familiar with, which gives us a sense of security. "You hem me in behind and before," and He knows the steps that we take.

- 1 Peter 5:7 is a verse that has helped a lot of people to calm anxiety, "Cast all your cares on him because he cares for you."

What is fascinating about this is that these are consistent with anchoring resource states. These come from a cultural tradition that most of us are familiar with, and yet we have never thought about in the context of NLP. When we study NLP, we can see how the ancient wisdom were explanations and attempts to help us replicate the success of other people and step into the abundance that we have been promised in this life no matter what the source.

It Works

Let us take a look at an idea that doesn't come from thousands of years ago, and it's not directly related to anchoring, but I wanted to point out it's a good example of NLP before NLP was articulated.

In the late 1920s, Roy Herbert Jarrett wrote a book titled *It Works*. And if you are familiar at all with the Law of Attraction and the literature in this genre, you are probably familiar with this red book. Millions of people have read this book and created success. They have replicated the success of Roy Herbert Jarrett by following the three simple steps that he offered in his book:

1. The first is to create a list. Create a list of everything that you want. Focus on that list. Take the things off that you do not really want. Add the things you really do want—the material things, the spiritual things, the psychological things. Get that list down to ten things you truly want. Take a few days to cultivate that list.

2. Meditate on the list. Read that list. Enforce that list. Bring your attention to that list from the morning, through the noon, and the night.

3. The third step is keeping it a secret.

What Roy Herbert Jarrett discovered was that it works. What is *it?* That when we focus on what we want, we can create what we want. This is an axiom that is true throughout time. Nobody is going to give us what it is we want. It must be created from within, and NLP gives us a skill set to do that.

Guiguzi

I want to introduce you to some outstanding ideas related to the Sage of Ghost Valley, known as Guiguzi in Chinese history. He was an ancient Chinese writer who lived thousands of years ago. When I first became acquainted with the work of Guiguzi, I was amazed at how the ideas of Guiguzi can change our experiences and give us wisdom in our current era. (Note: Nobody is sure when Guiguzi lived or if he even existed. His scrolls could be from another writer or even several writers. For our purposes, we will assume the story of Guiguzi at face value. If not historically accurate, there is no doubt these words have carried wisdom and weight for billions of people over the years and deeply influenced Eastern thought, business, politics, and psychology. So powerful were these words that certain political leaders have even banned access to these writings at various times in history. These facts are not part of the academic dispute over the existence of Guiguzi.)

It was many ago that I was teaching an NLP certification course in my office. People were coming from all over the world to earn their International Certification Board for Coaches and Hypnotists (ICBCH) training in professional hypnosis in a live seminar format. I was getting ready the night before by reviewing some notes on what I wanted to talk about. I was looking at my books and my notes, and my wife, who is Chinese and was new in the country at that time, said to me, "What are you studying?" I replied, "I'm studying Neuro-Linguistic Programming, NLP. Do you know what NLP is?" She said, "No."

I explained to her that NLP was a system for understanding interpersonal communication, understanding persuasion and leadership, business, psychology, and understanding our conscious and our subconscious mind.

She looked over at me, and she said, "Oh, like Guiguzi!" I looked around, and I said, "Like what?" And she said, "Like Guiguzi. He taught NLP." I said, "Who is Guiguzi?" She said, "You don't know who Guiguzi is? Everybody knows who Guiguzi is. He is the Sage of Ghost Valley. He was the teacher of Sun Bin Laozi, *The Art of War*. He was famous." I had never heard of Guiguzi. In retaliation, I asked, "Do you know who Aristotle was?" She had no clue. We were even. In her school, they did not teach "Western Civilization," just as in my schooling, they did not teach "Eastern Civilization." And we wonder why the world is so divided.

I grabbed the laptop, searched Guiguzi, and I came up with very little. I found a couple of web pages with some references to Guiguzi, a couple of videos that were in Chinese, some books here and there that were written in Chinese, and very little in English about Guiguzi.

In talking to my wife about who Guiguzi was, she explained that his ideas were so powerful that when China, 5,000 years ago, was broken up into tiny kingdoms, the strategies of Guiguzi were used to create a vertical alliance and eventually Qin dynasty (the first dynasty of Imperial China). Some of those kingdoms were conquered by war. Some of those kingdoms were integrated with agreement and with peace.

I started to study the history of this. It was fascinating to me, and my wife was right. It is NLP. It is NLP from 5,000 years ago. When I finally found a translation done by a University of Texas professor of the scrolls of Guiguzi, I was amazed.

I started to read what Guiguzi had written into scrolls thousands of years ago. And he wrote some basic strategies for communication. He wrote them in colorful ways. The art of listening is an important strategy in NLP. We call this calibrating. We want to calibrate the folks with whom we are working so that we understand where they are, their point of action. Guiguzi spoke about calibrating also, and he put it in the context of listening to other people. One of my favorite quotes from the scrolls on Guiguzi is, "When you are listening to a competitor, you should listen as a tongue seeking the marrow from the center of a bone." We know hypnotic language is filled with metaphors, but Guiguzi compared the art of listening to people to the action of a tongue.

How is it that we can listen in a way to effectively NLP calibrate? According to Guiguzi, it is to listen with the interest of a tongue seeking the marrow from the center of a bone. The ideas and the scrolls of Guiguzi are fascinating concepts that can help us understand effective interpersonal communication.

Here is a short passage from the scrolls of Guiguzi about how it is we should align our speech with those who we are speaking to be more effective communicators:

When you speak to an important person, show your knowledge.

When you speak to a knowledgeable person, employ judicious reasoning.

When you talk to a debater, stress key points.

When you talk to a person of power, speak with authority.

When you speak to a wealthy person, speak about loftiness.

When you talk to a poor person, speak about benefits.

When you talk to a low-class person, apply humility.

When you talk to a brave person, speak about courage.

When you talk to a person who has made mistakes, speak to the point.

When speaking to intelligent people, Guiguzi says, use these methods to enlighten them.

And when speaking to unintelligent people, and we all must do that at one time or another, speak with intent to teach the methods to truly impact, reach, and help people.

Guiguzi says these are the methods, but we almost always do the opposite.

If you are interested in applying NLP to copywriting or using NLP as part of political or persuasive speech, you can see how these communication patterns articulated by Guiguzi 5,000 years ago still have practical applications today.

The scrolls of Guiguzi, like the ideas articulated in NLP, are practical strategies to help us more effectively communicate with and influence other people.

Ever since I read this passage, it has been on a piece of paper that I printed out and posted over my desk. I think it is a fascinating way to conceptualize how it is that we can speak to persuade, to create agreement, and to influence other individuals. This applies in business, therapy, in our families, and in our community—every area of our life.

The scrolls of Guiguzi are summarized in two books. There are two scrolls, and there are twelve key points that I have identified from the scrolls of Guiguzi that I think are fascinating. And I think that by sharing these with you, you will find them fascinating also. Understand how by looking at ancient wisdom, we can discover strategies that help us with our modern communication.

The first six points are put in the context of the Tao. The Tao is the idea of yin and yang (duality or coexistence). The two sides. (For those wondering about my word choice, the Dao and the Tao are the exact same thing. Tao is the westernized version of Dao when transliterated into Pinyin.)

The first six points that Guiguzi wrote about help us understand that there are two sides to every equation. This is balance. Neuro-linguistic programming helps us to understand ecology; it has an ecology check pattern. We find out if the change in a person's making is the change that is going to be most beneficial to them. It is a very Tao concept or idea. We can look back at our ancient wisdom and find applications for today.

Six Strategies of Guiguzi

1. **A door might be open, or a door might be closed.** Either way, there is opportunity that can be found on either side of it.

   That is profound because as we are working with people in therapy to try to help people make change, people often think that once a door is closed, the opportunity has been lost. We can show people by using the principles of Guiguzi that open or closed, yin or yang, there is opportunity on both sides of the door.

2. **Create connection everywhere.** Guiguzi taught us to reflect and respond to the spoken word to know about other people.

   We can create connection. We can maximize impact by reflecting or responding. In other words, there is a pattern here of being able to utilize either side of the experience that we are in.

3. **The intent of others can be used to get an advantage.** We can enter or exit any situation or scenario. We can do this at will. We can cause other people to pursue us.

   Alcoholics Anonymous calls itself a program not based on promotion but on attraction. In social media marketing efforts, I rarely spam the world with things that I do or with discounts on programs. Rather I simply engage and answer questions. In other words, what I am doing is looking at being able to enter and exit a wide variety of different scenarios and situations in a way that attracts people in the language of Guiguzi so that they miss you like a "mother trapdoor spider." Colorful language in the scrolls of Guiguzi.

4. **Breaking or mending.** This is significant in the context of relationships that sometimes break or are sometimes mended. It is important in the context of business. There is a beginning of business, and sometimes there is the end of business. Guiguzi tells us that connection can be created either by mending or breaking and suggests how to do this. He says earth and sky come together, and they come apart. They start somewhere, and they end somewhere. Connection can be created by understanding the natural laws of making, breaking, or mending.

5. **We can either agree or disagree.** Guiguzi tells us that captivating words are persuasive speech. How do you create in your communication the ability to truly develop rapport? Rapport is one of the key concepts of NLP. But 5,000 years ago, Guiguzi was writing about captivating words as a way of creating rapport. He says that to establish authority and manage business, one must investigate both differences and similarities, differentiate truth from a lie, and tell the essence of a speech from the embellishment of speech.

6. **Resisting or reconciling.** Guiguzi reveals it is impossible to make plans and strategies loyal to two sides which necessitates converting one side to the other. We can do that by either choosing to change and enter somebody else's frame of reference or by drawing them in, again with rapport, something NLP has focused on.

These are the first six principles in the scrolls of Guiguzi. And they are really fascinating to explore in light of our current understanding of NLP. These are all strategies very congruent with our ideas of NLP.

The next six ideas are singular ideas.

1. **Weighing, assessing capacity.** This is a strategy to calculate the big or the small and then strategize in accordance with the size of something. We do this in business. We can do this in love or romance. We can do this in the community and in relationships.

2. **Gauging.** Subtly gauging the desires of others and measuring the depth of our ability to probe them could be in the context of NLP as either the Milton model or the Meta model—very similar relationships here to gauging and assessing.

The scrolls of Guiguzi give us some remarkable ways to do

this because Guiguzi tells us that what is occurring as an internal response to somebody who will show external signs. We are looking for the signs of how it is that others are relating to us.

3. **Assessing.** The mouth is a mechanism, according to Guiguzi, which means one can shut down or open feelings and ideas. The eyes and the ears lend aides to the heart by which one can discern treachery or malevolence. And the three—the mouth, the ears, and the eyes—move in coordinate response and move in harmony to strengthen the Tao.

    Think of this in the context of what Bandler and Grinder taught: our primary representational system. Do we see the world auditorily? Do we see the world visually? Do we see the world kinesthetically? This is really an idea expressed by Guiguzi 5,000 years ago. We can understand and develop a deeper understanding of NLP, not by limiting our study of NLP and that which we know since the 1970s, but by applying it to the writings and the teachings of wise leaders from the beginning of time.

    The ideas of Guiguzi were considered to be so powerful that during the Mao Zedong era in Chinese history, the scrolls of Guiguzi were banned from being taught for fear that it could give people the wisdom to challenge the ideas of the ruling class.

4. **The principle of practice.** Guiguzi tells us that two parties who share the same aversion are close, but both of them get hurt. When two parties who share the same aversion estrange each other, one of them gets hurt. Therefore, when two people benefit each other and become close, people who cause losses to one another are estranged. And this is Guiguzi's explanation for what divides and what unites people. This again is directly related to the NLP ideas of motivation and the ideas of being able to move with or against different people.

5. **Begin with questions.** One of the key ideas of NLP is the transderivational search. When we are connecting and building rapport, we want people to look inside of themselves. A primary strategy for doing this is *questioning*. This is a technique that is very effective in psychotherapy, and professional hypnosis, and life coaching. Guiguzi tells us that all decision-makers begin with questions. He tells us that prudent use of questions brings about good fortune. Improper utilization of questioning brings about adversity. NLP shares this idea that questioning is a pathway to creating influence, creating rapport, and building alliances, which is what happened as the warring states were unified largely due to the philosophies of Guiguzi. His ideas really created a culture, changed a nation, and set history in motion. In fact, the ideas of Guiguzi are still used in the highest levels of political negotiation and business acumen in China today.

6. **Regions are governed by the principles of civility, savoir-faire, scrupulosity, and serenity enjoy prosperity without exception.** This is the sixth principle offered by these ancient scrolls. As a hypnotist, as a therapist, as a father, as a community member, I am trying to create serenity. Guiguzi gives us the principles that we can bring to our clients to help show them this.

There are so many traditions that come from ancient wisdom that we can apply with the lens or the model of NLP to find effective solutions for the people that come to see us and that we are working with on a professional level.

One of the classic books, which has long been on my desk, is *The Art of War* by Sun Tzu. Most people are familiar with it even if they have not actually read the book. What's fascinating is that Sun Tzu was a student of Guiguzi. The ideas that come from *The Art of War* come from understanding the Tao in the context of the way Guiguzi taught it.

Ancient to Modern Application

When you read *The Art of War,* it is in the context of military strategy. But why has this book endured for so long as a book that people have turned to for individual wisdom to help them experience success in life? Justin Deol at freedominthought.com has a podcast and an essay about *The Art of War.* In fact, I want to quote the first part of his essay without any edits because I think it is powerful. It shows us how a connection from ancient wisdom to modern applications is truly possible. He says,

> "I find my life fluctuates between two internal states, between war and peace. War feels like being fired, or falling sick, or getting a divorce. It feels like stress, wanting, desire. War feels like dissatisfaction, danger, being off-balance. Peace feels like finding a new job, becoming healthy again, or entering a new and loving relationship. It feels like satisfaction, commitment, satiation, or love.

> "War feels like being asked a question, and peace feels like finding an answer. And although I want everlasting peace, I find war to be the dominant state of my internal life. War acts as a necessary precursor to peace."

The essay, or YouTube animation, then goes into taking quotes from Sun Tzu's *The Art of War* and combines them with his personal experiences to create a set of nine principles. And this is what NLP does. Neuro-linguistic programming looks to exemplars. Sun Tzu helps us to identify a set of scalable, actionable patterns. You have probably heard of NLP patterns. Justin Deol did this by identifying nine key principles and then applied them to the war and peace we find daily:

1. War is always possible.

2. Look for the signs of war in your life.

3. Avoid war at all costs.

4. Pick your battles wisely.

5. Spend energy in war wisely.

6. Adjust the battle plan to end the war as soon as possible.

Think about this in the context of therapy and people who are warring with depression. This is what I love about NLP, the fast phobia cure. It is a strategy to end that war with anxiety quickly.)

7. Be prepared for loss.

8. You are stronger than you think.

9. Appreciate, enjoy, and nurture peace.

This is essentially a pattern, a strategy from *The Art of War* that has a modern application.

The Art of War is another ancient text with wisdom for us that we can quantify, replicate, teach to our clients, and act on.

It is exciting to me to see how ancient wisdom is filled with ideas from exemplars that we can still model today to find solutions to our real-world problems.

SECTION TWO

Concepts, Processes, and Approaches to NLP Life Coaching

Chapter 9
NLP Presuppositions

The beginning of understanding NLP is in understanding the assumptions that NLP practitioners make to utilize it in effective ways. It does not matter the context that NLP is being provided. This could be in communications between individuals. It could be in therapeutic environments, life coaching, or even parenting. It could be in business, sales, and leadership development. It could also be in working with the community. These assumptions are the assumptions that most NLP patterns, techniques, and ideas are rested on.

Neuro-linguistic programming is sometimes questioned by those in the academic community—can we prove that these techniques actually work? The problem with that approach is a multiplicity of techniques and an array of arenas or worlds, and the result is it is impossible to put everything in NLP to the test. There would have to be hundreds, if not thousands, of tests, and it would be almost impossible to quantify.

Neuro-linguistic programming is not theoretical. A theoretical approach looks to prove a hypothesis. Rather, NLP begins with certain assumptions. It is believed that most people who practice NLP would share the validity of these assumptions, but these assumptions are not trying to be proven by NLP. Some of these assumptions might be disregarded by some practitioners. Instead, these are simply accepted as guiding principles to help us do the work of NLP. It is this kind of flexibility that allows NLP to be so adaptable in so many different situations.

NLP Presuppositions

1. The map is not the territory.

We have an assumption about the world and the experiences that are in front of us. This is our mental map, but the reality is when we find ourselves engaged with individuals or situations or in the world around us, we discover that the territory sometimes is different from the map.

Have you ever taken out your phone's Global Positioning System (GPS), put in a location, and you start to head there, and you notice that the map or the GPS is deviating from a way that your intuition tells you that you should go? This is because Waze or Google knows that maybe there is an accident up ahead, or a road is closed ahead. The reality is the territory is different from the map. In NLP, this is a very important assumption because NLP can be flexibly applied in a number of different situations. If we find that one approach does not work, unlike the theoretical model, the presumption model allows us to simply flow with a different set of resources and skills to adapt to the situation that is in front of us in the real world.

That is why NLP practitioners in therapeutic environments, hypnotherapy, and life coaching find it such a valuable tool because we can equip our clients to function within the territory, not just with the projections based on what the map looked like to them.

2. It is better to have choices than it is to not have choices.

This means that everything we are doing in a coaching model and everything we are doing using NLP should be designed to give us, as leaders, flexibility and choices. The way we work with somebody can change in the middle of a session. But what this means for our clients is that we can help them open doors so that the only choice they thought they had in front of them becomes one of many choices they can access because of the techniques or the patterns or ideas of NLP.

This is one of my favorite things about NLP because it helps a person who often realizes that they are stuck between a rock and a hard place recognize that there are many opportunities for them and that the place is not so hard, and the rocks can actually be moved. Without a doubt having many choices is always better than having no choices. And in NLP, this is a presupposition that we work from so that we can help people to brainstorm, use their creative capacity, and tap into the resources that they did not know existed within them. We help them access new choices in just about any situation, whether that is personal, business, therapeutic, or within their community, family, or even in self-reflection as they look at the choices they have within their own life.

3. When people have choices, they will choose the choice that is best for them.

This is important because we might not perceive the choice they have made as being the best for other people, but people will choose the choice that is actually best for them. Sometimes we see somebody make a choice, and that choice does not seem to be good for them. It is important to realize this presupposition tells us that with the tools they have, at the moment they make that choice, they are ultimately choosing the option they believe is best for them. Perhaps it is the easiest to make or the most accessible to make. And it gives us understanding, empathy, and compassion. Those are the tools for helping people make change. The good news is that in life coaching and NLP, when people try and they make a choice that might not be the best choice for them in the future, we come up with tools, patterns, and ideas, to help them make different choices.

Each moment is independent of each moment. This gives us the ability to operate under the presupposition that people make the best choice they can at the moment that they make that choice.

4. People work perfectly.

People making the best choice they can at the moment is related to this fourth presupposition. One of the viewpoints that comes from the work of Milton Erickson was that people are not broken. People work perfectly. It is amazing to see people in our world who have had extremely difficult circumstances and scenarios and yet be able to rise from these experiences and these occasions. This is a presupposition that is important because what it means is that we can approach life coaching, not from a psychological or a psychiatric perspective, where we are trying to fix broken people and help them to become well after being unwell. In NLP modeling, what we do is see people as working perfectly. This means making the best choices they can in the scenarios that they can. We have a role in helping them to work perfectly and work efficiently and work in a way that can help them rise to their highest level of potential.

This is one of the things that really separates life coaching from psychotherapy. Psychotherapists are taking people with a diagnosis who are not functioning adequately and trying to get them to function at an adequate level. But in life coaching, we are taking people who work perfectly, people who are functioning at an adequate level, and we are helping them rise to their highest level of peak performance.

5. All actions have a purpose, or as the psychiatrist, R.D. Laing, said, "All madness has meaning."

In life, even the things that do not appear to be beneficial to a person are beneficial to them if they have taken action on that. Let us take an obvious example here, cigarette smoking. The side of the pack of cigarettes tells you it is not healthy. It says the product causes cancer, lung disease, emphysema, and may complicate pregnancy. In other words, this is not a good thing, and you shouldn't do it. But if you ask any smoker, who has that message in their pocket on their pack of cigarettes why they smoke, they will tell you they need to relax or need a break, or it helps them control stress. The reality is all behavior, even behavior that is unhealthy behavior meets a legitimate need.

In our coaching, this can inform us because when we see somebody who is doing something that we perceive as unhealthy to them, we can discover the legitimate need and then ask if there another way to help this person meet this legitimate need. No matter how maladaptive the behavior is or how bad the behavior is, in the language of psychiatrist R.D. Laing, the reality is that madness has meaning. That meaning should be honored and embraced so that we can help the clients we work with find ways of meeting their deepest needs through healthy behaviors and choices that help them live their best life.

6. All behavior has positive intention.

This is one of the more controversial presuppositions. In NLP, we look at short-term thinking versus long-term thinking. We look at *toward* motivation and *away from* motivation. The presupposition here is that when our clients are engaging in a behavior, the goal of that behavior is positive intention, not malevolent intention. This is an essential presupposition that can help us to understand the best ways to work with the clients who come to see us for life coaching, NLP, and therapy.

7. The meaning of communication is not just the message sent but the response that we get from that communication.

Many people will read this book because they want to become more effective communicators in business, in the community, the family, and in therapy. A lot of people look at NLP as a tool for enhanced communication. It is important to recognize that communication is not simply the words that are said but the way the receiver experiences the communication that was given. This is a good tool to help someone in self-reflection understand how their communication with the world around them can be more effective. They can study formula sentences, like a sort of communication—I feel, I want, I need—but the reality is the receiver's response to one's communication tells a person what the content of that communication was.

8. We have the resources within us, or we have the ability to create the resources within us.

This presupposition comes directly from Milton Erickson. That is that we have the resources within us, or we can create the resources within us that can serve us in any situation at any time. This book is going to be helping you to develop internal resources, resource states, and strategies that, to this point, you have not activated yet in your life. And then you will be able to passionately share those with other clients.

It is important to realize that when Milton Erickson was doing his work in medical hypnotherapy psychiatry, he wasn't trying to bring something from the outside to people to help them function at their best, but rather was trying to draw out that which was in them into their world so that they could live their very best.

9. Mind-body, conscious-subconscious.

These are divisions that we use to help us understand different ways of how we experience the world around us. The reality is, mind and body and conscious and unconscious are inseparable. The mind-body connection is a unified whole. This is an important presupposition because, in learning, we like to say this is the subconscious mind, this is the unconscious mind, and this is the conscious mind. But the reality is, mind is mind.

I have always said that if I were to ask a room full of people to draw a picture of the mind, most people would draw a picture of the brain, but the reality is mind is in every cell of the body, and mind and body are inseparable from one another. This is the idea of the Tao. This is not a new idea. This is a 5,000-year-old idea from the scrolls of Guiguzi.

10. We experience the world around us through our senses.

This is my favorite presupposition. We often talk about auditory, visual, and kinesthetic—sound, sight, and touch. These are the primary representational systems and the primary sensorial systems in which we engage in the world around us. But we also have many other senses. We have the five senses we learned in second grade. We have our touch, sight, sound, taste, and smell. But we also have additional senses. There are not just five senses. Seventh-grade science was wrong. We have proprioception. We have many other senses that we can tap into as ways of understanding the world around us. In NLP, a large emphasis has been placed on the auditory, visual, and kinesthetic model.

We are going to spend a lot of time in this book focusing on that and teaching that. But we are also going to recognize that there are many other ways to understand the world around us. But we have ultimately come from sensorial experiences, whether it is visual, auditory, or kinesthetic, the five basic senses, or the many other senses that we have.

11. Modeling success leads to excellence

If I want to know how to do something excellent, I should model and do the same things that people who are successful are doing. This is a presupposition of NLP. When a client wants to do something better, all we have to ask is who the exemplars are and who the models for success are in this endeavor. Then we can tap into the methods, approaches, techniques, experiences, and ideas of those who are successful, and we can then create excellence in our own lives and with the clients with whom we work. We can replicate those who are successful and create excellence in our own lives. We do not have to reinvent the wheel. People have gone before us in these tasks and created high levels of success.

12. The way to understand is to take action.

It is not enough to simply think in our own mind, but rather to have true understanding, to have depth in our lives. We need to take action because action creates repetition. The repetition leads to learnings, and these learnings lead to an understanding that can truly help us create success. You have probably heard it said that mastery of any task—playing the violin, the piano, or something else—takes 10,000 hours of practice. And that is why *to understand requires action* is a presupposition that not only NLP practitioners use, but teachers from around the world have focused on.

13. We can't *not* communicate.

We are always communicating. We are always communicating with those present with us, and sometimes we are communicating with those who are not present with us. Think of a family that has become estranged, and one person says, "I will never talk to you again." And five years or thirty years go by, years of silence, yet something is still being communicated. The reality is we cannot not communicate. We can be silent. We can close our mouths. We can choose to not speak, but we still communicate. Maybe three percent of our communication is, in fact, not the contents of the words that we use. Neuro-linguistic programming recognizes this.

In this book, I am looking forward to sharing more ideas from Chase Hughes on body language. Right now, he is the world-leading expert in really understanding behavioral analysis and body language. And I have learned so much from him over the years that these ideas, I think, should be shared in an NLP training program.

14. The person with the greatest level of flexibility is the person who holds the most power.

The person in any system, whether it is at work, in a family, or in a community, the person who has the greatest flexibility is the person who actually holds the power in any given situation, encounter, or experience. In life coaching, part of what we will be focusing on is helping people develop psychological flexibility.

15. There is no such thing as failure. There's only feedback. We learn from our mistakes.

The reality is there are no failures—only feedback and lessons that can be learned. I hear many people talking about their previous failed marriages. I was once asked how many failed marriages I'd had. The question caught me off guard because I never thought of any previous marriage as a failure, only as experiences that brought me to where I am today. This is important because many people are hard on themselves because they view their mistakes as failures, and their decisions as failures, and their life as a failure. There is no such thing as failure. There is only feedback. In life coaching, and business coaching, and in our families, we can help people realize that no matter how far down the scale they have gone, we can see how our experiences can benefit others.

These presuppositions are all very helpful, but they also have a very practical element to them.

Try this exercise now:

Think about a situation that you are facing right now, a choice that you need to make. Maybe it is one where you feel a little bit between a rock and a hard place and can only come up with one or two choices, and neither of them appears to be great for you. Or perhaps you recognize that there are a couple or even five choices, but the reality is endless choices abound in our world. It might feel like we only have one or two choices and that no option is a good option, or that we are limited to a couple of choices, of which some of them might have some upside.

This exercise is to brainstorm what your options are. One of my favorite things to do with a client when they are faced with a choice is to give them a blank piece of paper and a pen.

Write down thirty things, and I know it sounds like a lot, but thirty things you could do in this situation. They're not necessarily things you are committed to. They are not even necessarily things that you want to do or that you think are good, but I want you to write down thirty things that you could do in this situation. Some of them might even be absurd such as setting the couch on fire or never going back to that scenario or situation. Perhaps you are thinking you could release your anger, meditate, or communicate more assertively. The possibilities here are endless, but really most of us haven't stretched our brains when faced with choice. Consider the many choices that abound beyond those that are obvious.

When I write down thirty things that I could do, it always creates the resource state of creativity.

Now, look at those thirty things. Are there any things on that list you would be unwilling to do, or that would be unsafe, or illegal, or dangerous to do? Cross those out. Now maybe you have twelve or fifteen things left on the list. Of those things, is there anything on that list that you could do if you wanted to? Considering the twelve or so things that are left on this list, there are a couple of things that you could do if you wanted to. Circle five of those things and cross off the rest. Now you're down to five options. Of those five options, is there anything here that you would be willing to try? Is there anything on this list that you would be willing to lead with that could be your first attempt? Well, *it* is this one.

This was a simple brainstorming exercise in creating options, and it comes from the NLP presupposition that having options is better than not having options.

These presuppositions give us useful tools and exercises that we can engage in.

Let's go back to presupposition 14. The person with the greatest flexibility is the person who holds the most power. There are five things we can do to increase our psychological flexibility:

- First, we can engage our minds in new things, new learnings, and new opportunities. Often, flexibility comes from expanding our horizons and making our world bigger.

- The second principle for developing psychologically is to do something we have been doing but do it differently. It could be as simple as the way you dress. It could be as simple as a habit of putting your watch on the right wrist instead of the left. It really does not matter. The idea here is to do something differently.

- The third component of developing psychological flexibility is to do different things. Maybe try not wearing a watch, and instead use a pocket watch. What we are looking for is a way to do things differently.

- And the fourth principle is to do something different somewhere else, expanding our world, making the repertoire of possibilities much larger.

- To develop psychological flexibility, we can put this into practice by doing something different in different places, with different people, which gives us an opportunity to use a popular NLP pattern, T.O.T.E.—Test, Operate, Test, Evaluate.

Psychological flexibility and the techniques of psychological flexibility can be harnessed and accessed by really understanding these NLP presuppositions.

Chapter 10
Life Coaching Models

In this section, I will introduce some of the key ideas surrounding the idea of life coaching, executive coaching, health coaching, family life coaching, community coaching, and really any other type of coaching that you are going to be doing.

Coaching is a broad subject, and the reality is you can use coaching in a wide variety of different contexts using the skills that you are going to learn in this book.

The Role of the Coach

In this chapter, I will cover what the role of the coach is, what coaching model I utilize with my clients, and then begin to set you on a path of attaining some of the skills required to do effective coaching.

The role of the coach is that of a teacher and a trainer. That is really what a coach is if you think of an athletic coach, a little league sports coach, or a basketball coach. What they are doing is they are coming alongside the players. They are not playing the game themselves. What they are doing is teaching and training skills. The coach is looking at global skills such as the ability to run and have endurance. They are looking at micro-skills, the ability to hold a ball in a certain position or swing in a certain position.

As coaches, our role is to stand behind somebody making changes in life, help them attain the changes they want to by teaching them the macro skills, and to teach them the micro-skills that will help lead them to success.

As a coach, it is really important that you have done these things yourself first, which is why one of the hallmarks of transformational leadership versus any other form of leadership is to transform yourself first.

I am going to share a lot of ideas that you can utilize to coach your clients, but we want to apply these in our own lives. We want to test them out. We want to experience them ourselves so that we can find success in our own lives and then pass those along passionately to the clients that we work with.

The Focus

The focus of coaching is to help a person move toward the desired outcomes, the intentions they have, and the goals that they have. This is as opposed to the *whys* of what has been holding me back. Therapists spend time trying to figure out the whys.

And although this could be a relapse prevention tool to help people make lasting changes in any behavior, whether it is behavioral health, or whether it is in a behavior in business, or a strategy in communication, it is essential that we recognize that the primary aspect of how it is that we are going to be conducting our coaching sessions is by focusing on coaching toward reaching outcomes, intentions, and desires, rather than figuring out the whys of what has held a person back from success.

The Audience

One of the wonderful features of life coaching is you really have infinite ponds to fish in. When I was primarily doing family therapy, as a licensed marriage and family therapist, I was working with couples, or I was working with families in the context of addiction treatment, or I was working in community development within the context of family systems. Largely I was working with people who were not performing well and trying to move them to an adequate level of functioning.

The coaching model is entirely different. What it means is that we are often working with people who are functioning adequately and trying to move them to the highest level of peak performance. Because of this, my audience expands. I am not restricted to simply working with families or a specific role like the oldest child, or husband, or wife, or leader of the family system. Instead, I can use the skills that I have to work with executives. I can use the skills that I have to work with leaders and mentor people in business. I can use the skills that I have to work toward helping people to achieve sales growth. I can work within the context of the community, helping to foster a sense of cooperation and help an organization, not even just a simple individual, but an entire organization, to function more effectively and move at a speed required to adapt to change.

Therapy vs. Coaching

The wonderful thing about life coaching is that we can apply the skills that we have in NLP, the skills we bring to the table, whether that's business and accounting, finance and management, or whether that's communication and empathy, and emotional intelligence to the table, really in a wide variety of different situations. That means that rather than working within a limited scope, you can work with a multiplicity of people across a broad range of situations and circumstances and coach them to reach their highest level of peak performance.

As a therapist, I worked with dysfunctional individuals. I worked with people who were in crisis, trying to help them to resolve a situation that was at hand.

Coaching is a different model. If you go into coaching with the idea that you are going to coach people with post-traumatic stress disorder (PTSD) to no longer have PTSD, or you are going into coaching with the idea of coaching depressed people to no longer have depression, or helping addicted people no longer have an addiction, really what you are doing is therapy without a license.

Rather, we are working with non-diagnostic individuals. We do not have a diagnosis for these folks because there is no pathology. We are not trying to fix anything that is broken. Rather, we are endeavoring to help people achieve new levels of skill and apply those in the situations they encounter in the real world. As I mentioned before, this opens up our opportunity to help people achieve success. A coach focuses on performance and outcomes, whereas a therapist is almost always focusing on diagnosis and dysfunction. We could put this another way. We, as coaches, are dealing with self-improvement rather than with the idea of healing.

If you are going into coaching hoping to heal broken people, the reality is you are going to have a difficult time. But if you go into coaching with the idea that you are going to help people to improve themselves and to rise to their highest level of performance, you are going to find success as a life coach.

As a life coach, I find that this is not only a more enjoyable task for me, it is also a more profitable task for me. The dysfunctional client is often unreliable. The dysfunctional client often wants a third party to pay the bill for them. A person seeking self-improvement is by definition motivated, and they're willing to invest in their transformation. In 2006, I decided that I would no longer provide any form of psychotherapy, referring my clients who need psychotherapy out to somebody else, that I would only provide life coaching to individuals. The result? My fees increased dramatically with a motivated self-paying group of individuals because I had a bigger pot to fish in, and it was easier to fill my schedule.

Life coaching is a solution for those looking to help people to work, rise to their highest level of performance, and work with individuals in ways that help them improve themselves no matter where they are in the stages of life.

One of the aspects of coaching is we are working with stable individuals who are experiencing the natural processes of change and transformation and adapting their success to the ever-changing world that we live in. In my book, *Transformational Leadership* that I wrote in 2014, I talked about change being the natural state of things. Nothing ever stays the same. For my mental health clients in the past, this resulted in crisis. For my coaching clients, change, transformation, and even challenges are opportunities that they can seize upon to again rise to their highest level of peak performance.

I am going to share a coaching model with you. It will take some of the considerations that I just mentioned and put them in the context of a coaching model. What does coaching look like? How does it integrate with NLP? Why do these skills coexist? It is important to recognize that the skills coexist because rarely does anyone make an appointment with an NLP practitioner for NLP only. They are not seeking to have NLP "done to them." Rather, they make an appointment with a life coach to apply the principles of NLP within the context of a coaching model. There are other models that we can use NLP in. We can apply it in business. We can apply it in sales training. We can apply NLP in psychotherapy. We can apply NLP in leadership development and training. But essentially, I represent myself as a life coach helping people to achieve their highest level of peak performance.

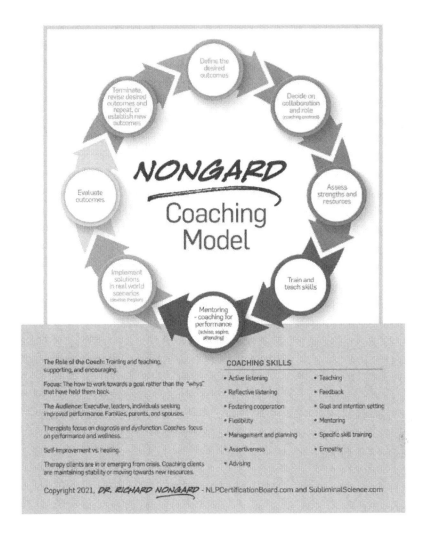

NONGARD
Coaching Model

Define the desired outcomes

Decide on collaboration and role (coaching contract)

Assess strengths and resources

Train and teach skills

Mentoring - coaching for performance (advise, aspire, attending)

Implement solutions in real world scenarios (develop the plan)

Evaluate outcomes

Terminate, revise desired outcomes and repeat, or establish new outcomes

The Role of the Coach: Training and teaching, supporting, and encouraging.

Focus: The how to work towards a goal rather than the "whys" that have held them back.

The Audience: Executive, leaders, individuals seeking improved performance. Families, parents, and spouses.

Therapists focus on diagnosis and dysfunction. Coaches focus on performance and wellness.

Self-improvement vs. healing.

Therapy clients are in or emerging from crisis. Coaching clients are maintaining stability or moving towards new resources.

COACHING SKILLS

- Active listening
- Reflective listening
- Fostering cooperation
- Flexibility
- Management and planning
- Assertiveness
- Advising
- Teaching
- Feedback
- Goal and intention setting
- Mentoring
- Specific skill training
- Empathy

Copyright 2021, *DR. RICHARD NONGARD* - NLPCertificationBoard.com and SubliminalScience.com

This is the model I use or the conceptualization of how I provide services. Here is the cool thing. Although there are probably ten stages or steps in this model, the reality is that we have the flexibility and the adaptability to alter this cycle at any time that would benefit the individual with who I am working.

It all begins with intake, and the intake process in coaching is about helping a client define their desired outcome. By entering into a coaching relationship, what do they hope the result is? Do they hope the result is increased sales? Do they hope the result is helping to develop a cadre of other leaders within an organization? Within the context of a family, is the desired outcome improved communication?

One of my favorite coaching clients was a couple who I worked with. Let's refer to them as Bob and Bertha. Traditionally in family therapy, Bob and Bertha would come in because they fight too much, or because Bob looked at internet porn, or because a child was acting up and they were fighting and could not agree. I was not doing couples therapy with them. I was coaching. Bob and Bertha had no diagnosis. There was no family dysfunction. Bob and Bertha came to me because, essentially, they had been highly successful in life. Bob was sixty-three years old, and Bertha was fifty-seven years old.

Thirty-five years before this, they started a dry-cleaning business with one shop. Over the years, that shop expanded in their geographic region, and they had seventeen shops, and they cashed out. They sold their business after thirty-five years for multiples of millions of dollars. The children that they had raised with the money they earned in the dry-cleaning business went to college, and all got married and started their own families.

By all accounts, it seemed to be the perfect family. Why would Bob and Bertha come to see me? Bob and Bertha came to see me because now they were in the next phase of their life, and they had created wealth because of their previous experiences in life. The outcomes they were trying to establish were multifaceted. How could they benefit the community with the wealth they had? How could they utilize their wealth to help their family in ways that would actually help the family rather than harm the family? They wanted to know how they could become involved in and create entrepreneurial studies and leadership opportunities for other young business people to learn the skills they had learned. They had spent so many years working together; how could they spend the last part of their life enjoying being with each other, rather than working with each other and the changing dynamics of their relationship?

There was no diagnosis. There was no dysfunction. There was no crisis. They were looking for specific desired outcomes, and we were able to enumerate what those outcomes would look like in my initial session with them.

When I do life coaching with people, my initial assessment is typically anywhere from an hour and a half to two and a half hours with either an individual or a couple. Or, if I am coaching with a C-suite, with a group of leaders, I will probably block off a three-hour time block for that. What I want to do in this phase of the coaching process is to find out where they are, where they would like to go, and what resources they are bringing to the table to move there. I also want them to have a chance to get to know me and decide whether I am the right person to help them on their journey.

Contract

When we decide to work together after the initial meeting, we move into the phase of creating a coaching contract. Life coaching requires a written contract.

In psychotherapy, I use a form called Informed Consent. It tells folks what my licensure is, what services I offer, and what the limitations of confidentiality are. In a way, if you are a therapist, this is a type of contract that you are familiar with. (To download the actual forms I use with my clients, visit

SubliminalScience.com/NLPbook.)

I use something similar but different in the coaching contract. I spell out and articulate clearly what my methods are, what the plan is, how we will utilize this, what my fees are, and how often it is we are going to meet. Because I am doing coaching, not psychotherapy, in my Coaching Contract, it details, "Although Richard is licensed as a marriage and family therapist, Richard provides no form of psychotherapy. In the event that psychological dysfunction must be addressed, Richard will refer you to a licensed provider who addresses those issues." In other words, I stick to my scope of practice, which is a coaching model rather than a psychotherapy model.

Once we have a contract, and we have clearly delineated roles, and the client knows what to expect, and I know what to provide, then we move into an assessment phase where I assess my client's strengths and my client's resources because I want to work from a strength-based perspective. I want to help people rise to their highest peak performance level, but I want to do that not by trying to fix what is broken or give them something from the outside that they do not have. But rather, I want to utilize the strengths and resources that my client brings to the table.

This is in alignment with our NLP presuppositions. Our clients have within them or can create within them the resources needed to address any issue.

We move into a phase where I, as the expert coach, am teaching them skills. I am teaching them and training them in the skills and the tasks necessary to achieve their desired outcomes. Just like a basketball coach will teach a kid how to dribble a ball right and shoot a basket, I am teaching and training the skills that will help them achieve their desired outcome. The skill might be creating a foundation or finding board members for that foundation in the case of this couple. For Bob and Bertha, I might be teaching them the skills of communication without task administration which is different than the communication they had for the last thirty years as coworkers. Now they are working as lovers. Now they are working as a couple.

I might be teaching them communication strategies and styles that are different from the habits they acquired in the workplace and applying those in the context of their morning coffee. I am teaching and training people in the life skills required to achieve the desired outcome. As I teach and train, it is not enough to simply show somebody, "Here's how you do it." We must supervise them. We must mentor them. We must be with them. We must attend to them. I always say that coaching is not about doing something *to* a person—it is about doing something *with* that person.

I remember my little league coach running up and down the basketball court. I remember my swim team coach walking up and down the side of the pool as I did my 500-yard freestyle when I was ten years old.

We are going to mentor these individuals. Mentorship is an essential skill. As we mentor them, they will hone their skills and abilities, whether these are emotional intelligences, social intelligences, business strategy, and communication strategy. There is a whole range of different skills that we can teach a person and mentor them. We are then going to be with them as they implement the solution. The coach doesn't say, "Well, I coached you. Go to the big game. Let me know how it goes." The coach goes to the game. The coach cheers them on. The coach continues to mentor and teach and encourage from the sidelines. And we are going to be there with our clients as they implement the solutions in business, family, community, social relationships, dating, and the world around them.

And then we go back to the NLP pattern T.O.T.E.—Test, Operate, Test, Exit. We are going to have them evaluate the outcomes. Did this work? And if it did, we are going to terminate the coaching relationship. Or we are going to revise the desired outcomes, teach and train different skills so that we can achieve what is most important to them. Or, we are going to say, hey, great. We accomplished those things. There are new goals to set, new outcomes to achieve, new vantage points to study and to look at and to implement. And we are going to enter back into an ongoing or a maintenance phase of the coaching relationship with them. Coaching can be short-term. Coaching can be over a period of six weeks or a month. Coaching can occur over the context of a year-long agreement or even a multi-year agreement. With some of the executives I have coached, it has typically been eighteen-month coaching agreements where we went through the cycle multiple times during the coaching experience or process.

The great thing is that the NLP skills that we will learn will help us define outcomes. The NLP skills are going to allow us to assess the strengths and the resources. The NLP skills will teach us what skills and strategies to teach a person, rapport, and specific patterns like a Swish Pattern. I can teach or train them in auditory, visual, and kinesthetic acuity. In my mentoring process, I am going to be mentoring from an NLP perspective, implementing solutions from this perspective, and be evaluating outcomes from this perspective. And so, you can see that NLP is not one part of this training, and life coaching is another part. Rather, the two coexist as one.

Coaching Skills

What are coaching skills? Coaching skills are the skills that we need as coaches to take somebody successfully through this process. They include skills of active listening, reflective listening, and fostering cooperation. Life coaching is a cooperative endeavor rather than me being the superior individual who is going to magically make you like me. I see myself as cooperating with an individual. I am the best me that I can be, the best coach possible, but I am helping them become the best them they can be, rather than the best me they can be. And I do that by fostering a spirit of cooperation with them. Flexibility is one of the skills that coaches need to guide somebody through this coaching model and assertiveness. It is very important that we use effective communication. We are more likely to get what we want or what we need or express our feelings when we use assertive communication. We will use effective and assertive communication throughout the coaching process to help people meet their deepest needs.

Depending on the type of coaching you do, you might need management, business, or supervisory skills. The reality is those skills come into play in any dynamic or any scenario or situation with an individual. Some management, leadership, and mentoring skills are all important parts of the coaching contract. Advising, teaching, training, and giving feedback are all skills that the life coach needs. The great thing about NLP is it gives us methods for giving effective feedback by understanding our client's primary representational system, how they view the world around them. And it gives several strategies for providing feedback in a way that is most likely going to result in the client adopting those ideas as useful tools for them.

How do you set goals? And, importantly, what is the difference between a goal or an intention? I am a big fan of intention setting, and I am less of a fan of goal setting. But do you know how to set the intention and set a goal, and do you know how to teach people to set a goal and to set an intention so they can activate their highest level of potential? Specific skill training is essential for the life coach to have as well as empathy. The work that we do should always be grounded on compassion, empathy, and wanting the best for those who are around us so that we can help people achieve their greatest level of potential.

We now embark on the pathway of implementing a coaching model with the clients that we work with.

Chapter 11
NLP Model of Communication

This is a foundational understanding that is really required to utilize NLP and life coaching to your greatest potential. The communication model begins when we have a real-world experience. It could be alone. It could be with other people. It could be something outside of our self. It could even be something within ourselves. But this is an awareness or a realization that this moment is different than any previous moment.

Filters

When these external events happen, what we do is take them through the filter of our five senses. The five senses are auditory, visual, kinesthetic, olfactory/smell, and gustatory/taste. The five senses are how we interpret and experience the world around us. We know there are more than five senses, but we will get into some of those as we proceed in this book. These other senses filter the experiences we have as well.

But we understand our world through a representational system or multiple representational systems. Every experience and every external event is filtered through the five senses that we have. This is why one of our coaching strategies isn't going be to simply match the primary representational system of the clients we work with, but actually to help them increase their acuity in the representational systems where they might lack functioning to their greatest level of potential. When the world experiences are filtered through the five senses, what we do is delete some of our thoughts, experiences, feelings, ideas, and interpretations. Or we distort our recollection or our memory. This is why two people can have the same experience and recall it completely differently. It is because it has been distorted through the filters that each one of us has.

We generate new ideas and new experiences. Some of what we believe to be true is not true because through the filters of our five senses, we have generated new understandings and insights, and some of them lead to a higher level of thinking. Some of them can lead to faulty thinking as well. We change our understanding or interpretation of external events. We transform these experiences, and this is what results in memories, decisions, beliefs, values, meta-programs, learnings, and experiences. All these come from how we filter through the five senses, the experiences of the world around us.

There is an important component of the mind here: the metaphor of the conscious mind and the unconscious mind. And as we filter the world around us, we delete, distort, generate change, and transform our understandings of the experiences into memories, decisions, meta programs, beliefs, values, learnings, experiences, either consciously or subconsciously, we create internal representations.

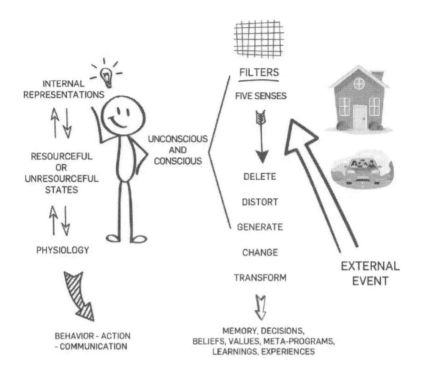

Internal Representations

Internal representations are really our worldview. Our worldview is how we see the experiences that we have experienced and how we would describe them to ourselves first and later to others. As we experience the internal representational systems that come about from receiving this information, filtering this information, deleting, distorting, changing, and transforming this information, processing it through the unconscious and the subconscious mind, we enter either resourceful states or unresourceful states. And an important concept in NLP is the idea of state and the ability to access both conscious and unconscious, resourceful and non-resourceful states in any given situation.

This results in a physiology of experience. This is where body language comes into play. In fact, ninety-three percent of our communication is nonverbal. It is not the contents of the words we use but the result of these internal representational systems. Are things near? Are they far? Are they heard? Are they felt? The resourceful or unresourceful nature of the states that are created because of this, and the physiology we have, is it congruent or incongruent, in any situation results in behaviors, communication, and action.

The way this model works and the way it is helpful for us is to understand that our clients in coaching have external events, things outside of them that become a part of their world. But every time our client experiences the world around them, it is immediately filtered. And as soon as it is filtered, it is changed, deleted, distorted, generated, transformed, becomes a memory, becomes a decision, becomes a meta-program, becomes a learning, and becomes an experience that is then filtered through the conscious or the unconscious mind. This results in lasting internal representations, resourceful or unresourceful states, physiology that produces action, reaction, communication, and behavior. Let's put this in the context of a specific experience.

As I was working on this book, I let my dogs out into the backyard. I wanted them to come inside quickly, but they wanted to bask in the beautiful sunlight of the day. So, I said, "Come on, dogs, come on, dogs." And the dogs did not want anything to do with listening to me. I marched out there, and I said, "Give me that stick. Stop playing with that stick. Come in the house!"

Eventually, I had to bribe them with a little piece of meat to come in. They did. They scampered in as soon as I had a little piece of meat for them. They were so excited they forgot they were enjoying the outside. I closed the door behind them. But that simple experience is filtered through our five senses. Could I feel the slimy ham in my hand? Could I see the dogs far in the distance? Could I hear the panting of the dogs who were busy playing? Could I even taste the ham residue on my hand? Could I smell the sweaty dog fur? All these experiences are filtered, and then we begin to delete, distort, generate, and transform. Perhaps one of the ways we do this is by scanning our previous experiences. I knew better than to simply let them out when I needed to accomplish something else.

Maybe it is filtered through our previous experiences of my dogs never seeming to listen to me or never seem to mind me. Or maybe it was filtered through my experience that these dogs are still puppies, and this was what puppies like to do. My memories, decisions, beliefs, values, and meta-programs about being a dog dad all come into play here, and it is filtered through both what I am aware of and what I am not aware of. The internal representation of this is an experience of being frustrated because I wanted to write before I had another appointment. And the internal representation is that anxiety that I knew I could have done something different. I could have put the dogs on their leash and just taken them for a short walk. It would have been faster and accomplished the same objectives. And, they would have been just as happy.

My internal representation was seeing myself walking the dogs, rather than frustrated by the back door, listening to the voice in my head telling me, *Richard, you never do anything right.* The states that were produced, in that case, were the *resourcefulness* of deciding that maybe some ham would trick them into scampering in the back door of the house and the *non-resourceful* state of being frustrated that I would not be able to write until later today. How was my physiology in that experience? I became authoritative. I stood up, and I told those dogs, "Look, I have a treat for you." The behavior I engaged in caused the dogs to go through the same communication process and respond with the response I wanted, which was to come in the door.

This is a very simple explanation of how this process works, but we can apply this to answer the, why are people acting unmotivated and yet say they are motivated? It is going to be a deletion, a distortion, a filter, the conscious, the subconscious mind, or the representational system. Why is it that people are on the precipice of success and then create fear and anxiety and respond by not following through? This communication and behavioral model answers a lot of questions for us. In this book, as we learn NLP and life coaching skills and strategies, we will return to this NLP communication model numerous times to truly create interventions that will be the most helpful to the clients we work with.

Chapter 12
NLP V.A.K.O.G.

R epresentational systems are a primary strategy and way of approaching people in NLP. This is expressed in NLP with the acronym V.A.K.O.G., which stands for our five senses. The first is **v**isual, the second is **a**uditory, and the third is **k**inesthetic. This is what we see, what we hear, including self-talk, and what we feel, including tactile sensations as well as experiences of emotional content that are felt from a somatic perspective.

Often in NLP, we focus on the V.A.K. because these are the easiest and most predominant sensorial experiences that people have. We often say people are visual, auditory, or kinesthetic. But there are other senses. The O is **o**lfactory, what people taste. And the G is **g**ustatory, what people smell. Those are the five senses that we learned about when we were in second-grade science. There are additional senses that we have, but when we are focusing on NLP, we are focusing on these five, and we are often focusing on really the first three, the V, the A, and the K.

Sensory Input

The way this works is simple. We have our sensory experiences, and we have sensory input. We have something that comes along, and we experience that visualization, those words that we hear, the feelings that we have, the smells, and the tastes that we have. And all of that comes into our conscious mind. We process that. We have already discussed distortions, deletions, and all sorts of things that change and transform the quality of our content. Experiences in the now become experiences in the past, and they are literally stored in what we refer to metaphorically as the subconscious mind. What is amazing is the power of the subconscious mind.

For example, think about the room where you lived when you were in first grade when you were six years of age. What was that room like? Close your eyes down for just a moment. Look at the wallpaper or the paint in that room. Look at the bed that was in that room. What were the bedspread, sheets, and pillow like in that room? What toys might have been in that room? Did you have ceiling molding in that room? Was the ceiling smooth, or was the ceiling textured? Was there a window? Was there no window?

It is amazing how easy it is to see the sights of that room when we were six years of age or even to hear the sounds of that room, the air conditioner, or music from down the hallway, or from a radio in the room. You can even smell that room. It is amazing how we can feel the kinesthetic qualities of that room, almost imagining ourselves being able to crawl in that bed and feel the weight of that blanket. Go ahead and open your eyes if your eyes are not open yet, and I imagine that room where you lived in first grade was probably thirty or more years ago.

You have not given any thought to that room, probably in the last twenty or forty years. And yet, when I suggested close your eyes and recall the room where you lived when you were six years of age when you were in first grade, it was instantaneous. We store our experiences in our subconscious mind, but what is amazing is they are literally on the tip of the tongue of the subconscious mind, and the subconscious mind is a vast reservoir of experiences that we can access at a moment's notice. It is really amazing. The sensorial input, the sights, the sounds, the touches, the scents, and the smells are stored experientially from a sensorial perspective.

This means that any time we can have an output, that output is almost always going to be based on these senses.

Our emotions are expressions of our sensorial experiences. We take the actions that we take because we can see ourselves doing something, or we can hear ourselves doing something almost always based on the sensorial output. It is the same with our communication. We communicate by saying to somebody, "I'd really like you to look at this. Look closely. I do not know if you can see what I can see, but you can visualize yourself five years from now, having taken action on this." The content of that communication was very visual. What does that tell me? That tells me that the primary sensorial experience that the conversation is relating to today comes from visual acuity. The conscious mind experienced the value of visual representation. The subconscious mind has stored the value of visual representation, and the output of my communication is primarily visual in nature. We say that people are primarily auditory, visual, or kinesthetic learners. They are also primarily auditory, visual, or kinesthetic communicators.

It is important to note that different senses can change in different situations and in different periods of time. A person might be very visual in one context and more auditory in another context, but we all probably have a primary or a favored predominant representational system. And this representational system is how we see the world, hear the world, taste the world, smell the world, or feel the world, and describe our experiences to others, how we interpret the world around us. We are probably drawn to others with whom we are in congruence because they are also functioning on the primary representational system plane. They are also visual, they are also auditory, or they are also kinesthetic.

In coaching, I find that almost everybody has a predominant representational system. Later I will share a test that I developed to help me with a new client in coaching to understand what their most likely predominant representational system is. It is a very useful tool and strategy. We can understand this by listening to them and hearing what they have to say and the way they describe scenarios and situations. They might come in, and they might say, "Failure to me feels like I have a boulder on top of me." There is our kinesthetic person.

Or they might say, "I'm always hearing myself say this . . ." There is our auditory person. When I am working with clients, I want to listen to the words that they are using that describe their problems because they are also telling me what their primary representational system is and how they experience the world, and how they predominantly relate to solutions. That does not mean that I cannot increase acuity in certain areas so that they have a more well-rounded approach to the world around them. But when I am first meeting a new client, I want to create rapport with them. I want to create congruence with them. And I want to be able to match their primary representational system in the instructions that I give.

You hear about miscommunication all the time. Put this in the context of couples. Bob says to Bertha, "Bertha, I don't know why you can't see it. It's right in front of your face. It's as if there's writing on the wall, and you can see it, but, but, but you just . . . you just don't understand what it means." And Bertha says, "Bob, you just don't listen to me. I'm sad time after time after time. It's almost as if your ears are closed. You're not hearing a word I have to say." Bob is very visual. He is using visual language. Bertha is very auditory, and she is using auditory language. What is interesting is that Bob and Bertha probably are not in disagreement. I have sat across the room from people who argue and argue nonstop, but they both would like the same thing. They are both actually on the same page. But because he is visual and because she is auditory in their communication, they're missing their points.

One brilliant avenue for working with couples in coaching is to help them understand the value of primary representational systems and how they can contribute to improving communication strategies.

V.A.K.O.G

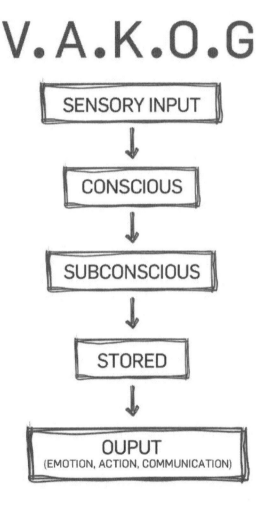

PREDOMINANT REPRESENTATIONAL SYSTEM
(SUBMODALITIES)

One of my favorite ways to describe the auditory, the visual, and the kinesthetic, or identify them is to ask them about shopping at Ikea. Even if you have not shopped there, you have probably, at some time or another, bought furniture in a box. And you bring the box home. You take the things out of the box. And there are fifty different pieces. When you build something like this, how do you do it? Do you look at the picture of the box and look at all the pieces on the floor and try to match the pieces on the floor to the picture on the box, and then build the picture? That is our visual learner.

Or are you the person who puts the pieces on the floor, grabs the instruction manual, and immediately starts to read step one, step two, step three, step four. That is our auditory learner. They are literally hearing. It is called transliteration. They are literally hearing the words that they read as a voice within their head, giving themself instructions, like somebody telling them what to do.

Or are you a kinesthetic person? Do you take the pieces, put them on the floor, kick the box off to the side, throw the instruction manual over the shoulder, and hold out which piece is the longest, which piece is heaviest? You hold the screw in your hand. Is this a longer or shorter screw, a narrower screw, or a smaller screw? You build the piece of furniture based on feeling the pieces. This is the Ikea furniture test that can help you to determine whether you are or whether your client is auditory, visual, or kinesthetic. It is not likely that you have somebody who is primarily olfactory or gustatory as their primary learning style, but there are some people.

It is interesting when people with primarily olfactory or gustatory styles find the perfect profession. A profession for them may be, for example, a wine taster or a chef where taste and smell become the way that they primarily see and experience the world around them. And we are grateful that we have those people in our world.

Something that is significant that we are going to get into later is the submodalities. These are the way the primary representational systems can become chunked down. For example, visual. Is it far? Is it near? Is it big? Is it small? Visualization. Is it colorful? Is it black and white? Submodalities are the qualities or the attributes of the primary representational systems, and they give us a tremendous number of different tools that we can use in coaching to elicit different responses.

"See," I might say to my client, "the color of the problem that you're experiencing—or an image of a previous life event, or the image of where you would like to go—and what your goal is, what if you change the image? What if you move it back? What if you move it closer? What if you make it colorful? What if you take the color away from it? And auditory. What if you add sound to the image? What is it? What would happen if you added feeling to the image, and it was three-dimensional, and you could feel the image? What would it feel like? Would it be soft? Would it be hard?" These are the submodalities. These are all important aspects of helping to communicate with individuals within the context of primary representational systems.

Later I will share with you a quiz that I use as a test or a tool that I developed to help me determine quickly what my clients are presenting with and how I can best build both rapport with them and help them to communicate, act, and feel in ways that are beneficial to them.

Chapter 13
NLP Swish Pattern

Now I want to share with you an adaptation of the famous NLP Swish Pattern. The Swish Pattern is where we take one representation of a person's experience, usually associated with a negative representation, and we swish it mentally into a new positive experience. This is often done in NLP as follows,

> Imagine you're in a movie theater. A movie is playing on the screen. It is the trauma, the difficulty, the stress, the things that you do not like, the things that are irritating you. Imagine a movie of that situation is playing on the screen. And right when it gets to the difficult part, freeze the screen. As you freeze the screen, look at the colors. Are they vibrant? Look at the people who are in this image. Look at the situation that is on the screen. Now that you are looking at the screen and you see that image imagine this to be a representation of the difficulty that you are trying to overcome. Now imagine in the very corner of that movie screen is a small postage stamp size image. And that image is a positive picture, a picture that is the antithesis of the stress that you're experiencing.

If a client, for example, was afraid to fly, that mental picture on that screen could be a jet flying through turbulent air, people screaming, stuff falling. That is their mental representation. They can hear the sounds. They can see the sights. They are praying in their head because they imagine the plane is going down. That is the representation that was so stressful to them. Over here in the corner is a little tiny image, a very small image that is positive. It is them flying through clear and unlimited visibility blue skies. They are in first-class rather than coach. They are comfortable. They feel secure. It is a great flight.

The NLP strategy is to have them put their finger on that postage-stamp-sized image of the positive experience and to *swish* it over the negative association or experience. We are instantly replacing negativity with something positive.

I use this variation of the Swish Pattern with many clients. For the last thirty years, I have used this with hundreds of people, and they all have a lot of fun with it.

A client might say to me, "When I try to look at one aspect of solving a problem, every problem is there. And it is bigger than I can comprehend. I have a sense of overwhelm."

I'll say, "The sense of overwhelm that you're saying is really all coming together in one experience. I would like you to take a piece of paper, and I would like you to take this box of colored markers and pens. And I'd like you to draw the image that you're seeing in your mind." It does not matter if these drawings are abstract or if they are very specific. It does not matter if they are art gallery quality renderings or if they are simply stick figure drawings. I will continue, "I want you to draw the colors, the shapes, the people, the scenarios, everything that feels like that sense of overwhelming."

Give them as much time as they want. They can have a lot of fun with this. I will give them another piece of paper. I'll say, "Now, I want you to draw the antithesis of that stressful picture. Draw the opposite of it. If you woke up this morning and everything was exactly the way you hoped it would be, what would that picture look like instead?" The same box of markers, another piece of paper, and let them go at it. Let them draw.

We are all very familiar with the remote control for the TV. We can change the channel at any time. So, I will ask my client to hold up the picture and to take a look at the images. To look at the images, to look at the stress, the overwhelm, the difficulty. Remember the difficult images on top of that antithesis image. And I will let them know that they can stay stuck picturing this in their mind, hearing those sounds, feeling those feelings for as long as they would like to. Or, if at any time they are ready to, they can click the remote control. They can simply change the channel to the antithesis image, to the image that would bring them a sense of security, an image of success, an image of confidence, an image of whatever resource state it is that they are trying to acquire.

Then, as my client leaves my office, I will usually crumple up that first picture and let them know that they have a homework assignment. And the homework assignment is to take the second picture, to stick it on their refrigerator, or tape it to the wall next to their computer monitor, or anywhere, and at any time they are having that sense of overwhelm or they feel trapped, they can change the mental channel to the antithesis experienced.

It is a valuable resource state to them rather than the non-resourceful resource state that they have been holding onto. This is just one application. I have used this in psychotherapy. I have used it in coaching. I have used it in professional hypnosis. I have probably used this, at one time or another, in a sales meeting. I'll say, "Draw a picture of you at the end of the month, when you haven't reached your sales goal. What does it look like? Is your boss in the picture? What else is going on? Draw an image now of wildly exceeding your sales goals. What would that be like? What would that image look like?" This can be a powerful interactive experience, where a client is literally putting the solutions in their own handwriting.

That is an effective strategy and technique that you can apply with your clients immediately to help them discover success.

Chapter 14
NLP Assessment of Primary Representational Systems

Before I begin my work with my clients, I almost always use two assessment tools. The first one is the Nongard Assessment of Primary Representational Systems. This is a tool that I use to help my client assess their own primary representational systems. Are they primary visual, auditory, or kinesthetic? The form is relatively easy to complete. The very first thing you should do is to do the assessments yourself. Discover your primary representational system.

The instructions that I give are very clear. "Each question has three choices. Although you may utilize any of these three choices in any of these situations, I would like you to pick the one and only one answer that would either be your first choice or the obvious choice or the one you would gravitate to first. It may be true that you would probably do some of the other things as well. But which one would be your first inclination, your first choice? Only one answer for each of the ten questions."

For example, question one. "When you are injured, what is your immediate response? Would you see the wound as if it were magnified? Would you hear the sound of the impact? Would you feel the sensation of pain?"

Or question nine, "When you give a speech . . . Do you talk with your hands? Would you hear yourself telling you what to say? Or would you speak slower than other people?

There are ten questions, each with three answers. Pick the one that is your first inclination, the one you would do first. Then add up all the As, add up all the Bs, and add up all the Cs. The group that has the highest number is your preferred or your primary representational system.

UNDERSTANDING
The Nongard Assessment of Primary Representational Systems

Use the following quiz to find out if your client is operating primarily from a visual, auditory or kinesthetic representational system.

Instruct the client to read each statement and consider the 3 responses A, B and C. Have them X or √ the response that most closely matches their thoughts on the subject of the question.

Once complete, you will add up the number of A answers = _____ the B answers =_____and C answers =_____. If the majority of the answers are A, their representational system is primarily Visual. If most are B, they are primarily Auditory, and if C, they are primarily Kinesthetic.

Of course, all people can access and use all representational systems, but we can usually identify the strongest.

This is information can be very valuable to you. For example, if you are trying to communicate or create a new induction for a new client, knowing their style can help guide the development of an induction that utilizes visualization, or auditory triggers, or feelings, to increase effectiveness. Matching representational systems of our clients is an effective tool for building rapport and overcoming resistance.

The Nongard Assessment of Primary Representational Systems Questions

The following quiz to find out if you operate primarily from a visual, auditory or kinesthetic (feeling) representational system.

Read each statement and consider the 3 responses A, B and C.

Mark an X or √ the one response for each question that most closely matches your thoughts on the subject of the question.

1.) When you are injured, what is your immediate response:

___a.) See the wound as if it is magnified.

___b.) Hear the sound of impact.

___c.) Feel the sensation of pain.

2.) When you spell a new or difficult word, do you:

___a.) Visualize it on a blackboard.

___b.) Sound it out.

___c.) Start writing it out.

3.) When you read, do you:

___a.) See images of what you are reading.

___b.) Have conversations with thecharacters.

___c.) Seek stories with action andbehavior.

4.) When you think, do you:

____a.) Imagine your thoughts as a movie.

____b.) Hear yourself talking to yourself.

____c.) Become distracted by external activity.

5.) When driving, do you:

____a.) Daydream in pictures.

____b.) Listen to talk radio.

____c.) Rock out and dance.

6.) If you buy an assemble-it-yourself project,what do you do:

____ a.) Look at the picture on the box.

____ b.) Read the directions out loud.

____ c.) Just start building and complete it by trial and error.

7.) Which is more appealing or interesting to you:

____ a.) Artful Images of beautiful people.

──── b.) The sounds of a sensual voice speaking.

____ c.) The feeling of human touch.

8.) When you go to movies or watch TV, do you:

____ a.) Prefer rich scenery of distant places.

──── b.) Enjoy the dialog of heavy movies like courtdramas.

____ c.) Get bored and wish you could go dosomething else.

9.) When you give a speech, do you:

____ a.) Talk with your hands.

____ b.) Hear yourself telling you what to say.

____ c.) Speak slower than other people.

10.) When relating to others, do you:

____ a.) Imagine them taller, fatter, further, closer,or different in any way; or pay particular attention to unusual features they possess.

____ b.) Find it easy to follow the stories, jokes and conversations with others without feeling lost.

____ c.) Move toward them, feeling their energy.

A answers =____ B answers =____ C answers =____.

I have my clients complete this online before they ever make an appointment because it gives me a good insight into their primary representational system.

It is an excellent tool for you in coaching, using the V.A.K.O.G. method or approach that NLP teaches.

You can access a free easy to print version of this on my webpage at: SubliminalScience.com/NLPbook

Strengths and Resources Inventory

The Nongard Strengths and Resources Inventory is a tool that I developed in either 1993 or 1994, and I updated it probably about six years ago. The Strengths and Resources Inventory asks clients to identify the strengths they have in six categories of their life. The strengths are the internal characteristics and qualities: trustworthy, loyal, helpful, friendly, courteous, cheerful, thrifty, brave, clean, reverent.

What attributes about them do they have that can help them to problem-solve? Resources are the things outside of myself. I have a car. I have a résumé. I have a professional license. I have a certification from the ICBCH. I have references. What are the resources that I have—the things outside of me—that can help me problem-solve.

When I have a new coaching client, I want to do what I want to do right off the bat because I want them to tell me what is right with them. I use an approach called Positive Psychology, or Appreciative Inquiry. Positive Psychology is the term we use in coaching individuals. Appreciative inquiry is the term that we employ in corporate situations and scenarios, which is an approach that does not try to fix what is broken.

Therapists—mental health professionals—are trying to take a person who is at a dysfunctional level and move them to an adequate level of functioning. In coaching, we are trying to take what is right and help them rise to their highest level of peak performance.

I am focusing on what is right rather than what is wrong. I am not trying to fix what is broken but rather compensate for deficits or difficulties by activating and utilizing my clients' strengths and resources.

It is a whole lot easier to use what is right with a person than to try to fix what is wrong with a person. For example, if you were to ask me what my greatest deficit is, I would tell you that I struggle with organization. I am one of the most unorganized people on the planet Earth. My strength is delegation. I see big pictures and leave the details to somebody else.

I have learned to overcome or compensate for my deficits by using my strength and then partnering with those who are resources to me to help me solve any problem.

The Strength and Resources Inventory is a self-assessment. Your clients can complete it and bring it to their session or scan it and send it back. Or you could create a custom form using Gravity Forms— a WordPress plugin to create forms to collect information—out of this if you wanted to. You can access a printable version of this at SubliminalScience.com/NLPbook.

- The first area is: What do you possess or have access to? These are resources.

- Area number two: Make a mark next to any of those. These are strengths that apply to them.

- The third are things that they have or can do. There are twenty-four things in the fourth box. I want them to pick the six that describe them best.

- Area number five: Read the entire list first. Pick the four that describe your best areas of interest or ability.

- And number six: Put a mark next to any or all the statements regarding those people who you think would be willing to help you to reach your goals.

This helps me to define the situational supports that are available to them. I have found that the information it provides serves me well. And it aligns with my approach of trying to use what is right rather than to fix what is wrong. I am using NLP under the assumption that people work perfectly, have strengths and resources, and have the resources inside of themselves to reach any goal that is important to them.

NSRI - Nongard
Strengths and Resources Inventory
Copyright © 2014, Richard Nongard.

Name: _____

Date: _____

ID #: _____

1/PUT Make a mark next to any and all of the following that you possess or have access to:

- [ ] Close friend
- [ ] Reliable transportation
- [ ] Pet
- [ ] Internet access
- [ ] Stable living environment
- [ ] Uniforms and clothing
- [ ] Healthy food sources
- [ ] Primary care physician
- [ ] Source of income

2/ISO Make a mark next to any and all of the following that apply to you:

- [ ] Can solve problems
- [ ] Can follow directions
- [ ] Can give clear directions
- [ ] Can work well in team
- [ ] Can work well independently
- [ ] Can listen well
- [ ] Can express thoughts or feelings
- [ ] Can create plans
- [ ] Can develop creative options

3/EJS Make a mark next to any and all of the following items that you have or can do:

- [ ] High school diploma or G.E.D.
- [ ] Military training
- [ ] Vocational or technical certificate
- [ ] College degree or higher
- [ ] Resume
- [ ] Management or supervisory experience
- [ ] Volunteer or charity work
- [ ] Job history more then 6 months
- [ ] Job history more than 2 years
- [ ] Can pass alcohol or drug screenings
- [ ] Able to use typical business communication skills
- [ ] Appropriate attire
- [ ] Able to learn new skills easily

4/PAA Read this list of 24 items before marking any spot. Then mark the 6 items that you think best describe you:

- [ ] Creative
- [ ] Curious
- [ ] Open-minded
- [ ] Inquisitive
- [ ] Wise
- [ ] Brave
- [ ] Persistent
- [ ] Honest
- [ ] High energy
- [ ] Loving
- [ ] Kind
- [ ] Aware
- [ ] Team player
- [ ] Fair
- [ ] Leader
- [ ] Forgiving
- [ ] Humility
- [ ] Careful
- [ ] Impulse control
- [ ] Appreciative
- [ ] Grateful
- [ ] Optimistic
- [ ] Humor
- [ ] Spiritual

5/PIA Read the list first. Then mark 4 of the following which best describe your interests or abilities:

- [ ] Cooking
- [ ] Playing sports
- [ ] Exercise
- [ ] Building things
- [ ] Music
- [ ] Arts and crafts
- [ ] Games and puzzles
- [ ] Singing
- [ ] Reading
- [ ] Writing stories or poems
- [ ] Dancing
- [ ] Travel
- [ ] Family time
- [ ] Community involvement
- [ ] Religious services

6/SSS Make a mark next to any and all of the following who you think are willing to help you at this time:

- [ ] Mother
- [ ] Father
- [ ] Sister
- [ ] Brother
- [ ] Step-parent
- [ ] Grandparent
- [ ] Other relative
- [ ] Best friend
- [ ] Close friend
- [ ] New friends
- [ ] Boss or supervisor
- [ ] Co-worker
- [ ] Religious leader
- [ ] Neighbor
- [ ] Support group
- [ ] Mentor
- [ ] Coach
- [ ] Counselor or therapist
- [ ] Spouse
- [ ] Medical professional

Chapter 15
The Coaching Agreement

I am providing you with the text for a sample Coaching Agreement at the end of this chapter. It is a sample because you need to adapt this to the type of work that you are doing, the type of fees you have, and the setting or situation where you are working with clients, whether it is an office or online. It is important to note that all forms can be adapted to online work. When I am building a website, and I want to use online forms, I will use Gravity Forms as my tool for creating an online version of this. It asks for the questions and answers and an electronic signature. Electronic signatures are as valid as real signatures.

The coaching contract is important because what the Coaching Agreement does is really lays out our role as a coach. It separates our work from other consultants or psychotherapists, or others who are helping a client make decisions. This can be adapted based on your own experiences, the type of clients you work with, and the settings you see people.

The sample Coaching Agreement is between the client and you. And you can edit the text of my Word document and use it as a template to generate your personalized coaching form. It is really important that you use a Coaching Agreement form. You want what we would call in therapy "informed consent." In other words, I only provide services that my clients know the price of and what it is that they are going to be doing, and the methods that I use.

In the first session, because of this coaching agreement form, my client will not mistake professional coaching for psychotherapy or counseling services. The very first statement is, "The three primary outcomes from this coaching agreement that I desire include [one, two, and three]." I want to know, straightaway, what my client hopes to accomplish entering into this coaching relationship with me, their coach.

The next paragraph or two defines the nature of coaching, understanding that the coaching service is informed consent.

> The techniques and the methods that I use include problem-solving training, modeling success, intention, goal setting, and exploring options for moving toward my goals. The services Dr. Richard Nongard provides are considered non-therapeutic. And no form of diagnosis, psychotherapy, or counseling will be provided. If either my coach or I determine the need for mental health services, I agree to ask for a referral to a licensed healthcare provider or agree to accept the referral provided to me by my coach.

> I understand that coaching is a partnership that requires collaboration, honesty, and effort on my part to manifest the outcomes. The purpose of our sessions is to engage in creating options, both personally and professionally, and to learn new skills that will help me to acquire the desired outcomes through this service. My coach will support me in creating strategic plans and actions to reach the goals. I understand it is my responsibility to implement the strategies and plans. And I will request of my coach any support or guidance needed to assist me in this outcome.

Remember, they are signing this agreement. And then, there is a line that describes the client's ability to terminate the relationship. This is important too. At any time, my client can terminate the coaching relationship. They can ask for a referral. They can simply no longer participate in the coaching process.

The next section deals with my schedules and fees. It is critical that your client knows, at the beginning of services, how often you are going to meet, where it is you are going to meet, and for how long. What is the duration? Is this a six-week commitment? Is this a six-month or twelve-month commitment? And how long will each of the coaching sessions be?

I outline in the Coaching Agreement exactly what my fees are, how many dollars per hour they are going to be paying me for the service, or what the total cost of the solution is going to be.

I also let them know that there are additional fees. These could include communications, texts, emails, consulting, preparing reports if I am providing business coaching, and that they will be billed in one-sixth of an hour increments, rounded up to the nearest one-sixth of an hour, for any other form of communication or work that I am doing, for example, traveling. With many of my business and executive coaching clients, I am actually meeting them in their place or wherever they're engaged in business. And that can be in other cities. Clients agree to be charged for travel time, mileage, meal expenses, and lodging at the per diem price that has been established.

Confidentiality and Release of Information are also part of the Coaching Agreement. I want to spell out that a life coach, an executive coach, is neither a priest nor a lawyer.

You might be a priest, or you might be a lawyer. Even if you are a priest or a lawyer, or a therapist, you are providing services in the context of life coaching. And so, you do not have the same level of confidentiality that you might otherwise have. It is not considered a privileged relationship. Whereas an attorney has the attorney-client privilege and does not have to reveal to the court the nature of their conversations with their client, the reality is courts, in the discovery phase, will require you to provide information.

I let my clients know that I will keep business and personal information acquired confidential. I will only discuss or disclose when there is written consent to a third party that my client provides in advance. But I let them know that the courts likely will not protect the confidentiality of life coaching services.

And, in the unlikely event that information records are required by a court or subpoenaed, information will be provided. Again, I want to discuss confidentiality at the outset. They can have full confidence that I am not going to talk to their husband or their wife or their boss about the coaching contents unless written permission to provide that information exists before I provide that information.

There is a cancellation policy. This sets out my policies about whether there is a no-show or if they are late.

There is a section disclaiming my liability for actions taken, decisions that are acted on it, and limiting my liability to the fees paid for the professional coaching services. That being said, I am not a lawyer, so do not take legal advice from me.

As I understand it, to a large extent, these forms that the client signs—waivers that release me from liability—really are not enforceable on a practical level, but they do set a precedent or an agreement that my client has agreed to, and that could be helpful.

The next paragraph is particularly useful for dispute resolution. If there is a dispute, we will mediate that dispute. If a dispute between my client and I is not resolved through mediation, then the prevailing party will be able to cover the costs of defending themselves in the event of a civil suit.

It is important because it is something the client has agreed to and is very helpful in determining whether or not an aggrieved client will pursue, which, by the way, has never happened to me in thirty years.

A paragraph on where the applicable law will be applied is essential to include. I live in Texas, and I file in Texas even if my client whom I meet on Zoom is in Montana.

Finally, the document includes a spot for the client's signature and name.

The purpose of the Coaching Agreement is to create professionalism. It creates clear expectations about the services that will be provided. It is to make sure there are no disagreements regarding fees or billing for ancillary services or missing a session.

The more we can discuss ahead of time, the more problems we can alleviate later. One of the great benefits of this coaching form is it helps establish a cooperative relationship.

As a coach, I view myself as doing something with my clients. I see myself as coming alongside them, coaching, sharing, and encouraging them, but it is the client who is doing the work. And this Coaching Agreement reflects that.

Sample Coaching Agreement

I, _____ am choosing to participate in life-coaching with Dr. Richard Nongard. The purpose of this coaching will be to focus in this area of my personal performance: _____.

The three primary outcomes from this coaching agreement that I am desiring include:

1.)

2.)

3.)

I understand that these coaching services include problem-solving training, modeling success, intention and goal-setting, and exploring options for moving towards my goals. The services Dr. Richard Nongard provides are considered non-therapeutic and no form of diagnosis, psychotherapy, or counseling will be provided. If either I, or my coach, determines a need for mental health services, I agree to ask for a referral to a licensed healthcare provider or agree to accept the referral provided to me by my coach.

I understand that coaching is a partnership requires collaboration, honesty, and effort on my part to manifest the desired outcomes. The purpose of our sessions is to engage in creating options both personally and professionally and to learn new skills that will help me acquire the desired outcomes of this service. My coach will support me in creating strategy, plans, and actions to reach my goals.

I understand that is it my responsibility to implement strategy and plans, and that I will request of my coach any support or guidance needed to assist me in this outcome.

I understand the I may terminate or discontinue the coaching agreement at any time.

Schedule and Fees:

All fees have been explained to me in advance. This agreement will commence on _____, and will continue through _____.

My meeting with my coach will occur:

_____ Daily _____ Weekly _____ Monthly

The time will be limited to: _____ Minutes per session.

Additional fees will be charged at the hourly rate of _____ billed in 1/6 of an hour increments for phone calls, online meetings, email, texting and any other form of interaction and rounded to the nearest 1/6 of an hour increment.

Clients will be charged for travel time, milage, meal expenses, lodging fees, and other travel expenses related to providing these services at the daily per diem established.

Confidentiality/Release of Information:

I understand that my coach will keep business and personal information acquired about me confidential and will only disclose information to a third party about the content of the coaching sessions when written permission is provided by the client in advance. Clients should know that there are limits to confidentiality and that courts will likely not protect the confidentiality of this service, and in the unlikely event information or records are required by a court, information about these services may be subpoenaed and requested information will be provided.

Cancellation Policy:

If I am unable to meet at the designated time, all cancellations not within 24 hours, or no-shows will be charged the full amount of the service.

Limited Liability:

Except as expressly provided in this Agreement, the Coach makes no guarantees, representations orwarranties of any kind or nature, express or implied with respect to the coaching services negotiated, agreed upon and rendered. In no event shall the Coach be liable to the Client for any indirect,consequential, or special damages. Not withstanding any damages that the Client may incur, theCoach's entire liability under this Agreement, and the Client's exclusive remedy, shall be limited to theamount actually paid by the Client to the Coach under this Agreement for all coaching servicesrendered through and including the termination date.

Dispute Resolution:

If a dispute arises out of this Agreement that cannot be resolved by mutual consent, the Client and Coach agree to attempt to mediate in good faith for up to 45 days after notice given. If the dispute is not so resolved, and in the event of legal action, the prevailing party shall be entitled to recover attorney's fees and court costs from the other party.

Applicable Law:

This Agreement shall be governed and construed in accordance with the laws of the State of _____, without giving effect to any conflicts of laws provisions.

Client Name: _____

Client Signature: _____

Date:_____

Coach Name: _____

Coach Signature: _____ Date: _____

Chapter 16
Client Personal Information

The Client Personal Information form is a couple of pages, and it asks my clients some questions. Before I provide any service to my clients, I want them to answer these questions. What is interesting is that not all the questions are always answered by all clients. We can adapt or change these questions depending on whether we are doing life coaching, executive coaching, providing hypnosis coaching, or any other form of service, such as community development coaching.

It is important to note that what is on the form is important, but what is not on this form is also very important. The client will usually talk about some of the things that are missing. The form simply asks for the date they are completing it, their name, address, email address, preferred telephone contact, date of birth, age, employer, and the type of work that they do.

I am interested in the work that they do. A person typically spends a third of their life asleep, a third of their life at work, and a third of their life doing something else. A lot of people have issues and difficulties in managing the boundaries of their work life world.

The questions begin with asking what their three most resourceful personal strengths or characteristics are. Notice I do not ask what the three problems are that they are facing. I am far less interested in the problems a person has than the solutions they have.

I always lead with, "What are your strengths?" I'm asking what's right with them rather than what's wrong with them. What I have noticed, though, is that my clients give me this form back, and they have written one, two, or three things down. They're able to identify three strengths, resources that they have. But a lot of folks struggle with looking at what's right. I *require* my clients to complete all three things. The three answers are very important.

When I get stuck in coaching, when I am not sure what to do next, I review their strengths and resources. It is easier to teach somebody to use the resources they have in the context of new situations than to bring outside resources they do not yet have or possess into the new situations and scenarios.

One of the points that I want to stress here is what is not on this form. I do not ask about their medical history, recent surgeries, or medications they are taking. Those questions are not on my intake form because I am not providing any form of healthcare. I am a life coach, an executive coach, a business coach, a community development coach, a personal development coach, or a trainer. I am not a healthcare provider in this context.

If I have these questions on my form, it could be construed that I must be providing some type of medical intervention or diagnosis or answer or support. It is not essential to me in the beginning, and my client will tell me those things that are important.

Let's take a look at some other questions found on the form. "When completing our coaching, how will you know that life coaching has been successful to you?" That is one of the most significant questions on this form. How will they know that this was successful to them? Their answer to this question tells me what my coaching should be aiming for.

In NLP coaching, we are always using our client's resources and helping them to become the best them they can be, rather than the best me I think they can be.

"What outcomes would you like to accomplish through coaching?" "Have you engaged in life coaching in the past? Describe for me that experience." "What's your primary goal in meeting for life coaching?" "Do you understand the nature of the relationship that coaching is a goal-directed collaboration to help you accomplish your goals, and that is not healthcare, psychotherapy, or counseling?" I have documented, again, that the work that I am doing is not a form of healthcare regulated by state boards.

"What are your current limitations in achieving your desired goals?" "Who are the situational supports, the people in your world, both personal and professional, that can help you to accomplish your goals?"

I am a paid temporary professional in my client's life. My goal ultimately is to help my clients become a part of the world around them, the people in their families, their community, and their work. I want them to identify right here at the outset who those people are. And if they cannot identify anybody, I know one of the tools that I need to use in coaching is to help them build these relationships. If they are able to identify people, I now know as I go through the process of NLP coaching with them who can be situational support so that when I practice with them in my session, they can implement it in their real world. "What do you want me to teach you?" "What skills do you think will help you move toward your desired outcomes?"

You can adapt the Client Personal Information form. You can make it as long as or as short as you want to. I do not ask if they are married, divorced, or have children. I do not ask about their sexual orientation, shoe size, and religion they grew up in. These may be very significant in the process of life coaching but, in my very first session with them, I really want to focus on their strengths, the resources, the situational supports, the who that are in their world. What desired outcomes do they have? How would they know if they were successful? And what skills can I teach them to achieve that which is most important to them?

The Personal Information Form and the Coaching Agreement are written records, both completed before we have our first session, that shows that you have clearly not represented yourself outside of your scope of practice.

Client Personal Information

Date: _____

Name:

_____

Address:

_____

_____

Preferred Contact Telephone# _(_____)_____

Email: _____

Date Of Birth: _____/_____/_____ Age: _____

Employer: _____

What type of work do you do?

_____

What are your three most resourceful personal strengths or characteristics?

    1.)

    2.)

    3.)

When we complete our coaching, how will you know that life-coaching had been successful for you?

What outcomes would you like to accomplish through coaching?

Have you engaged in life-coaching in the past? Describe the outcome of that experience:

What is your primary goal in meeting for life-coaching?

Do you understand that life-coaching is a goal directed collaboration to help you accomplish your goals and is not healthcare, psychotherapy, or counseling?

What are your current limitations in achieving your desired goals?

Who are the situations supports in your personal or professional life that can help you accomplish your goals?

What skills would help you move towards your desired outcomes?

Chapter 17
Transderivational Search

This is one of my favorite concepts in NLP and one of the concepts I find to be most valuable. I can use this with a lot of different coaching clients. I can use this with therapy clients. I can use this with my own family, or even when I meet somebody new. It has also been a useful tool for me in sales and elsewhere in business.

A lot of ideas that we call NLP are ideas that have been developed within other organizational systems of understanding behavior and communication. The book *Psycho-Cybernetics* by Maxwell Maltz has long been one of my favorite books. This book articulates a lot of ideas related to the power of the transderivational search.

The transderivational search is what is sometimes referred to as the "fuzzy match." It is where a person has to look inside of themself. It is abbreviated to TDS. When you see TDS in NLP, it is referring to the transderivational search, the fuzzy search inside.

Literal Match

What I mean by a fuzzy search inside is that if we are looking for a literal match, for example, two plus two equals four. If I ask somebody what two plus two is, we know what answer they should give, and they know what answer they should give. What we are really looking at here is contextual math, even though it is linguistics rather than mathematics, where a person has to look inside of themselves and find the context where the match is. What I mean by this is for them to consider "[This] means [this] in this situation." And it could be different in every situation.

Contextual Matches

Contextual matches mean this is the match in the context of this time or this experience. These are tools that help us to understand what transderivational search is all about.

Hallmarks

A hallmark of a transderivational search in communication is ambiguity. We are intentionally being nonspecific when we are interviewing or speaking with others because we want them to attach the meaning that is most important to them. This was an idea that Milton Erickson discussed in *Professional Hypnotherapy*. It is the idea that the client has the answers inside of them, and it is up to us to elicit them so we can give ambiguous hypnotic suggestions. The result is that the client will attach the meaning that is most important to them.

Ambiguity is our friend in transderivational search. Rather than asking questions that allow for yes/no answers, always ask open-ended questions where a person must look inside of themselves before they can draw the answer out. The concept here is having the client look deep inside of their experiences, their five senses, their previous learnings, and their subconscious mind to find the answers.

T.D.S.

TRANS-DERIVATIONAL SEARCH
(THE FUZZY MATCH)

LITERAL MATCH	CONTEXTUAL MATCH	HALLMARKS
2+2=4	(This) means (this) in (this) situation	• Ambiguity • Open-ended • Looks inside

QUESTIONS:

What will you be thinking tomorrow?
The many options you have....

What emotion do you struggle with most?

You need something, don't you?

WORDS

• Recall
• Find
• Discover

Words

Words and phrases that are very powerful or that can elicit a transderivational search are words like, "What experience do you recall when . . . ?" This causes a person to have to look inside of themselves to see if there is an experience that they recall, or an emotion, or anything else related to whatever the topic is. A phrase like, "I wonder what you would *find* if . . .?" is very powerful. *What is it I am finding?* I must look inside myself to discover what it is that I find or what I found and discover is another powerful world. In the context of sales, "What could you discover if you owned an electric vehicle?" In another context, "What could you discover if you allowed yourself the freedom to experience emotions differently now than you have before?" The client would have to look inside of themselves to see what they could possibly discover. The book *Encyclopedia of Positive Questions: Using*

Appreciative Inquiry to Bring Out the Best in Your Organization by Diane Whitney, David Cooperrider, Amanda Torsen-Bloom, and Brian S. Kaplin has long been one of my favorite NLP books, even though the word NLP is nowhere to be found within its pages. Almost every question used as an example in Appreciative Inquiry in the book creates and fosters a transderivational search.

Here is an example of one of the questions: "What was it about you, your coworkers, and your organization that facilitated the seamless service in those positive customer reviews?" I must look inside and see *me*. I must look inside and see my coworkers. I must look inside and see the organization to answer the question.

"What is it about the situation that most supported you in delivering on this one success?" Again, I must look inside of myself. I must review the situation to determine what it is. And by looking inside of myself, that comes from the deepest levels of awareness. The answers we get are higher quality answers that help us help people make connections to choose options and develop pathways into success.

Let me give you a few examples of other questions that we might ask—in therapy, coaching, business, sales, and even in our family structure. "What will you be thinking tomorrow when . . .?" "What will you be thinking tomorrow when you get out of bed after you've made this big change?" I must look inside myself to see what it is that I will be thinking tomorrow. This is powerful because if I can think it, I can create it. And if I can create it, I can step into tomorrow already with action having been taken at least on a mental or metaphysical level.

Here is another excellent question or a way of phrasing that is particularly useful: "The many options you have include what things?" Well, I must look inside of myself to find the answer. *I thought I was between a rock and a hard place. I didn't know that I had multiple options. Let me look inside of myself and see the options.* As the questioner or the speaker, I have asked this transderivational search. This is a technique that is often used in the opening line of a TEDx talk or the opening line of a keynote speech, asking participants in the audience to internalize what the result of the talk is going to be.

"What emotion do you struggle with most?" I have to do a scan of all of my emotions which puts me in touch with all of my emotions to determine which one I struggle with most. You see, it is not just a yes or no answer because although I may elicit a specific response—anger, depression, hopelessness—whatever it is that we elicit, they have to scan all their emotions.

This helps me when I am providing therapy with individuals to recognize that they are not a human *doing* and that they are a human *being* with a full range of emotional expressions available to them, even if they found themself to this point, stuck in anger, or stuck in depression, or stuck emotionally with some other predominant non-resourceful emotion.

Another excellent question is, "You need something, don't you?" I will write about language patterns later, but "don't you?" is a compelling language pattern. It causes a person to look inside of themself and ask, *Do I really need that? Do I really want that? Do I really feel that?* If I said to somebody, "You really need something, don't you?" They must look inside to answer the question and determine, *Yes, I do need something. Here is what it is.*

We can put a transderivational search in the context again of therapy, sales, business, or any form of effective communication. Let's take a look at a couple of quick examples here.

In the context of new car sales, the salesperson might ask the client, "What will you be thinking tomorrow when that new Honda is in your garage, and you open up the garage door and have this realization, this car is mine?" Well, I must look inside of myself. *I will be excited because I have reliability. I will be excited because I have affordability. I will be excited because I have comfort.* So, I am going to look inside of myself and discover all these things with this question.

In the context of therapy, the therapist might ask the client, "What will you be thinking tomorrow when the problem that you came here for feels less defeating than it has in the past?" What would I feel? I would feel freedom. I would feel relief. And if I can create through a transderivational search awareness of freedom and relief, I do not have to wait for change to occur to experience it. I am actually experiencing it right now, here in the therapist's office.

Again, in the context of new car sales, "The many options you have include competitors' vehicles, but what is it about this car that really matches your needs better than any of the rest?" This is great for overcoming objections. I must consider why the others are not as good to answer the question and look inside of myself to answer. *It is because this one has a furry steering wheel.* And so, because we have elicited that transderivational search, we have elicited commitment to this stage or this product in the sales process.

Again, in the context of a therapy session, "Of the many options you have, which of these options would appear to help you manage your anger the most effectively?" I must look inside of myself and consider all my options to answer the question, which means I'm choosing the best one. And when I choose the best one, it is going to be the one that is most effective for me.

Returning to the new car sales, "What emotion do you struggle with most when driving that lemon of a Buick that you bought seventeen years ago?" *Oh my gosh, I feel despair, hopelessness, embarrassment!* The reply will come from within. So, a pain point has been created, and we know that can be a sales strategy to elicit the next question, "And what emotion do you think you would feel most if you were driving a brand-new Honda Civic?" *I'd be feeling empowerment! Excitement! Security!* So, I am eliciting the deepest emotional commitment level answers to these questions with a transderivational search.

"You need something, don't you?" "In order to overcome the transportation difficulties you've had in the last year, wouldn't you. . .?" *Wouldn't I? Well, let me look. Yes, I would. I would need a new Honda.* "You need something in order to overcome the depression, don't you?" I must look; I must see. *Is there anything I need to overcome the depression?* To answer the question, I have to tell you what I need. And once I tell you what I need, the needs can be met. And once the needs are met, I can overcome my depression.

Transderivational search is a powerful tool in NLP, coaching, therapy, hypnosis, parenting, or being a good friend or community leader.

Transderivational search is something that we are going to come back to time after time in this book, which is why I have covered it here already. You can understand the power of having people look inside of themselves to find the answer.

One of NLP's presuppositions is that people work perfectly. One of NLP's presuppositions is that we have inside of us all that we need to solve any situation, or problem, or experience that is causing us difficulties. And transderivational search is what brings that to the top so that we can effectively help other people.

Chapter 18
NLP Trance and Hypnosis

The relationship between hypnosis and NLP is essential to discuss because people often confuse NLP and hypnosis. They think that doing hypnosis is NLP or that NLP is a form of hypnosis. The two are different, but they are related.

States

Let's take a look at what trance states are. Most of you have seen a Hollywood movie where Frankenstein casts Igor under a spell or into a trance. And he simply moves forward mindlessly like a zombie. That type of scenario is typically what we think of when we think of trance, or we think of an altered state of consciousness, something from the super-normal, not possible except through some sort of magical or mystical trance state.

The reality is that trance is a natural phenomenon. Every person and every creature experiences trance. We experience some form of trance all day long, every single day. It is for this reason that when I am working with my clients, I am not trying to induce trance. The reality is my clients are always in some form of a trance, no matter what they are doing. It could be their driving trance, their parenting trance, their anger trance, their relaxation trance, their meditation trance. Trance states are states of being that are actually not super-normal. They are normal. And they could be in the category of resourceful, something that benefits us and is useful to us like a relaxation trance. We know there are numerous physical and emotional benefits of deep states of relaxation. A resourceful state might be absorption into learning.

We know that high levels of stress and disorganization are non-resourceful states. A non-resourceful state might be inattention and daydreaming, a distraction.

Trance can be looked at as *resource* states or *non-resourceful* states. And these are naturally occurring all day long, every single day in every one of our lives. We can have our sleep trance, our dream trance, our awake trance, our alert trance; all of these are either resourceful to us, or they are not resourceful to us.

Trance states can fall into the bio-psycho-social-spiritual model. We can have emotional trance states that are either resourceful or not resourceful. We can have, for example, a happiness trance that was resourceful to us. We can have an anxiety trance or a panic trance that is not resourceful to us. We can have physical trance states, a comfort trance, a painful trance. We can have spiritual or metaphysical trances.

These are trance states associated with awareness and meeting our deepest and most profound needs.

Needs

Let's take a look at a couple of my favorite ways of looking at our deepest needs, our metaphysical needs, our spiritual needs. A person's religious faith might be a way to meet their deepest spiritual or metaphysical needs, but I am not talking here about religion. I am talking about spiritual needs at the most basic and most profound level.

William Glasser, in the 1960s, was a renowned author in psychotherapy. He wrote a book called *Reality Therapy,* and he said, "At our deepest need, at the core of who we are, we have the need to love other people and to receive love in return."

One of my favorite authors, a Christian author named Robert McGee, wrote *The Search for Significance: Seeing Your True Worth Through God's Eyes*. He put it into a religious context. He said that through a particular brand of Christianity, you could have your deepest needs met. And he identified one of those as being security. We must feel secure, and we have to feel significant. I happen to think that we can probably experience security and significance without adhering to this specific brand of Christianity, but broadly those are good words to describe our deepest spiritual needs.

Glasser came along in the 1980s and said (paraphrasing), "Hey, I wrote all that stuff in the 1960s. And I have actually reduced it down to one word. Our deepest need is a sense of belonging." Really profound stuff here. We can have a belonging trance. You felt that when you have had full unconditional acceptance at one time or another, not only from others but from within yourself. We have had our security trance where perhaps because of your religious faith, or perhaps because of other experiences, there is a sense of security, a sense of significance. We are talking here about trances that occur because of our deepest spiritual or metaphysical needs. And we can have social trances as well. Birds of a feather flock together. The reality is I see people arguing about politics on social media. We have this side and that side. We have our social trances that either bring us together in unity or cause division.

Those can be resourceful and non-resourceful as well.

Trance is a broad term. Trance is not a mystical or magical state, even though it might have mystical and magical qualities. Understanding emotions, and being in touch with emotions, and expressing emotions can be mystical in our experiences.

There was a movie in the 1980s called *Altered States*. I never saw the movie, so I do not know what it was about, but I remember the poster, and it had somebody lying on a gurney. Their hands were clenched, and there were green veins. It was about altered states of consciousness. A supernatural movie. Trance is normal. We all experience trance every day.

Getting our client into trance is not anything difficult. They come to us in a trance. What is difficult is teaching people in coaching how to direct their trance states so that they are resourceful rather than non-resourceful.

Hypnosis is the mechanism by which we help people to create resource states or trance states with intention. This could come in the form of self-hypnosis or hetero-hypnosis, where I am hypnotizing somebody else. It could even be mass hypnosis where one person is hypnotizing a large group of people, whether that is entertainment or whether that is from the pulpit or the political bully pulpit.

We can see hypnosis in a lot of different forms.

What we are discussing in this book, though, are the traditional approaches used predominantly by Milton Erickson.

Milton Erickson was a medical hypnotist from the 1950s to the very early 1980s when he passed away in March 1980. Milton Erickson was a psychiatrist who was a medical doctor treating people with psychiatric disorders. He used hypnosis as a tool.

How does this fit into NLP? In the late 1960s, Richard Bandler and John Grinder went to Phoenix to observe and study Milton Erickson to find out why he was having such superb success with his patients. They wanted to know what separated him from other psychiatrists who were also treating the same types of folks. John Grinder, the linguist, studied the hypnotic language of Milton Erickson. Richard Bandler studied the processes of Milton Erickson.

And the two of them created, using Milton Erickson as an exemplar, replicable patterns and language components that could be taught to other people so that, ideally, those other people could get the same results in applying these methods of hypnosis to their patients. And much of NLP is based on the work of Milton Erickson and his language patterns, helping people access resource states and use hypnosis as a tool for intention.

One of the interesting aspects about Milton Erickson is he sometimes used conversational hypnosis. He did not have the client sit in a chair, put on headphones, and count backward from ten. He used conversational hypnosis. The client did not really know when the session was beginning or when the session was ending. Rather, Milton Erickson guided and directed the individual to create those transderivational searches, to look inside of themselves and find those resources through what we call conversational hypnosis. But make no mistake, even if there is formal hypnotic induction, it utilizes trance experiences and directs somebody into the resourceful trances that can benefit them.

There are also indirect methods of self-hypnosis where we ask a person to reflect on the moment, to look inside of themself. We want to make analogies, comparisons, use other linguistic techniques to elicit the resource states indirectly. And there is simply direct hypnosis. Go ahead and close your eyes down now. With your eyes closed down, take in a breath, relax the muscles of your body. We might associate this with what we would call the formal process of hypnosis.

Indirect, direct, conversational hypnosis, the formal process of hypnosis, one is not better than another. They are all tools that we can tap into and that we can utilize.

You do not have to be a professional hypnotist to use NLP or to be an effective life coach, but by enhancing your skills in using professional hypnosis, I am confident that you can find numerous applications for NLP as well as enhance the quality of your life coaching experiences.

Conscious, Subconscious, Unconscious Mind

Let's explore the ideas of the conscious mind, the subconscious mind, and the unconscious mind because these are related to trance and hypnosis.

We often hear that hypnosis is a way of speaking directly to the subconscious mind. While we can speak directly to the subconscious, we can also directly speak to the conscious mind. I think it is important to realize that conscious versus subconscious is just a metaphor. It is a useful way of understanding how the mind works. Imagine the mind is like an iceberg, and the very top is the small part that is sticking out of the water, that is the conscious mind. That is what we are aware of at this moment.

It is said that the conscious mind has a limited capacity of up to seven things at any given moment, and then something must go. An example of that is, you are cooking rice and beans. You are boiling the water. You are talking on the phone. You are adding some seasoning. You are doing all these things simultaneously. You are watching TV because there is something on the news you do not want to miss, so you have seven things going on.

That is when someone comes walking into your kitchen and says, "Hey, can I take twenty bucks out of your purse or out of your wallet?" And you simply shake the rice and beans and focus on the TV and say, "Huh." And then later, you discover your twenty-dollar bill is missing, and you wonder who took your twenty-dollar bill. The person who did, reminds you saying, "I did." You respond, "Why didn't you ask for it?" "Well, I did ask you." The reason why you were not aware of that is that the conscious mind was overloaded.

I think we can reduce it to the conscious mind really only having the capacity for one thing in any one moment. It really is limited. It is short-term. It is temporal.

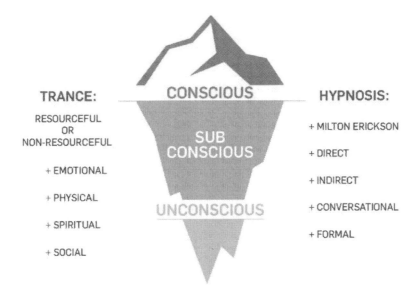

TRANCE:	CONSCIOUS	HYPNOSIS:
RESOURCEFUL OR NON-RESOURCEFUL	SUB CONSCIOUS	+ MILTON ERICKSON
+ EMOTIONAL		+ DIRECT
+ PHYSICAL		+ INDIRECT
+ SPIRITUAL	UNCONSCIOUS	+ CONVERSATIONAL
+ SOCIAL		+ FORMAL

But the subconscious mind is different. It is our vast reservoir of all of our previous experiences. Most of our mind is like the huge underwater part of the iceberg that we do not see. This is the vast reservoir of our experiences, of our learnings, of our emotions, of our thoughts, of our physical state of being. And the interesting thing about the subconscious mind is that no matter how far down the iceberg it is, we can bring it to the conscious mind almost instantly.

Close your eyes for a moment. Think of the very first car that you owned. What color was that car? How many miles were on that car? How much did you pay for that car? Go ahead and open your eyes. That picture in your mind that showed up—that recollection of the price, or the miles on the car, or the color of the car—those were things you had not thought about in years. But instantly, the subconscious mind was able to bring up $500. I paid $500 for my first car. It was a 1974 Pinto, white with orange pinstriping; it had a gray primer door. I am instantly able to bring that to the conscious mind.

The great thing about the subconscious mind is it contains our wisdom, learnings, experiences that really last a lifetime, and we can tap into that subconscious mind of ours. We commit to the subconscious mind the learnings that help us to act instantly in any given situation. This is what gives us the ability to drive a car. We do not drive a car with our conscious mind.

Have you ever taught an adolescent how to drive? I remember when I taught my son, who was fifteen at the time, how to drive, and it was nerve-wracking because he had to pay attention to the brake. He had to pay attention to the turn signal, all the other traffic, the stick shift—all these things were overloading the conscious mind. I drive subconsciously. In fact, it was Milton Erickson who said he would not want a New York taxi driver that was not in a trance state.

What is the unconscious mind? The unconscious mind can be thought of as the back of the head. That is where the old brain is, the amygdala. It is the least developed part of the brain, but it is also the most well-protected part of the brain. It is an unconscious process to breathe. It is an unconscious process to blink. It is an unconscious process to have blood flow through our hearts and our lungs and into the cells of our body.

The question is can we change our unconscious mind? And the answer to that is yes, we can, but the unconscious mind is very limited as well. It does not have strategic thinking. It does not tap into the past experiences to decide on the present as the subconscious mind does. Instead, the unconscious mind just does what the mind is programmed for.

It is also essential to realize that the mind is not just brain. Mind is in every cell of our body. It is the essence of who we are.

Back when I worked in Houston in the early 1990s, I worked with a liver transplant program doing some substance abuse assessments for the liver transplant program. We would regularly hear these stories like this: The patient hated carrots with a passion, but they got a liver transplant, or a heart transplant, or a lung transplant or whatever it was that was transplanted. Suddenly, they loved carrots. Their goal in life now is to become a carrot farmer.

How did that happen? Then we discovered the person whose liver was donated loved carrots. It was their favorite food. How does that happen? The theory is that mind is literally in every cell of the body. And when we transfer somebody else's organs into our body, we are literally transplanting mind into our body. A pretty deep thought, a rather controversial idea, but certainly something interesting that, although unproven, is congruent with my experiences working there.

Hopefully, this has given you an idea of what trance is, what hypnosis is, and how it is used, as well as a clearer understanding of the unconscious mind, conscious mind, and subconscious mind.

Hypnotists use NLP techniques or coaching techniques to be more effective hypnotists. NLP practitioners and coaches can use methods of hypnosis to help create resourceful trance states. The two are complementary. They go together. It is important to recognize that when you are finished reading this book, you will have a vast repertoire of hypnotic skills, even if you are not practicing formal professional hypnosis.

Chapter 19
NLP Eye-Accessing Cues and Calibration

To begin a discussion on calibration, we need to talk about the world-famous NLP eye-accessing cues. And the reasons why this needs to be the first part of our discussion are:

1. It is going to be part of how we calibrate.

2. It is the most controversial area in NLP.

The idea here is that we move our eyes in congruence with whether we are remembering something and seeing something, whether we are hearing something and recalling something, or whether we are visualizing something and creating a new recollection (in other words, something that did not exist), or we are seeing something in our mind that we have already seen before. Our kinesthetic aspects can be measured here as well with the eye-accessing movements, called auditory digital, and it is the concept of self-talk. I will explain all these things.

Here is why it is controversial. In the early days of NLP, the eye accessing chart—showing if an individual moved their eyes this way or that way, meant one thing or another thing—was put to the test, and it failed it.

If it is controversial, why do we still teach it? There are a couple of reasons. This chart is for a "normally" organized person. Typically, we associate this with right-handedness or left-handedness. We must remember there are almost eight billion people on the planet Earth. There is always going to be somebody who is not going to match the assessment perfectly.

That is where the idea of calibration comes into play, and the direction to "always be calibrating." What do we do if we have a left-handed person or a person who is organized differently? Well, we can reverse the chart. We can turn our piece of paper around. You can flip the chart over. And it makes sense for the other twenty percent or so of people who are left-handed or might be organized differently.

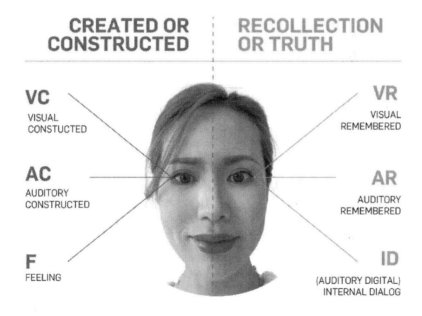

There are people for whom the chart simply does not work. It is not a useful guide for whatever reason, the way they express themselves emotionally, perhaps the shared dominance of various representational systems, or the lack of acuity in some representational systems.

Another reason why it is sometimes disregarded is that it did not turn out to be a reliable tool for determining truth or a lie in law enforcement interrogation.

Why do we still teach the NLP eye-accessing chart? The reason is simple. It is one more tool and one more guide that can help us. This is not something that should be used independently of other methods of calibration.

We should look for a primary representational system and its congruency across a wide variety of different settings and situations, but it should never be our only source of determining how we are going to go about calibrating.

A lot of these tools in NLP are exactly that, tools, and they work in some situations, and they do not necessarily work in other situations. When you are new to NLP and new to coaching, it is great having some resources that most people generally accept as a fairly useful or reliable tool to help us work with individuals.

Let me introduce you to the eye-accessing chart itself.

I wrote *truth* on the left, and I wrote *lies* on the right. This is only a guide. This is not a truth serum. This is not going to stand up in a court of law or police interrogation, but it can be a guide for us as to how it is that a person is expressing themselves and whether, because we are trying to calibrate with the eye-accessing chart, they are sharing something that is true or something they believe in or something that is fiction or something that they doubt. It can be a useful guide for us.

When the individual is looking right at you, that is visualization. They are seeing you. They are making eye contact with you. They are seeing something beyond you. This is generally associated with visualization.

We have lies on one side and truth on one side. This is a chart for when I am looking at the person. Because I am talking to somebody when I am calibrating, if I ask them a question, "What's your favorite type of dog?" and they look up, up, and to the left, that is visual constructed. That is not accessing a previous experience but constructing a new experience. In other words, they are creating a visualization in their mind of something they have not seen before. This is why it is associated with lies, perhaps. It is not something they are accessing from their memory. They are constructing it on the fly as they answer the question. Auditory construction is the same thing. What would it sound like if this were real or if it had happened?

In response to the question, "Richard, what's your favorite dog?" I look up, and to the right, before I answer the question, this is visually remembering. I am looking at my own mind, at what it is that my dogs look like. The answer to that question is Goldendoodles are currently my favorite dog, although I love all dogs.

Horizontally without going up or down to the right, is an auditory remembering. In response to the question, "Richard, what's your favorite kind of dog?" and I look to the right horizontally, I am hearing the dog bark in my mind. I am remembering the sound of something.

Now, if in response to the question, I look down and to the right, what I am doing is listening to my own inner voice. This is called internal dialogue. These things are generally associated with congruent or truthful responses.

In response to the question, "Richard, what's your favorite dog?" I look down to the left, the lower left; this is kinesthetic. This is the feeling. These are emotions, the weight and the feeling of joy, the weight, and feeling of depression. All these things that our clients can share with us nonverbally.

This eye-accessing chart is a fun chart to play with. It is just one more tool or one more guide. If the information that I gather from the eye chart does not match the other aspects of calibration, I will probably go with those as a whole, which most likely seemed to ring true. Now let's take a look at the others.

The reason I believe why calibration or congruency is an important topic in NLP and coaching is, as a coach, I am always calibrating those with whom I am working. I am not necessarily trying to determine lies or truth. I am often trying to determine their congruency with their stated goals and the actions they are taking. This helps me recognize whether we will have a hard time or an easy time reaching those goals. Calibration can be used in many different areas.

Typically to calibrate, we are going to ask some easy questions. "Richard, do you like dogs?" Yes or no. "Richard, do you like living in Katy, Texas?" Yes or no. "Richard, what are three things you are good at?" I'm a good dad. I am a good friend. And I'm a hard worker. These are things that we know to be true.

I will ask the person who I am coaching, the person who I am working with, some questions that give me a baseline for what their voice tone is, their posture, their eye-accessing cues, their breathing, their muscles, their position, do they lean in, do they draw back? These are the kind of things that I am really studying when I am calibrating as I am speaking with somebody.

In coaching, I may be asked, "Richard, you've described the goal that you would like to reach. Have you ever experienced success in that way before?" While you are going to be looking at my voice tone as I answer the question, you will also pay attention to my posture, eye accessing cues, breathing, muscles, body position, and body language to determine whether or not it is congruent with previous answers, previous actions, and previous experiences.

What is it that we can calibrate? We can calibrate truth statements. These are assertions a person makes, such as the ones I made above. We can calibrate whether the person believes those self-statements about themself or believes those statements about other people. "My old boss was lazy, he was no good, and he was a bad trainer." That is an assertive statement.

I can see the congruency here in the political arena. Trust me, NLP is widely used in politics. We might have somebody making true statements that they know factually to be untrue. And we see that untruth, no matter which side of the political aisle we are talking about.

We can calibrate emotions and feelings—congruency. He says he is happy, but does he appear depressed? Are they doing the things they do when they are depressed, but stating that they are happy, or are they saying that they are committed, but they are doing the things that are congruent with what they have done when they have been in periods of "stuckness" or inaction?

We can calibrate trust in the coaching relationship, trust in the leaders and mentors that are part of the client's world, trust in their own abilities, trust in their abilities to shepherd other people and mentor other people, whether that is their child, a coworker or a colleague or a new hire, or other people who are going to be on their team. We can calibrate their confidence in their knowledge. This is a little bit different from the true statements that are almost always assertations about oneself or a situation. This knowledge is when, for example, Richard starts talking about NLP, noticing where his eyes are directed. Is he constructing this and making this up, or is it visual remembering? Perhaps Richard remembers a client that he has been working with in the past where this technique or strategy worked.

You have been in an argument before where you have asserted your knowledge. This is different than a true statement. A true statement is about belief. The knowledge statement is about fact, but we can gauge whether there is confidence in those facts, which brings us to a whole other area of calibration.

We can calibrate global confidence. Does a person feel confident in themselves, in others, their world, their finances, their relationships? When they step up to the podium to do public speaking, what is their confidence level? We can calibrate their confidence in one situation and their lack of confidence in another situation. Then we can help them map over what causes confidence in this situation to the new situation. They can be confident there too.

I do a lot of public speaking coaching, and I have discovered that I am confident in a small group explaining one-on-one or to a couple of my peers. But when you put me in an audience in front of a hundred people, I do not have that same level of confidence. And we could easily calibrate that to be true.

When I watch a video of my client speaking in front of a group and compare it to how I see them speaking to me one-on-one, this is a strategy that can be used. This is why this is practical. I can coach the client that when they are confident with themself or me in the state of one-one speaking, they are confident here. Then I continue, "Now imagine yourself in front of that hundred-person group, continue to maintain that posture, that pose, that breath, the state of your muscles, and imagine being in front of that group. Do you feel more confident now in front of that group, even though you are not there yet?" "Yes, I do," they likely reply. I continue, "So next time you step up to the podium, bring yourself to that resource state of confidence you have here one-on-one. And step up to the podium, ready to speak to a hundred people with that confidence you have brought with you."

We can also calibrate behaviors and actions for congruency commitment. We can also, in relationships, calibrate their comfort level, or their intimacy, openness, respect, or other qualities of relationships. There are many others that we could add here. But these are some of the major areas where, in coaching, I am trying to calibrate and determine a baseline of a person. When I know where they are, I can discover congruency and coach my clients into success by mapping over from one scenario or situation into other ways to be truthful, ways to mask their emotions, ways to be confident, ways to trust themselves, and trust others, ways to be knowledgeable, and ways to increase our comfort and relationships with others. All great tools for NLP and coaching, as we seek the skills of being more effective life coaches.

Chapter 20
Socratic Questions

The Socratic method is a way of questioning and interviewing somebody. We use the Socratic method because it creates a transderivational search rather than confronting, educating, or leading a person with authority. We ask them to look inside of themself and make a decision about their beliefs, actions, or goals and help them transform from the inside.

That is why this model is a very popular model in teacher training programs. Chances are pretty good that any teachers at your local school have probably been trained in the Socratic method. Interrogators are trained in the Socratic method to find out the truth about individual situations or the ideas that people have. This is why the Socratic method is used in academia.

It is something taught to those in the legal profession—lawyers for questioning people who are on the stand.

What about it in the context of coaching? If I am working with somebody and they are sitting across the chair from me, or we are face-to-face on Zoom, I might use Socratic questioning as a way of helping the client to get in touch with their core values, those things that are most important to them and to take the actions that are probably most relevant to help them achieve their goal. Many clients might have a goal, but the methods they set out to achieve that goal might be less than resourceful or might be timewasting or might be over complicated.

Using the Socratic method to help someone sort through the options they have, they create more options. Remember the NLP presupposition that it is better to have more options than to have no options. The Socratic method can open those doors, but rather me imposing my options and my thoughts on somebody, it causes them to have that transderivational search to look inside of themself.

Socrates was a Greek philosopher, and he is considered the founder of Western thought and philosophy. He was born around 470 BC. He had many students.

One of Socrates' famous quotes is, "I cannot teach anyone. All I can do is cause them to think." And that is what we are trying to do as coaches. We are trying to help people think on their own rather than imposing our thoughts on them. This is an important distinction between traditional models of therapy, which often are crisis-oriented, and telling somebody what to do. The Socratic method asks them to look inside themself to determine what they should do.

SOCRATIC QUESTIONS

INFLUENCE, CRITICAL THINKING, LEADERSHIP, TEACHING, COACHING

It creates change from within not from outside.

1 CLARIFICATION QUESTIONS

"Could you explain further?"
"What do we already know about this?"
"Are you saying ____ or ____?"
"Can you rephrase with more clarity?"

2 ASSUMPTION QUESTIONS

"Is this always the case?"
"Do all ____ think like this?"
"What exceptions to this are there?"
"Please explain why/how..."

3 EVIDENCE QUESTIONS

"Is there any reason to doubt this evidence?"
"Can you give me an example of that?"
"Are these reasons strong enough?"
"How might someone refute this?"

4 VIEWPOINT QUESTIONS

"How else could you answer this?"
"What is the counter-argument?"
"How might (another person) answer this?"
"Why is this view better than ____?"

5 CONSEQUENCE QUESTIONS

"Then what would happen?"
"What would happen if everyone believed this?"
"What would happen if ____ happened?"
"Why is ___ important?"

6 QUESTIONS ABOUT QUESTIONS

"Why is this question important?"
"Why do you think I asked this question?"
"Am I making sense to you? Why?"
"What other questions could I ask?"

RAPPORT

Tone

Pitch

Rapport

Eye Contact

Proximity

The Socratic method is used in influence. When I see talented conversational hypnotists practicing conversational hypnosis and change work, I see them using Socratic questioning as a hypnotic method of causing people to look inside themselves, creating the ability to influence other people with their questioning. It is used in critical thinking, training science curriculums, etcetera. It is used in leadership development, and leadership development is an excellent area for coaches to expand their business opportunities.

If you are a life coach and you would like to work with corporate clients, work with small groups, or begin teaching and training teams, the Socratic method really gives you tremendous opportunities to share these skills with others who could also benefit from them. In life coaching, we are going to use NLP. Socratic questioning was not an idea that was foreign to the originators of NLP. Neuro-linguistic programming utilized the power of Socratic questions early on to help create rapport, help people create options, and help them step into a problem-solving mentality rather than a problem-oriented mentality. It is important to note here that as the Socratic method relates to NLP, NLP has always been focused on creating rapport and to use the Socratic method correctly and compassionately, and effectively with people, no matter what setting we are in. We have to establish rapport.

In this book, I cover the various components of transderivational search, the communication and coaching model. They give us some ideas related to rapport. In verbal communication, there are the words that we use. In nonverbal communication, we have a depth of communication far beyond simply the words that we are using.

We are looking at the tone. What tone do we have? Is it a tone that is authoritative? Is it a tone that is coaching and collaborative? Is it a tone that lacks confidence? We want to evaluate our tonality as we look to apply the skills of NLP with coaching clients, the pitch of our voice, the rate of our voice. Are we a quick talker, or are we a slow talker?

Are we creating rapport, which is two-way communication? Are we actively both listening and receiving? And when we receive, do we feed that back to make sure that the message we have received is the message the sender intended to send? Remember, in NLP, one of the first presuppositions is that the meaning of our communication is the message received by the receiver.

Rapport

Rapport investigates the quality of communication to ensure we are at a point where we can ask these deeply personal, sometimes challenging questions to a person. Rapport deals with the idea of eye contact as well. Too much eye contact can scare somebody off. Not enough eye contact can communicate a lack of confidence, or it could communicate mistruth. We want to have the right balance of eye contact and creating rapport, the idea of proxemics and proximity, and this is crucial as we deal with the technology we utilize to coach.

In my experience with rapport, creating it is different when somebody is sitting on a chair in front of me. When I can sit directly across from somebody, I can attend to them. Attending is a skill of being fully present with the person. There is plenty of research to show that when we are in the proximity of other people—when we are physically present with other people—it changes our neurochemistry. It changes the way we feel. We can create rapport simply by being present with somebody. The internet gives us a new opportunity to coach people in a different way. But if I am on a Zoom meeting, I might not have the same level of rapport.

This can be a little deceptive because I can see you, and you can see me. It almost feels like reality, but proxemics is missing. I must make sure that when I engage in Socratic questioning that the person with whom I am speaking is at a point where they are willing to be open and are willing to exchange these ideas with me. We also must develop rapport with empathy. Empathy is all about being fully present with another person. It does not necessarily mean agreeing with a person, but it does mean being fully present with a person. It means more than simply listening to them. It means attending to them. Ernest Rossi, a contemporary of Milton Erickson, described hypnosis and rapport in hypnosis as "belly button to belly button communication." That is a very powerful metaphor about the power of empathy.

The very first Ericksonian hypnosis training I went to was titled "Advanced Accurate Empathy." It was a course for mental health professionals, and it was taught by Bob Bullet from the University of Florida. It was the model for being able to compassionately attend to somebody and exchange ideas with them. That exchange of ideas with the client fosters the development of options from within themself.

I think that rapport requires curiosity. Do we genuinely have curiosity about other people? When I ask you a question that is a challenge statement, I am not doing it so that I can be right. I am doing that because I am generally curious if the person with whom I am working has the ability to be flexible.

Do they have the resources and the tools within to adapt to new situations? I am genuinely curious. What would the outcome be for them if their life were improved by releasing old ideas that held them back from having successful relationships, getting along with other people, or dealing with problems in a way that was not non-resourceful? Do we have a genuine curiosity about people? These are all elements of our nonverbal communication that are important as we use the Socratic method of questioning to help our clients create options.

The Six Types of Socratic Questions

Clarification Questions

Questions that we ask can require the person with whom we are speaking to have or create clarification. Some examples are, "Could you explain that a little bit further?" "Let me ask you, what do we already know about that?" "Are you saying this, or are you saying that?" We are asking for clarification here. "Can you say that again with a little more clarity?"

Let us put this in the context of somebody who we are working with who has anxiety. They have anxiety about making changes. They say to me, "You know, Richard, every time I come up against a problem, I'm always filled with anxiety." In response, I might ask, "Can you explain that a little further? What does anxiety look like to you?" I might ask them this question, "You've said you felt anxious in many other situations, so what do you already know about your ability to handle or get through anxious situations?"

I can adapt these questions to any situation. "Are you saying anxiety is what's stopping you, or panic is what's stopping you?" "Can you describe for me how anxiety fits into the problem that's holding you back, but with a little more clarity just so I can see the whole picture?"

We can adapt each of these questions for the type of client that we are working with.

Assumption Questions

When we are speaking with somebody about their situation, they are going to bring their assumptions. The second set of Socratic questions probes the assumptions that people have. Maybe the assumption is, *I will always be anxious when I find myself in difficult situations*, or maybe the assumption is, *Everybody is anxious when they have to face these difficulties.*

Those are assumptions, and we act on our assumptions. When we act on assumptions, sometimes we are right. Sometimes we act in ways that are non-resourceful to us. Here are some questions we could ask somebody to challenge their assumptions. "Let me ask you, is this always the case?" "Do all business leaders facing change have this same assumption? Let me ask, are there any exceptions to this?" "Are there times when you faced a change, but when you faced that change, you didn't feel anxious?" To challenge assumptions, I can simply say, "Explain this to me, please."

Let's put this in the context of business coaching. For me to move from being a publisher of my own books into a business where I publish other people's books and become a publisher, I have to transition from being a one-man-show to having many different people I am working with. If I found that to be difficult or unknown to me and asked you to coach me, you could ask questions that challenge my assumptions. "Richard, is it always the case that publishing books for other people is different than publishing your own book?" I would have to look inside. *I guess it is not. It is actually really pretty simple. It is the same steps.* "Richard, do all solopreneurs, do all self-published authors, wrestle with the same issue when they agree to help other people publish books?" I must think about that. *I know some other people who are self-published authors who then became publishers for other people's works.* "Let me ask you, Richard, are there any exceptions to the process when you're publishing somebody else's work versus publishing your own?" "Richard, explain to me the process of publishing somebody else's book and how it differs from publishing your own book."

Evidence Questions

The third category of Socratic questions is questions that go to the heart of reasons or evidence—everybody who has an argument. Someone's politics are right, their religion is right, their favorite dog is right, dogs versus cats is right, there are people in outer space, or there aren't people on outer space. Anything that a person has a belief about, they will have an argument about. An argument inside that helps them to support their belief. Sometimes we might want to work with an individual to help them determine if their beliefs are resourceful to them. This is where having a level of rapport is essential before we start asking some of these questions, where we have empathy, where we are genuinely curious, rather than trying to make me right at the expense of their beliefs.

Here are some examples of questions I might ask. "Let me ask you, you've said that this is true, and you believe it to be true because of this evidence. Is there any reason at all that one would doubt the evidence or might question that evidence?" Notice, I didn't say, "Is there any reason why I should, or you should, doubt the evidence?" That personalizes it too much. We've added a third party here. "Is there any reason why somebody outside of this situation might doubt the evidence or wonder if the evidence is valid?" "You said this is your belief, your belief Goldendoodles are superior to all other dogs. Let me ask you this question, Richard. Can you give me an example of how Goldendoodles are superior to other dogs?" I don't know. They're both fuzzy and curly. They're both big, and they're small. But in the process of giving you my answer, I have to question. It doesn't even make sense. Other dogs have these characteristics also. So, I have to compare them to other dogs to decide if my argument is correct.

Another question that can be asked to challenge evidence and arguments could be, "Richard, let me ask you, are these good enough reasons to believe that Goldendoodles are the best dog of all?" Well, now that I think about it. They are really based on my opinion rather than on fact. Again, we are asking a person to look at the evidence and decide if it really supports the belief that they have.

We could ask, "How might it be refuted, the evidence that you've presented? I'm just curious here. I'm not saying your evidence is wrong, but let me ask you, if somebody were to refute the evidence that you have given, how would they go about refuting it? What do you think they might say?" That causes somebody to listen to an opposing argument.

Viewpoint Questions

Now to questions that explore alternate perspectives or questions that explore viewpoints. "How else could this be answered?" is a question that asks a person to increase options. Other questions like, "What's the counterargument to that?" "How might a cat lover answer this question?" "Why is the dog better than the cat, or why is the cat better than the dog?" "How might a Nissan salesperson answer that?" "Why is the Nissan better than the Honda, or why is the Honda better than the Nissan?" Again, I am asking questions from an alternate perspective. The purpose of this isn't so that I can be right and they can be wrong. It is so that ultimately my client can create options and determine what is best for them.

Consequence Questions

The fifth area of Socratic questioning is a series of questions that ask them to consider the implications or the consequences of the options, choices, desires, beliefs, whatever it is that we are questioning. Some examples of questions here might be, "Then what might happen?" "What would happen if everybody believed the same thing and did this?" "Tell me, why is that important?" "What would happen if something happened?" "What would happen if you found a stray puppy that you really loved that wasn't a Goldendoodle. What would happen then?" Again, we are challenging the implications and the consequences.

Questions About Questions

The sixth type is questions about the questions. A lot of times, people are asking the wrong questions. This is certainly very true in business coaching. They are asking the question, "How do I move from this level to this level?" When the questions are, "Should we even move to a new level? Should we move in a completely different direction rather than to a new level? Should we start an entirely new project?" This is sometimes true when we are coaching individuals dealing with emotional aspects. The individual keeps asking, "How is it I can stop being depressed, or how is it I can stop being anxious?" But I wonder if the real question is, "How can we be happy, or how can we create security?"

Some questions we might ask to help us question the questions include, "Tell me, why is this question important?" "How come this one has to be answered before we can go forward?" "Why do you think I asked this question?"

In other words, we are asking them to determine whether the question we asked was even relevant or important. I might ask them for clarification and question the question, "Am I making sense to you with what I just said? Why or why not? Are there any other questions that I should be asking you?" I use this a lot in my coaching, so when I get done with the pre-talk in my first session, we are still going to do interventions, probably hypnosis, NLP, all these sorts of things. But I always say to my clients, "Now, before we go any further, I know I've asked you a lot of questions. Do you have any questions for me? Are there any other questions, things that we haven't yet considered that we probably need to be taking a look at in order to make this time that we spend together so helpful to you?"

I think that for you to truly benefit from the Socratic method and increase your ability to be an effective coach, you can practice using these questions in your everyday life. Practice being aware of what Socratic questions from these six categories you can use. Who can you use these with? Can you practice Socratic questions with your partner, spouse, neighbor, child, teacher, coworkers? How and where can you practice asking Socratic questions?

You will probably discover something that is true when you practice this. You create deeper levels of rapport with the people that you already have relationships. You will become closer to the people you already have relationships with. You will probably have a lot of fun being curious about other people using the Socratic method.

I also want you to pay attention to my teaching style. I was trained early in the Socratic method. I probably use the Socratic method fairly unconsciously in my communication while I interview and speak with people because I've been aware of these questions for so many years.

This skill is one that you can use to increase your acuity in life coaching, NLP, and helping people to draw out from within themselves using transderivational search, discovering the options that help them to live their best life.

Chapter 21
States and Circle of Excellence

In this section, I will share with you what I think is one of the most valuable concepts in NLP. We will also explore an application or a way to apply that, first in your own life and then also with the clients you work with and the various settings where you work with people.

States

The mathematical formula is our internal representations, plus our physiology equals the state—the resource state or the unresourceful state. Earlier I wrote about states, and now we are going to explore this idea a little bit more.

What is a state, and how do we elicit states? We do this consciously and subconsciously. As we go throughout the day, we are simply producing various states. We manifest our happiness states, perhaps our attraction states, or perhaps our scarcity states.

These can be either resourceful or unresourceful states, but no matter what state it is, it is always a combination of our internal representations coupled with our physiology, which equals the state which we have created, which we are experiencing in any given moment. Throughout the day, we could have multiple states.

In fact, we can probably have multiple states simultaneously. You can both have grief and happiness at the same time. When my grandmother died years ago, and my grandfather, who had been with her for more than seventy years, said to me that he felt sad. He felt grief, but he also felt joy and happiness because it was a life well-lived, and he believed that she was in a better place. So, we can have conflicting states even simultaneously.

When we talk about states, we can probably break states down, probably into more than just these four, but these are four broad categories of states that we are eliciting and working with in coaching and in NLP:

Emotional States

This is the state of joy, the state of happiness, the state of excitement, the state of exuberance, the state of productivity, the state of depression, the state of sadness, the state of loss. All of these are emotional states. We elicit these as a result of both our internal representations as well as the physiology we hold. It is pretty hard to be truly depressed when there's a smile on your face, and you're feeling a high level of energy. You can fake it and hide it from other people, but the incongruence will be obvious to the observer.

Physical States

These are a representation of our internal representations coupled with our physiology. Pain is an example of a physical state. Comfort is an example of a physical state. Strength is an example of a physical state. Energetic could be either an emotional state or a physical state or both of those states. Fatigue is a physical state. We have an internal representation—this is how we know we are fatigued—coupled with a physiological profile for that.

Focused States

These are our attentional states. A learning state, an attraction of the abundant state, a motivational state. Or on the unresourceful side, our focus states could be distraction, disinterest, inattention. Those are all examples of states that are a combination of an internal representation coupled with our physiology that results in a state that we can apply a label to.

Created Resource States

These could be created non-resourceful states but, generally, if we are going to spend the time to create a state, we are going to create one that is resourceful. These could also be called projected states or *as if* states. These states are important because the emotional, physical, and focus states are almost always, at one level or another, something that we can revivify. In other words, we have previously experienced what the state is like, and we are stepping into it again in the current moment or planning to step into it in the future moment. This is based on our experiences, subconscious reservoir of learnings, and experiences that we have had.

But sometimes, it becomes important to create a new state. A state that we have never experienced before. This is something that we want to experience, and so these states, rather than being revivified internal representation systems, are created representational systems. The visualization of what it would be like, or as if I am doing something, or I am projecting what that visual imagery would be like, or what the auditory message would be like, or what the kinesthetic feeling would be like, or the smells and the tastes of those sorts of things. I am projecting what I think or what I hope to be the outcome of attaining this resource state.

These resource states are important because when we are coaching, we often work with people trying to move from where they have been to where they would like to go. Because they have never been there before, these resource states can be very real. When we can achieve the resource state in the office, we can step into it in the future, in the real world. This fourth category is often overlooked by a lot of trainers and teachers, but these projected resource states or created resource states, or *as if* resource states, are of particular value. It is easy for me to wonder, *What would it be like if . . . ?* and to visualize that, to hear that, feel it in my body, taste it, smell it, touch it. Then, because the mind is infinitely creative, to experience it, that fantasy, as if it were reality.

Circle Of Excellence

Our amygdala, that part of the brain where the unconscious mind lies, is the stupid part of our brain. It cannot really tell the difference between fantasy and reality. Close your eyes down for a minute and imagine that I was slicing open a fresh lemon. I have a cutting board and a knife here, and I am slicing it open. I am slicing up a very thin slice of that juicy tart lemon, and I then put that slice of lemon between your pursed lips. You would probably instantly notice salivation. You would probably immediately be able to taste the tart, sour, bitter lemon. Now go ahead and open your eyes. As you know, there is no lemon, but you had a natural physiological response to an imaginary lemon that I simply talked about.

This is because our amygdala cannot tell the difference between what is real and what is not real. If we create an *as if* state, our unconscious mind brings us into congruence with the ability to take action on that. This is really good news for those who set intentions and set goals.

That is one way of helping clients and helping yourself to be able to shift states, move states, create new states, revivify old states. Rather than go through life unintentionally experiencing life, intentionally go through life creating resourceful states rather than non-resourceful states.

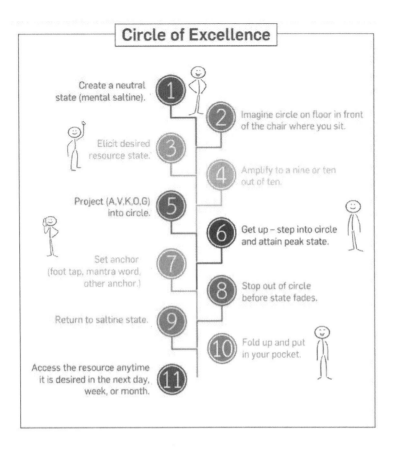

Exercise: Circle of Excellence

Create a Neutral State

Begin with what I always call in my coaching work, a mental saltine. At a wine tasting, they will have you eat a saltine between the glasses of wine, so everything is clear. Simply take a breath and create what you would associate with as a neutral state, an average state. Set aside any stress from yesterday, any fears of tomorrow, just be fully present.

Take in a breath and achieve here a neutral state, a mental saltine state. You can do this either with the eyes open or with the eyes closed, but I was enjoying doing this with the eyes closed.

Before you close your eyes, look at the floor in front of you and imagine drawing a circle on that floor. Imagine a circle on that floor. Now, go ahead and close your eyes down.

Elicit a Desired Resource State

With your eyes closed down, think of a desired resource state that would be beneficial to you. Perhaps confidence, perhaps learning, perhaps the state of recollection, perhaps the state of committed memory, perhaps the state of helpfulness to others. Whatever resource state that would be of value to you, identify what you would label that resource state as right now.

Breathe in and breathe out and say the word associated with that state. I am going to say, "Excellence, excellence, excellence."

Amplify

As you say this word that you have created to associate with the state, allow yourself to amplify the feelings of being in this state. Notice your body. Does your posture become better? Notice your breathing. Does it change in any way? Notice your visualization. What movie is playing in your mind right now? Is it near, is it far, is it in color? What is the soundtrack of the resource state that you have created? Is the song one that you have known before or a song that you have never heard before? Is it a song with singing? Is it voices talking? Is it your own breath, that moment of success? It could be any number of things, but amplify that state, both the physiology and the emotional experience of that state that would be of value to you, that *as if* state, or that previous state that you would like to be able to utilize in any situation.

Amplify it from a level six to a seven, from a seven to an eight, amplify it from an eight to a nine, and all the way to a ten, and allow yourself to hold the state at the highest level.

Project the Resource State into Circle

Now project from your mind that resource state into that circle in front of you. Remember that circle we drew just moments ago? Picture yourself being able to channel or direct that energy, that vision, that thought, those words, those sounds, those experiences, those tastes, those smells, from where you are in the part of the mind that creates awareness to that place outside of you simply in that circle on the floor in front of you. Pretty amazing how we have the ability to do that, isn't it?

Step into the Circle

Go ahead now and stand up for a moment and step into that circle in front of you and allow yourself as you step into that circle to be surrounded by this peak resource state.

Set an Anchor

While standing in the circle at a level ten, set an anchor. You could do that by just tapping your foot. You could do that by touching your thumb and your index finger together. Or you could do that by simply saying a word. For me, it was excellence, excellence, excellence.

Step Out of the Circle

Before that resource state that you have created fades, step back a little bit out of that circle. You can return to the chair where you are.

Return to the Mental Saltine State

You can open your eyes if they are still closed. Allow yourself to return to that mental saltine state. Taking a breath and taking another breath while your hands rest on the armrest of the chair.

Did it feel incredible to be able to, on command, create that resource state? Sure, it did. The good news here is that any time in the next day or week or month, when you need to tap into that resource state if you touch your thumb and index finger together, or you tap on the floor, or you say whatever your word was (in my case the word was excellence), you will be able to experience that resource state at the highest level of peak performance.

Fold and Keep Handy

The best thing is you can take this with you. See that circle on the floor in front of you. Visualize it there in front of you. Imagine folding it up, folding it up as small as you can. Put it in your back pocket, handbag, or wallet, being able to carry it with you anywhere you would like to go.

Access the Resource State at Any Time

Test this in the next day, week, month, in any situation where this resource state would be of value to you. In your mind, imagine taking it out of your back pocket or out of your handbag, setting it back on the floor, and stepping into it. Actually do this, step into it, fire that anchor—tap, tap, tap, "Excellence, excellence, excellence," thumb and index finger together—whatever anchoring mechanism is helpful to you.

Notice how easy it is to step into this resource state, which can be a problem-solving tool in business, family, community, personal and peak performance, athletic or academic performance, and in any area where you would like to live your best life.

This Circle of Excellence exercise is a fun thing to do. My hope is that you will actually practice this. But what is most important is that you put this into action in a way that benefits you. Practice stepping into that resource state at any place and at any time, so it would be beneficial to you in the real world where you live.

The result of doing that is that you will then begin to share passionately with your clients the things that have been beneficial to you.

Chapter 22
The Disney Strategy in NLP

This has long been one of my favorite patterns or strategies in NLP. The reason why is because, in its truest form, this is what NLP is all about. It looks at somebody who has created success, and it models that success, and it asks the question, why is this person so successful? In this case, we use Walt Disney as our exemplar, who undoubtedly was one of the most creative individuals in the field of animation, in the field of bringing stories to life. Disney was able to tell those stories, create theme parks, and saw a vision for swampland in central Florida, turning it into a gigantic moneymaker.

There is a lot we can learn from somebody like Walt Disney. The interesting thing about this pattern is that the earliest NLP courses did not teach the Disney strategy. The reason why is this was developed by some associates of the early founders, Robert Dilts and Todd Epstein. They articulated this idea of the Disney strategy and used Walt Disney as an exemplar in the late 1980s early 1990s.

What I really like about this is that rather than modeling excellence in psychotherapy, they look outside that field of psychotherapy to find out where we can model excellence? Walt Disney is an impressive model for us when it comes to enhancing creativity.

Would you like to increase your creativity in any area of life? Would you like to increase your creativity in solving mathematical problems? Would you like to increase your creativity when it comes to being a songwriter? Would you like to enhance your creativity in the way that you conduct teachings and trainings, and classes? Creativity is something all of us can use, no matter what our primary profession is. We can use it in therapy. We can use it in coaching. We can use it in parenting. We can use it in every arena of life. The Disney strategy offers something for all of us.

The Dreamer, the Realist, and the Critic

Walt Disney, his colleagues, and employees described three aspects or three phases or the three people of Walt Disney. These were the dreamer, the visionary, the person who could see a swamp and create a theme park in his mind, the person who could take a stick figure mouse and turn it into a global brand, and the critic.

The dreamer is the person who looks up. Their physiology is consistent with the dreamer.

The employees of Disney described these three aspects of the creative genius Walt Disney, using the descriptors of the dreamer, mentally, the way he spoke, the way he articulated his vision, the way he carried himself in his emotions and his physiology.

The second aspect, the second person, Walt Disney, is the realist. Walt Disney, the realist, would look you in the eye. Walt Disney, the realist, would put his hands on his hips. Walt Disney, the realist, would say there is not a lot we can dig here in a swamp, and so we're going to have to use different construction methods in order to turn this into a global giant theme park. The realist looked at the problems and what was in the way and began to apply creative solutions and new ways of thinking to the dreams that the dreamer had.

The third person, or the critic, is the person who looks at what has been decided, might look down in contemplation. There is a famous painting, the official portrait of John F. Kennedy, and you cannot see his eyes. He is looking down in that picture, really showing that thinker, that person who went beyond the dream, went beyond the realism and into a kind of the minutia of how to problem-solve, which was a big part of his approach to leadership in the presidency.

Walt Disney did this as well. The employees at Disney would describe the dreamer that came in, looked up, and created a vision. The realist who would look forward put his hands on his hips and look at the specific issues, creating solutions based on the dream.

And that third component or that third aspect, that third person, the critic, looks down in contemplation, sees the roadblocks in the way, and finds a way past and through those roadblocks. There are hurricanes and crocodiles in Florida. Any of these could be roadblocks in creating a dream. One aspect of the critic and one area where I criticize the Disney company is in copyright. We want to preserve the mouse. We want to own this mouse. Our modern copyright law is directly related to what I call protecting the mouse. And this is something that has benefited Walt Disney. But I think it sometimes stifles our creativity in both leadership and literature, music, and other creative areas.

You can see in Walt Disney these three characters, the dreamer, the realist, and the critic. And Dilts and Epstein referred to Disney as a great exemplar. If you want to enhance your creativity, enter into your creative assignment with each of these three personalities or each of these three characteristics. What is interesting is this was not just a hypothetical that Dilts and Epstein came up with. It was when they came up with it, but people have put it to the test.

Study

There is a recent journal article from 2020 from a university in Malaysia where they studied students in mathematic programs. They sought to enhance their creative ability in solving mathematics by elevating their thinking to a higher order of thinking, also called higher-order thinking (HOT).

Could they teach the Disney pattern to mathematics students to help them think in a higher order and creatively solve problems? The answer to that was yes. And they put it to the test. They used assessment tools and measurements and higher-order thinking. They taught the Disney process to some and not to others, and they studied the outcomes.

The journal article is interesting. It shows that this is an evidence-based approach to helping people enhance their creativity. Think about an area where you would like to improve your creativity. Is it in your music? Is it in your writing? Is it in your communication? Is it in your art? Is it in your mathematics? What area of life would you like to be more creative?

Without a doubt, we really admire the creative person, the person like Jeff Bezos or Elon Musk, who has the idea, the dream to put people on the planet Mars, for example.

Creativity is essential to humankind's progress. And you can be a part of that by increasing your acuity in creativity using the Walt Disney process. Whether it is coaching, counseling, or consulting, we can apply creativity to solving problems in family therapy. We can apply creativity to helping managers creatively embark on new ways to manufacture, distribute, or install the products and services that they offer and that they deliver. This crosses the spectrum of skills for coaching.

Imagine that I have you across from me. I would like you to think for a moment about a dream you have, a creative endeavor that you would like to participate in, something it is that you would like to accomplish in your life. And as I share the hallmarks or the elements of this process with you, think about these things in the context, in terms of your own desires and your own experiences. The result of doing this will be more than if I simply articulated or listed it out here. You will be going through the Disney process as I describe it. And the results will be increased success in your level of creativity.

I could have somebody across from me in the coaching office. I could have somebody I am meeting with on Zoom, helping them to enhance their coaching. I could have somebody in my family or really anyone else that I was guiding through enhancing their creativity but, for our purposes here, just think of what it is that you would like to create.

What would you like to accomplish? What would you like to be better at?

Last year, my friend RJ (Rob) Banks and I made a bunch of silly songs. We released some cover songs that we made, and I am not a particularly good singer. Although he is a masterful guitarist and a wonderful audio engineer, Rob is certainly not an expert on being in a cover band either. But we created these songs, and we released them, and people loved these songs.

When July 4th came around last year, Rob and I decided to write our own song. I said, "Rob, we've sung some of these cover songs. And we have had a lot of fun doing that, but let's write our own songs, something that nobody else has said before." And so, we wrote a song together called *I am America*. Rob wrote the music, and I wrote the lyrics. We videographed it and put it all together, and it was a lot of fun. And ever since then, one of my creative outlets has been writing some verses, writing some songs, in addition to writing my books.

That is an area, for example, where I would like to enhance my creativity.

Where would you like to enhance your creativity?

To enhance your creativity, the first step of this process is the dreamer phase. And it begins by eating that mental saltine. Wherever you are right now, just take in a breath, breathe in, breathe out and create what we call an NLP, neutral state. Set aside the difficulties of yesterday, the fears of tomorrow, and just be fully present in this moment, breathing in, breathing out. Now that you have created a neutral state setting aside those things, think about past creative achievements that you have had. You can do this with the eyes open or with the eyes closed and think of a time that you were at your creative best when you made that music video or that song. Or when you wrote those amazing words in that book. Or when you were speaking from the stage and doing your best. Or when you were creative and problem-solving really in any area of your life.

It might have been recent. It might have been a long time ago but access, recall, revivify that experience of being your creative best.

As you revivify and you recall that experience, what were you seeing? What were you hearing? What were you feeling? What were you tasting? What were you smelling? What was the situation like? Look at all the internal representational systems that you can associate with that previous creative endeavor and notice your physiology as well. What was your posture at that time of creativity? Bring yourself to that posture now; feel the creativity that you felt and that you created before in another previous successful experience. You can say out loud; you can speak to yourself with your voice. What was it that you were feeling? What was it that you were sensing? What was it that you saw?

Speak out loud. This is what I saw; this was what I heard; this is what I felt. By speaking it out loud, we take the past creativity, and we bring it into an experience of the present.

And now we can move to the realist position. Do that by opening the eyes if the eyes are closed, taking in a breath, creating that neutral state again. Shake it out, shake out that dreamer. We are going to be the realist here. And you can do this with your eyes open, or you can do this with your eyes closed. How did you achieve number one? Ask yourself that question. The realist asks a question, and that question is how. *How did I do it? How did I write a complete song? How did I produce an entire music video?* How was it that you did that? What were the steps? What were the strategies? Who did you partner with? How did you implement the ideas? The realist then evaluates their intentions and goals in the present moment. *My intention is to be creative. I am creative. I am creative. I am creative.*

My goal is to write a new song for Christmas. What is your goal?

This is a strategy that is a little bit different than what Dilts and Epstein first articulated, but I would like to utilize this in the realist phase here, and that is to map the previous experiences into the present.

If your eyes are not closed down yet, go ahead and close your eyes down for a moment. And imagine the dreamer, internal representational systems being mapped over to this moment and this experience. See a new project with new goals and new intentions, and let yourself right here right now feel once again the same thing you felt before. Hear the same things you saw before, the same smells, the same type of experience. And amplify that experience right now in the present, mapping the previous creativity over to the present scenario. And notice you have the ability right now to be as creative in your state, your physiology, and in your mind, and in your emotions as you were before.

Now we go into the third phase, the critic. Go ahead and open your eyes if your eyes are not open. Take in a breath, a mental saltine. Shake it out. Feels pretty good to enhance your creativity. Take in a breath. Make your body posture neutral, your emotions neutral. Close your eyes down again. With your eyes closed down like Walt Disney—who put his hand on his chin and looked down at the desk—what roadblocks might you see stopping you from being creative? What obstacles could be in the way of being able to reach those goals? Are the obstacles from people or within yourself, or are they practical things that need to be resolved? Ask yourself these questions: In order to be your most creative and to reach your goal, what is it that you can add to your success? What would help you in the present that maybe you lacked in the past that could take your creativity to the next level? Who can you add to your success?"

Sometimes we can accomplish great things with teams rather than individually.

The last aspect this critic faces is, how can I improve the processes? The process I used before led me to a state of creativity. But I want to have another option, another opportunity to rise to my highest level of creative performance. What can I use to improve the processes? Can I dedicate more time? Can I commit more resources? Can I plan better? Can I implement more efficiency? All of these are questions that you can ask yourself. Now take in a breath, allow yourself to feel creative, both in mind and body and in your spirit.

Opening the eyes, feel fantastic and ready to be your best creative self.

This is the Walt Disney strategy. This is the strategy that when we model Walt Disney, we see somebody who has been a creative genius throughout his life, utilized in many different ways, in various situations from business to art, from communications and personality to every area of his remarkable life.

You can apply the same strategies that Disney used in his life to your life. And the good news is NLP teaches us that so you can replicate those successes.

THE WALT DISNEY STRATEGY
(DILTZ & EPSTEIN)

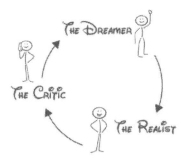

Dreamer	Realist	Critic (Self-questioning)
1.) Saltine state (neutral state)	1.) Saltine state	1.) Mental saltine
2.) Think of a past creative achievement	2.) How did you achieve this previously?	2.) What to do if there are roadblocks?
3.) Revivify (internal representational systems and the physiology)	3.) Intention and goals	3.) What can you do to add to your success?
4.) Speak out loud what you feel, sense, see, are, and do	4.) Map past into present	4.) How can I improve processes?

Chapter 23
NLP Mapping Across

An all-time favorite strategy of mine in NLP and coaching is the idea of mapping across. This is the idea or the concept of taking something from before and bringing it into the present moment. We know all the power comes from focusing on the present rather than the past, but each one of us has a set of previous experiences that might either indirectly or directly relate to a problem that we are trying to solve in the present moment or emotion that we are trying to become more comfortable with and amplify a behavior that we would like to step into.

Previous Resources

Because NLP's basic presupposition is that we have all the resources within us already to handle any situation, the mapping across strategy is about taking our previous learnings, experiences, feelings, and internal representation systems of value from previous life events and bringing them into the present.

Most of you know that when it comes to hypnosis, I have never been a big fan of regress to cause. In other words, going back and trying to find the cause of what our problems are today. The reason why is simple. We cannot actually change anything about the past, but I am a fan of what my friend, Kevin Cole, refers to as regress to resource. In other words, we can go back and discover the resources that we possessed at one time, with the assumption or the belief that we can map them across into the present time.

We have our present state, and this is where we are now, and we have our previous resources. This is what the subconscious mind is storing up. The subconscious mind is storing our previous learnings, experiences, internal representational systems, processes, steps, relationships, all these sorts of tools for us. They can be beliefs. They can be experiences. They can be feelings. They can be intentions. They can be skills from our previous experiences or more, and we want to map them into the present.

Present Resources

The big question is how do we go about doing that? What is the strategy for taking the past previous resources and mapping them into the present? When we do that successfully, the outcome of this is new directions, new opportunities, new levels of success. This is how you move into peak performance. You take your previous experiences, and you bring them into the present moment. You practice and rehearse.

Let's say you want to improve your golfing. You can create new directions where instead of being a ten handicap, now you are a three handicap or a scratch golfer.

We can really use this mapping across pattern in NLP with any situation. It could be about my relationships. How is it in the present situation that I can create a good relationship in my current relationship, especially if in the past I have had a history of difficult relationships? One way to do this is to see what your previous resources were. You might have had difficulty in those relationships, but did you do anything right? What was it you did right? What beliefs did you have that helped? What experiences did you have that helped? What feelings and intentions, and skills did you have that benefited that relationship? Even if the relationship ultimately did not turn out the way that you hoped it would be, that does not mean we can give up hope. We can believe that we can map across those tools and resources that were resourceful. Chances are, in that situation, you probably also have been mapping across non-resourceful previous experiences, but map those into the present moment.

New Directions

Once we have mapped those resourceful feelings into the present moment, then we move forward with new directions, new outcomes, new relationships. We can see that this could be a pathway to success in several different ways, but it goes back to the question of how to do this. What action steps can we take, or when we are working with a client, what action steps can we take to help them to do this?

I am going to give you three tools. These are three different scripts, or patterns, or tools to be able to map across. This answers the question, ow? One is auditory, one is visual, and one is kinesthetic.

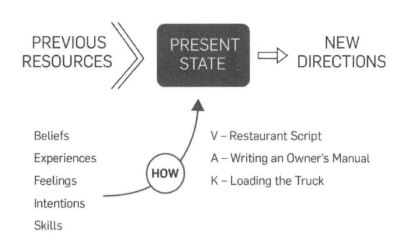

MAPPING ACROSS
— STRATEGY —

PREVIOUS RESOURCES → PRESENT STATE ⇒ NEW DIRECTIONS

Beliefs
Experiences
Feelings
Intentions
Skills

HOW

V – Restaurant Script
A – Writing an Owner's Manual
K – Loading the Truck

Visual

Go ahead and close your eyes down for a moment and think about your current situation. What is one thing you would like to do more of, or that you would like to do better, or a problem you would like to solve? And think about that.

And as you think about that and as you associate into the desired state, access the subconscious mind, that reservoir of our previous experiences and learnings. The beliefs you had, the behaviors you had, the challenges you had, the feelings, the intentions you had in other situations in the past.

Imagine you are going into a restaurant. This is your favorite restaurant, and this is called the Restaurant of Mapping Across. And imagine walking to your table. The hostess brings you to your table. It is a great table with a splendid view. And you are with your partner. You are with your partner of the present moment or the present experience.

And as you sit down and begin to read the menu, you will notice that there are things on that menu that you have tried and that you have tasted before. There might be skillsets, problem-solving strategies, or emotions, or even aspects of belief that are important. For example, if we want to change a belief, congruency might be one of the aspects that we want to map across to help believe truth.

If I want to map across my emotions, and I want to map across joy, one thing that I might discover on the menu is creating shared experiences. Because when I create shared experiences, I discovered it often brings me a sense of joy. Study the menu. I will give you all the time you need to go over the menu. There are appetizers, the things that you might do first. The salads might give you some extra flavor in your quest to map across the resources from your previous experiences to the present. And the main dish. Is there anything on this menu you think would be truly useful to you in the present scenario that you had not even thought about ordering? And the desserts. There is almost something that can top it off and lead to success in the long term.

Since you have your partner with you from the present moment, what are some of the resources from the present moment that you can tap into? Right now, in this moment, you might be trying to solve a particular problem, but maybe the resources of commitment or the resources of sharing experiences. Imagine the server comes over and asks a simple question, "What is it you would like to order today?" And imagine yourself ordering that five-course dinner of all those resources from your previous experiences, and they are delivered to your table one at a time.

As you bring them into the present moment, when dinner is over, you walk away from the table, and you step out the door of the restaurant into a new direction, a new future, where you feel full and satisfied from having brought from your previous experiences, even those that might not have led to the outcomes you wanted, a set of skills and strategies that in the present moment can lead directly to the options, the opportunities and the directions you'd like to proceed.

Go ahead and open your eyes if your eyes are not already open.

Auditory

I have always said that the person who builds Ikea furniture by reading the instructions is the auditory person. They are hearing the internal dialogue.

Go ahead and close your eyes down for a moment and see yourself as you are right now. What is it you would like to build? Would you like to build better relationships, sales success? Would you like to build a sense of community? Would you like to build happiness? What is it that you would like to build in your life? Imagine what that is, the outcome you desire. This is your intention in the present moment.

Scan your subconscious mind, your past reservoir, beliefs, experiences, feelings, intentions. And imagine you are sitting at a desk. You have three pieces of paper in front of you. You have a pen, and you are going to create the outline on these three pieces of paper of how to go about building the present moment that would be of the most value to you.

You can use pictures and diagrams if you want, or you can simply use words, and you can outline your steps. Perhaps step one, congruency. Perhaps step two, amplify a resource state of joy. Perhaps step three, share my commitment with others. I do not know what is in your owner's manual because I am not sure what it is that you are trying to build, but you know, and your subconscious mind knows. So, take as much time now as you need to write out this owner's manual, so somebody else or you can follow the steps, follow the directions here in their own mind, how the process works, to map across the resources from the past into the present moment.

And now, open your eyes. Look in front of you at the paper you have, the owner's manual you have written. You are going to fold that up, put it in your pocket, and you can take it with you. Anytime in the future, when you need to access this owner's manual and listen to the steps, you can do that.

Kinesthetic

Go ahead and close your eyes down, and with your eyes closed, imagine the present state. What is the immediate intention or desire, or situation? In the past, you have probably loaded something into the back of your car or the back of your pickup truck.

Imagine now that in the present moment, in order to map across the resources from the past, you have taken each one of these beliefs, experiences, feelings, intentions, and skills and put them in a bag, and you have loaded them in the back. And once the trunk has been loaded or the bed of the pickup truck is loaded, you are ready to start the engine and move forward in a new direction as quickly as you want to travel or as slowly as you want to travel, probably depending on how well you have secured the payload in the back. If your eyes are not open, go ahead and open your eyes, take in a breath.

There are three strategies for working with clients, conversationally, using examples and metaphors, to help them to map across resources that are already within them to new situations and new opportunities.

Let's talk about a basic principle in sales. It is a lot easier to sell things to your existing customers than to get new customers. It is less expensive, and you already have a warm lead. In business, they call this return on investment (ROI) or the cost of acquiring a new customer. It might cost me $50 or $300 in advertising to acquire a new customer. But once I have a new customer, it might only cost me $10 or $30 to create another sale.

Similarly, when we are mapping across, it is a lot easier for us to problem-solve in the present by utilizing the skills, strengths, and resources already within us than it is to try to find new skills and new resources and new ways of problem-solving. In the past, things might not have worked out exactly the way you wanted them to. It's okay. Life is a journey. Sometimes that disastrous relationship was necessary to create a wonderful relationship today. They say that good judgment comes from experience, and experience comes from bad judgment. Alcoholics Anonymous phrases it this way, "No matter how far down the scale we've gone, we will see how our experiences can benefit others."

Chapter 24
NLP Submodalities

Important to cover are the submodalities of primary representational systems. We have visual, auditory, and kinesthetic. That is where we spend most of our time focusing, but we also have taste and smell. What I am going to share with you are the submodalities of each of these. For example, within visual, there is near, there is far, there is color, there is noncolor. What we are asking a person to do when they are sharing their submodalities with us is asking them to share the qualities or the characteristics of the primary representational system.

It is very important that you as a practitioner become acquainted with the huge repertoire and the depth of potential descriptors for each of these different primary representational systems. These are the submodalities, the way we would describe visual or auditory or kinesthetic or taste or smell.

Within each of these is a range, and some of these descriptor words overlap. They can be used across the modalities because the word can either have a visual meaning or an auditory meaning or a kinesthetic meaning, or some other type of meaning.

Familiarize yourself with the word salad that I am giving you. There are more on the planet Earth than simply those that are on this list, so feel free to embellish your list to add things to the list that you think perhaps I might have overlooked or forgotten.

When you are working with clients, listen to their submodalities, the descriptors they use of their primary representational systems. To work with a client to help them increase their acuity in a certain representational system, we can share with them this word salad or some of the words, talk to them or teach them, or instruct them on creating acuity within these areas in these contexts.

It is really a rich exercise and is a lot of fun to do.

Visual Submodalities

We could be talking about the hue, think of a TV set. How much green, how much blue, how much pink, how much red? We might change the contrast. More black, less white, more white, less black. We can also deal with colors. What color is the visualization?

If I have a client who tells me, "I am so depressed every time I look toward to the next day, it's almost as if I can see gloom and doom around me," I know this is a very visual person. I will ask them about the qualities of those submodalities. Is the visualization they have or the experience they have framed, or is it borderless? If we live in a virtual reality (VR) world, is it at 180 degrees, or is it 360 degrees?

What is the location of their visualization as compared to where they are? What is the motion of the visualization? Is it moving, is it not moving? Is it far? Is it near? What is the angle or the viewpoint? Is the visualization associated or non-associated? What that means is that from their perspective, they are associating themself as them looking at something. Or, it is non-associated, viewing from outside of themself as if it is a picture or something.

Is the visualization hazy? Is it clear? Is it fuzzy? Is it to the left? Is it to the right? What is the movement or the direction of that movement? Does it move closer? Does it move further? Does it move left? Does it move right? Does it move top? Does it move bottom? What is the brightness of it? Is it very bright? Is it very dim? Is it easy to see? Is it hard to see? Is it focused? Is it unfocused? What is the sharpness of it? Is it in 4K? Is it in 8K? Is it in 720p, or is it 360p?

All of these are various submodalities, ways that a person might describe their experience from a visual perspective.

Auditory Submodalities

What is the pitch? What is the tempo? What is the rate? What is the strength? Is it verbal? Is it nonverbal? Is it heard audibly or not audibly? Is it clear? Is it fuzzy? What is the timbre? Is it thick? Is it thin? What are the distances? Is the sound heard in the distance, or is the sound spoken loudly into the ear? What is the duration of the auditory experiences? Is it long? Is it short? Is it muffled? What is the rhythm, the cadence, the tempo? What is the accent? And are there pauses? Is the sound from inside where I am or outside from where I am? What is the variation? Is it mono, or is it in stereo?

All of these are submodalities of the auditory experience. By exploring these at a deep level with your clients, you can really have them paint a very detailed soundtrack of their auditory experiences.

Kinesthetic Submodalities

A lot of people who are naturally kinesthetic have a wide repertoire of how they experience things from that physical perspective. Those who are primarily auditory or visual sometimes really wrestle with these. Knowing the different words on this list can help you to elicit a deep understanding of submodalities from your clients.

Direction comes into play. Pressure comes into play. Texture comes into play. Emotions can be a physical experience of depression, of joy. Then there is the weight of something. Is it balanced? Is it not balanced? What is the tactile nature of it? What is it that they feel? Is it soft? Is it hard? Is it high? Is it low? High to reach, low to reach? Is it large, too big to put my arms around? Is it very small? Can I hold it in my hands? What about movement? What about the quality of the kinesthetic experience? What comes into play here is proprioception, body position. What is their awareness of themself within the context of what it is that they are describing? Notice their facial expression, contorted, the form, the gesture. Do they speak with their hands? Movement, is it steady? Is it intermittent?

These are all hallmarks of kinesthetic traits or characteristics.

Taste/Gustatory Submodalities

We can break taste down into four different types: sweet, sour, salty, bitter. What is amazing, though, is that these four words could really be expressive. You hear this in the context of business all the time. "I've done business with him before. I had a salty experience." "I'm not looking forward to doing business again with that person because it left a bitter taste in my mouth last time." "I enjoy working with this person. They leave a sweet taste in my mouth every time I purchase something from them." "I hope this business deal doesn't go sour." We have those in relationships as well. "My wife is so very sweet." "The last time I broke up with somebody, I was bitter for months."

We can see these same words again in the context of relationships, business, community, parenting, helping other people, any of these sorts of things.

Smell/Olfactory Submodalities

What does thought, feeling, and emotion smell like? That might seem like a strange thing, but much of the world around us is interpreted through our sense of smell. Is it a camp floor, in other words, mothball sort of smell? Is it musky? A lot of perfumes go after that musky smell. Is it floral? Is it peppermint? Is it ethereal, a chemical smell, the smell of whiteout? Is it pungent? Is it putrid? Is it fruity? Is it nutty? Is it a woody scent?

If you are a wine tasting expert, you are probably familiar with all of these things, but most of us aren't wine tasting experts. We struggle to try to figure out what are the submodalities of the olfactory sense, the sense of smell, and these are them.

We can easily discover ways of enriching our clients' ability to describe their previous experiences, their current experiences, and their future experience when we incorporate the kinesthetic sub-modalities, the olfactory, and the gustatory submodalities well.

Now that we have had our word salad let's have our main course. The main course is what to do with all these submodalities. I am going to give you a fairly simple version of a classic NLP technique.

Think of something that you struggle with, something that is difficult for you, something perhaps that is either a situation, a person, a place, a thing, an emotion, an attitude that you are either currently experiencing or have experienced in the past.

It leaves a salty, or bitter, or sour taste in the mouth. And go ahead and think of that scenario or situation so that we have something for this exercise.

You can close your eyes down if you want to. You will probably find that it really lends itself to helping you experience this at a fuller or a richer level.

Imagine walking into a movie theater, and you are the only one in this theater, so you can pick the place where you would like to sit. Do not pick one of those movie theaters that is uncomfortable, but rather one of those new movie theaters perhaps that have those comfortable recliners. And you can pick close to the screen or far from the screen, off to the side, on an aisle, or in the center. It really doesn't matter. Simply pick one of the seats that you would find the most comfortable.

And imagine sitting in that seat and seeing a movie playing of that distressing or difficult scenario or situation that you just thought of moments ago. You can hear the sounds as it plays in the movie of that scene, scenario, interaction. You can see the sights. You can even feel. You can feel the kinesthetic experiences as that movie plays. The smells are filmed in, smell a vision, and then taste a vision. From this vantage point, pay attention to that movie playing that distressing, uncomfortable, or difficult movie. Now, in your mind, freeze the movie. Imagine the guy in the projector booth has stopped it. He has frozen it on a frame. Pay attention to each of the submodalities in the visual movie that you have been seeing. The motion, the location, the boundary, is it all clear? And the movement, the direction, the brightness? Really pay attention to this frame of this movie.

You can hear the sound of the movie. You can feel the feelings of the movie. You can smell the movie. You can taste the movie. Now we're going to begin changing these things. You have already frozen the motion from the visual perspective. Change the color, change the color from, perhaps if it was in black and white to color, or if it was in color, change it to black and white. If it was 180 degrees, change it to a 360-degree virtual reality. If it was clear, change it to hazy. If it was hazy, change it to clear. If you were in the movie, step out of the movie. If you were out of the movie, step into the movie. Change it from bright to dim, from focused to unfocused. Imagine the lens got moved a little bit, and the frame becomes a little bit less focused. The sharpness comes out of focus, the hue, the color, the depth, the shape; it all begins to change. In fact, you can even change it dramatically.

You can change it like you used to do on an old TV set so that it is all pink or all black and white. You can change the submodalities in any way you want to but play with that idea of changing the submodalities you first noticed when the movie was playing. When the movie was playing, there was an auditory experience; the dialogue on the screen, or the soundtrack in the background, the rhythm, the direction, the accent, the pauses, change those things. If there was mysterious music, replace it with calliope music. If there was calliope music, replace it with haunted castle music. If the people were speaking with an American accent, give them a British accent. If it was clear, make it muffled. If it was muffled, make it clear.

What you are doing here is you are changing the auditory aspects of this experience that was distressing to you. And as you begin to make these changes, do you notice something? Do you notice that it is different, maybe even more tolerable or better? What about your kinesthetic experiences? The pressure, the shakiness, the quality, the distance, what it is you feel. The weight, the texture of these things. Change these things. Change the leather fabric of the chair you are sitting in for a cloth or a metal chair. Change anything you can about the kinesthetic awareness that you had when the movie was playing now that it is on a frozen, still screen. And, you can change the taste from sweet to sour, from sour to sweet, from bitter to salty. And if there is a smell in the smell of the vision of the movie, you can change the smell. If the smell was an ethereal, chemical smell, let it become flowery, like a lilac. Or perhaps it was fruity like lemon or fruity like an orange and let it become nutty like a peanut.

It might seem strange to be able to change the submodalities of a real experience that you thought of, yet right here, you have actually been able to do it, and you can do it dramatically. You can drain the color from the visualization. You can change the soundtrack of the audio experience, or you could even make it silent. You could make the movement of the kinesthetic experience stop, or you can make the stopped bits move. You can change the smell. You can change the taste.

Now imagine the movie begins to play again, but this time it is playing with all of these changes. These changes are entirely different now than they were just a moment ago. It is a completely different experience. And notice your response to it. Is your response more intense or less intense? Is it attracted to it, or is it repelled by it? What is it that is changed in the way that you relate to this experience now that you have changed the submodalities? Chances are pretty good that the way you relate to it now is entirely different. Your visceral response, your emotional response, your kinesthetic response are all entirely different. Often the change we seek is not actually better or worse. Sometimes it is simply different. And by being able to change something that we disliked or disdained, or had difficulty with, into something that is simply different, we have then begun the journey of stepping into a new direction.

Let out a breath. Pay attention to the chair below you. You can continue to play the movie if you want to, or you can simply stop the movie and open your eyes. Opening the eyes, taking in a breath, feeling fantastic because you have learned the art of changing the experience to something, the relationship you had with a thought, a feeling, a sensation, by really focusing on the ability to change the submodalities.

You can use this in coaching and counseling, with PTSD, with business choices, you can use this with spouses and partners, evaluating relationships. You can use this within the community to discover new ways of interacting with people and previous experiences and new planning that might be going on by paying attention to the submodalities or our primary representational systems. More importantly, to those that our clients will share with us, it can be a tremendous tool for creating lasting and effective change with the people with whom we are working.

Chapter 25
The S.C.O.R.E. Approach to Coaching

The S.C.O.R.E. model has been one of my favorite techniques in NLP because it is a very practical strategy. It is not actually a technique; you can use a number of different techniques within NLP to apply the S.C.O.R.E. model. Todd Epstein and Robert Dilts originally developed the S.C.O.R.E. model, and an improvement was made by Judith DeLozier that really focused on the kinesthetic aspects.

One of the excellent aspects of the S.C.O.R.E. model is that it is almost universal. You can use this with just about any type of client. You could use it in academics, business, and parenting. You can use it as your own sort of roadmap for self-improvement and to help you overcome anything.

It is a noteworthy resource tool, and I am going to share something I think is really important in using the S.C.O.R.E. model in the context of positive psychology or appreciative inquiry.

First, let's take a look at the acronym S.C.O.R.E. It stands for **S**ymptoms, **C**auses, **O**utcomes, **R**esources, and **E**ffects. I want to point out that I do not really like the word "symptom" because symptom has a medical context, and I want to be practicing outside of a medical model. I almost always use the word "situation" when I am working with people and coaching. The situation is that which is distressing, irritating, bothersome, problematic, or in nondiagnostic language, something the client would like to resolve, change or transform because this is a tool for transformation. We can use it in several different ways.

THE S.C.O.R.E. MODEL

S - **SYMPTOM** (Situation)

C - **CAUSES** (The why behind the situation)

O - **OUTCOMES** (Desired state, action, intention)

R - **RESOURCES** (Internal, external, skills, intentions)

E - **EFFECTS** (Ideally, desired effects)

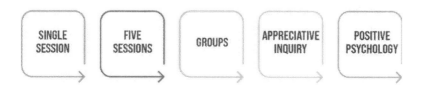

Symptoms/Situation

The first step is to help somebody to understand where they are now. We cannot go anywhere or do anything until we recognize what is going on in this moment, in this situation. What is it about this situation that is distressing or irritating? What is it about this situation that causes the client to want change? One of my favorite questions to clients is, how do you know that this is a problem for you? They may answer that they know that this is a problem for them because it affects their money or their relationships, or their motivation, or some other important aspect of functioning. At this level in my coaching, I am working with a person to describe and understand the current situation.

I will ask them questions, probably using the Socratic method, to help them really understand. And I am probably going to also focus on the auditory, the visual, and the kinesthetic.

When you think of the distress of this situation, what are you seeing? When you think of the distress, what are you hearing? I will ask my clients, and this is Judith DeLozier's idea, to model it. "Show me when you are the most stressed, what that looks like. Strike a pose." Physically have them model the kinesthetic state that they are in when they are finding themself distressed by this situation.

Now that we have identified the situation or the symptoms clearly so that we know exactly what it is we are working with, we want to ask clarification questions here. "Is there anything that we are missing that we want to add to this situation?" "Are there things you are describing in this situation that actually aren't a part of the situation but are part of somebody else's situation?" We could bring into this idea Stephen Covey's four quadrants, is it urgent and unimportant? Is it not urgent but important? Is it un-urgent and un-important. Or, is it urgent and important? Those are four quadrants from Stephen Covey that can help us understand this situation exactly what we want to be able to focus on or change.

Causes

Then we look at the causes. It is essential to note that these are the whys behind the current situation, but it is done without blame, and it is done without judgment. This is a crucial component because otherwise, many people will get stuck in the cause. We know there is a problem. Let's look at the causes of that problem and not try to find who is to blame or who is at fault, or why somebody is an idiot.

When we can externalize it, we can take it out of our experiences and shift blame. Doing this, we can spend all day long trying to solve somebody else, but not solving ourselves. So, we are going to bring it home. And we are going to look at our self in this situation. How is it that the client has contributed to the causes of this situation? Yes, we know there are other people who are probably players here as well. Things do not occur in a vacuum. There are probably some other situations that relate to this situation, but what are the causes? Is it my miscommunication? Is it my misinterpretation? Is it my distortion? Is it my deletion? Is it my generalization? We can look at what the causes are.

When I work with a client, to help them understand the causes, I take out a piece of paper and get them to write down the five predominant causes of this situation or the symptom that is so distressing. We do this with acceptance, without judgment, just acknowledging that these things are there. It is outside of them. It is on the paper. It is something we can acknowledge, and we do not have to become emotionally involved in the distress then.

I might even have them model this from a physiological perspective, asking them when they are in the cause of the problem, what they look like. Model it. It is like a game of charades and is kind of fun. By using the kinesthetic component and asking them to step into the physiological state, they are engaging at deep levels of awareness. This provides additional insight instead of simply questioning things or dealing with the visualization or the auditory aspects of things.

Outcomes

Then we move into the outcome. The outcome, in this case, is the desired resource state, or the action that would be preferred, or the intention of the goal.

Focus on intention rather than goals because you can activate an intention right now, whereas a goal is something you have to anticipate acquiring in the future. You need to brainstorm. You are in this situation, and here are some of the causes of the situation. You can ask yourself, What desired state would I prefer? What action would I prefer? What intention would be more resourceful? And again, you can visualize yourself with the desired outcome, with the desired action, with the desired intention. Hear yourself. Be that. Imagine right now that the outcome you desire is there. What would that look like? Model these things. And it may feel silly, but it is fun. It is interactive. People really enjoy that modeling or that kinesthetic aspect. Have them contrast the kinesthetic aspect of, I would be this, right now I am this. We can bring the kinesthetic experience powerfully into this process.

Resources

These are internal resources. Strengths resources. These are external resources. These are things that might help me solve a problem, specific skills, specific people. These are the resources. These are the strengths that can help me to activate the outcome that is desired.

Effects

The effects are ideally the desired effects from making the change by implementing the powerful resources available to us. The most valuable resources are those that are already within us. We can bring other NLP processes like the transderivational search into the S.C.O.R.E. model by simply saying to our client, "Imagine the desired effect. How can you find the resources that are within you to overcome the causes of the situation that's been so distressing to you?"

The great thing about the S.C.O.R.E. model is that it can be something accomplished in thirty or forty minutes with somebody conversationally in my office, maybe with a pencil and paper in front of us to write some thoughts out.

It can be a conversation that I have. It could be something I do with my clients in the first session. In much of my coaching, I have said, "I'm going to share with you a very powerful process that can help you to create change in our very first session." When I make that promise, I am almost always using the S.C.O.R.E. method in that very first session with them, whether it is a one-hour, two-hour, three-hour, or a full-day coaching session. I am going to use the S.C.O.R.E. model so that they can begin stepping into the effects, the ideal desired state, or change or transformation that is so important to them.

Five Sessions

We can also use this in what I would call a five-session protocol, either with individuals or groups. We take a dive deep into the S.C.O.R.E. model, moving from where they are to where they would like to be. We do that over a period of five sessions. The first session focuses on the situation. The second focuses on the causes without blaming, without judgment. The third on the outcomes, the fourth on the resources, and the fifth on the effects. When we are done the five-week transformation, they are able to set aside the situations and the symptoms that have been so distressing and step into lasting transformation. I can schedule five coaching calls on each one of these subjects. Or I can make it a weekly process or a daily process over the course of a week for an individual. There are a lot of different ways to configure this.

It is a valuable coaching strategy to use in groups. We can teach the S.C.O.R.E. model, and the group members look at the situations, usually within either their educational setting or their work setting. I could have five flip charts. I could have four flip charts with symptoms, causes, outcomes, and resources. And I could have a fifth one that is our effects flip chart, off to the side, away from the others. In other words, we are noting that there is a finality or difference to it. And I can give participants in the room flip chart markers, and I can have them map out their situations, their causes, their outcomes, their resources, their effects on the flip charts. The desired effect and the positive outcome being the final step. This puts them, without any effort, into the physiology of each one of these five components of the S.C.O.R.E. model.

Appreciative Inquiry

We can do a whole giant course just on Appreciative Inquiry. Volumes of books have been written on the subject. I like, what I would call, the reverse S.C.O.R.E. model in Appreciative Inquiry coaching. Appreciative Inquiry is a corporate application. I am simplifying this, but it is a corporate application or a business application of Positive Psychology that focuses on the individual. Rather than trying to fix what is wrong, we take more of what is right and increase the correctness or the rightness or the joy or the happiness. Instead of focusing on our depression, we focus on our happiness.

Appreciative Inquiry has been used by John Deere, British Airways, and educational organizations. It is a well-researched method. Case Western Reserve University has done a ton of research on the value of Appreciative Inquiry and Organizational Psychology. If you do any kind of corporate work or business consulting, you are going to want to study Appreciative Inquiry and learn as much as you can about it.

The basic tenant or philosophy is that if we have six percent of our customers dissatisfied, giving us one-star reviews and complaining, that means ninety-four percent of our customers are not doing that. Most companies focus on the problem, and the Law of Attraction says, "Focus equals fuel." And if you stay focused on the problem, you will produce more problems. Appreciative Inquiry does not try to figure out how we are screwing up six percent of the time. It asks a different question. It asks the question, what are we doing right ninety-four percent of the time? How can we do more of that? We can use the S.C.O.R.E. model within the context of Appreciative Inquiry or within the context of Positive Psychology in a different way. Rather than looking at the symptom or the situation that is a problem, we could look at the solution.

In this situation, customer satisfaction at a five-star level is eighty-two percent. Another ten percent are four-star level happy. Another three percent are three-star happy. And then, five percent are unacceptable with two-star or one-star reviews. But the current situation is ninety-two percent are giving us a high feedback rating. That is the current situation. What is the cause of it? Rather than looking at the cause of the problem, why are those five percent unhappy, ask why are these ninety-two percent satisfied? What is the cause behind that? What are we doing right? Who is doing things correctly? How can more of that be done? And so, we look at the desired outcome.

The desired outcome is to have ninety-nine percent because there is always somebody who is going to be unhappy. Ninety-nine percent of our customers leaving us three, four, and five-star reviews. The action we would like to take is to improve the communication between our sales, our delivery, and our installation teams so that we have a higher level of satisfaction.

We move from ninety-four to ninety-six to ninety-eight, and hopefully, to ninety-nine. Our intention is to make all our customers satisfied.

Then we look at the resources. Who are the people? What are the skills that we have as an organization? What are the internal systems that function, that work well, in our organization? Again, we are focusing on the solution rather than focusing on the problem. It is an entirely different way of looking at things, but it is an essential strategy that will set your consulting apart from other people's consulting. And then the effect, the ideal desired effect is to open our Google or Yelp reviews and find that there is nothing but five-star reviews. Wouldn't that be awesome? And then our customers refer their friends and family so they can become our customers.

Positive Psychology

We can use the same S.C.O.R.E. model in a Positive Psychology model as well.

Let's deal with physical pain. I have worked over the years with a lot of chronic pain clients. My first job in this field was probably in 1994, and I was doing substance abuse assessments within a chronic pain program at an inpatient hospital facility. People came to us with chronic pain. They know that situation. That is what they have been focusing on.

Let's look at this from a Positive Psychology perspective. "Where is your comfort?" "How much comfort do you feel?" They have never been asked that question before. They may respond that they only feel three percent comfort. Let's focus on comfort rather than the ninety-seven percent pain that is felt. They have been focusing on the pain. They have had doctors, surgeries, psychiatrists, medication, and all kinds of things focusing on the pain. Let's focus on comfort, the three percent of the time they are comfortable and what that comfort is like emotionally, as well as spiritually, as well as from a physical perspective. Let's look at the causes for the comfort.

My pain control clients have never done that before. When we ask them to consider what it is that causes them to be more comfortable, they may respond it is when they get some physical activity. "I don't get physical activity often," they might say, "because of my limitations, but I do notice that when I increase my physical activity, I do better." So, we are looking at what? We are looking at the why behind the situation that increases what is right with them—the comfort.

Then we can look at the outcome. The desired outcome here is they would like to be comfortable at a level twenty, or forty, or eighty. They would like to be comfortable when they have to stand and work all day. They would like to be comfortable when they sleep. They would like to be comfortable following the next surgery that is scheduled. Whatever the issue is for them, discover the desired emotional state, physical state, spiritual state, metaphysical state that they want so you can help them to define the desired outcome from a positive perspective.

Then we are going to look at the resources. What resources do you have? Do you have a massage chair at home? Do you have a prescription that you have found to be beneficial to you? Do you have access to high-quality health insurance that gives you preventative programs in addition to acute treatment care?

Every situation has a different set of resources, and you would be surprised how often people are leaving money on the table or, in other words, untapped resources until we guide them through this process. And it can make all the difference in the world to the final effect, the ideal desired outcome. And I might have my pain control client show me the situation where they feel comfortable three percent of the time. Again, act this out. Ask them to physically show you. "What does it look like when you increased your physical activity? And you know it is probably going to make a difference in the way you feel. Show me what that looks like." And I tap into the kinesthetic aspect of the S.C.O.R.E. model using a Positive Psychology or Appreciative Inquiry approach.

Chapter 26
The YES! Set

The YES! Set is one of the most useful NLP patterns or language patterns we can possibly use. It is applicable in coaching, therapy, and sales. It can also help you motivate your family members to clean the house and assist you in yard work. It is simply a fantastic strategy.

The idea here is to create alignment with other people so that their desires are congruent with what it is that we would like to suggest. This is also a handy tool in hypnosis.

We are looking for the opportunity to have somebody create agreement with us. This increases rapport, the desire to work together and provide cooperation, and the likelihood of acting on suggestions that we have made.

You have probably heard the universal Law of Attraction, "Like attracts like." We can say that the universal law in NLP is "Agreement creates agreement."

I am going to help you to utilize the Yes Set in several ways.

The fundamental principle is that when you can get somebody to agree with you, when you can get them to say yes, it is easier then to get the next yes from them. You can see how this could be truly useful in sales.

Let me give you a couple of examples here.

I am going to ask you some questions, and you can respond as you read this book:

- "So far, have you enjoyed the NLP learnings?" "Yes."

- "Have you applied anything from this NLP training to either your life or the work you do with your clients?" "Yes."

- "Have you discovered how truly useful these strategies can be?" "Yes."

- "Let me ask you another question. Would you like to commit to a year-long master class with me? The investment is only $2500 a month. Would you like to do that?" "Yes."

You can see how this can be used as a sales tool. It can be used as a tool for persuasion. It can be a tool for overcoming disagreement.

Now to a therapeutic example: I might have a client who struggled with anxiety for a long time. The idea here is that the first "Yes" that we're trying to elicit is an easy "Yes" for them to give. It gets easier for them to give yeses as we go into harder questions.

"Let me ask you a question. You've held onto this anxiety for a long time now, haven't you?"

"Oh, yes. Yes, I have."

"I've taught you a strategy. It was the 3-2-1 strategy for managing anxiety. Did you try that?"

"Yes."

"Did you find that was helpful to you?"

"Well, yes."

"Next time you experience anxiety, do you think that this would be a strategy that could help you to stop your panic?"

"Yes."

"Let me ask you one more question. Are you ready to give up the anxiety you've held onto for years and start stepping into confidence and comfort?"

"Yes."

I have always said that therapy is about the art of the close, being able to close the deal. If we are selling the idea that a depressed person could be happy or that an anxious person could be calm, they must buy it. This language pattern truly is a closing strategy.

The YES! Set is mapped out below:

For our desired agreement. What is it that we want alignment with? What do we want agreement with? What do we want them to say "Yes" to?

We create questions that elicit a "Yes." The easiest question, a more difficult question, a more complex question, maybe even four questions. The result is that we get alignment and agreement.

The reason why we get this alignment and agreement is that persuasion comes from three things occurring in this Yes Set.

The YES! Set

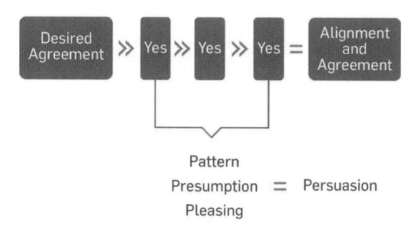

Pattern

Presumption = Persuasion

Pleasing

Chained Pattern:

We Have... and, and, and, so _____.

First, a pattern. Our minds are wired to love patterns. We act in the future the way we acted in the past. The easiest way to get somebody to do something healthy is to have something healthy that they did in the past. It is a lot easier to help them discover what they have been doing right rather than try to equip them with new strategies and new skills because we like patterns. We like things that we have done before.

This YES! Set also presupposes and creates a presumption on the part of the individual that they want to be in agreement with us. And it is human nature to desire to please other people. It makes us happier to give a yes answer than it does to give a no answer. The pattern, the presumption, and the pleasing equal the persuasion that comes from this YES! Set.

We can expand this YES! Set by using one more formula. Rather than asking questions, we can use what is called a chained

YES! Set. The language pattern here is it begins with "We have" or "We've," and then it goes "and . . . ," "and . . . ," "and . . . ," "so [conclusion]." This is the formula for the chained YES! Set, and it is a pretty cool strategy.

Let me give you an example of this. You spent time reading this book learning NLP. Now you do not have to say yes. It is a transderivational search. You are considering whether you agree with me. You are asking yourself, *Have I spent time learning NLP?* You are going to say yes. *And* we have discovered a lot of new strategies, *and* you have applied those in your own life, *and* you've learned how that could benefit other people. The next step would be to take an advanced practitioner course. Wouldn't that be good for you? And you will likely respond in the affirmative, "Well, yes."

Let's go through this again.

"We've spent time learning new strategies for managing anxiety, *and* you've taken it to the next level. You've used the 3-2-1 strategy in a number of different situations, *and* the result has been your panic attacks have ceased, *and* it feels good, doesn't it? And *so,* at this point, you are ready to give up the anxiety that you hold on to and step into calm and comfort and confidence." This is a chained YES! Set. This is a language pattern that I find extremely effective. We could use this in sales.

"We've just gone on a demo ride with three different cars, *and* you said that the X3 was the best size for the parking lot that you like to park your car in, *and* you really liked the white with the basketball-colored interior, *and* you said to me that having a car that had a high level of horsepower was important, but that you wanted to balance that with the price, and *so* it seems clear to me you would probably prefer to drive the X3 and neither the X1 or the X5. If we can get the numbers right today, would you like to park it in your garage tonight and drive to work tomorrow in your brand-new car?" "Yes."

This is how the YES! Set works. It is a remarkable strategy, one that you can use in just about any situation. We can do this with kids. I want them to clean their room. "Hey, kids, you like ice cream, don't you?" "Yes." "Do you remember last time you spent the afternoon cleaning the room how wonderful it looked?" "Yes." "I bet you kids would like some ice cream today, wouldn't you?" "Yes." "Do you know of a strategy that could help you get that ice cream today?" "Yes. Clean the room."

We can use this in a number of different ways. It is a phenomenal strategy in corporate coaching, sales, and leadership development. This is a fantastic set of strategies, whether we use questioning or whether we use a chained approach with one yes affirmation at the end. The YES! Set is a strategy every one of us can take to the bank.

Limiting Beliefs

We have beliefs about ourselves, beliefs about our situation, beliefs about our future. And these beliefs often limit us. For example, a person might believe that because they never graduated from college, that means they are not going to be able to make a lot of money. Or a person might believe they have been divorced a couple of times, and that means they are not going to be able to have a healthy relationship. Or maybe a person believes they are not very smart, and that means they are not going to be able to do a lot of things.

People are often limited in their beliefs. They might believe that they have risen high on the corporate ladder, and they are lucky and cannot rise any further. The reality is no matter what you believe to be true is true for you. We are held back by the beliefs we hold that limit us.

In NLP, particularly in NLP coaching, we try to break through these limiting beliefs and create unlimiting beliefs. This is a compelling strategy that needs to be at the center of much of the coaching work we do.

I will always be listening to what my client says about themselves, their situation, and their future. And when I hear beliefs that they have imposed limits on, I am going to address those and call those out. I am going to ask them how they know that is true and to consider that something else might be true. Have they sought options to get around these limits to the beliefs that they hold? In coaching and NLP, overcoming limiting beliefs is essential.

In 1994, I was driving a 1980s Mercury Monarch, and as I was going through West Texas, all the FM radio stations disappeared. This was before satellite radio, so I flipped over to the AM dial. There was not much to listen to other than radio preachers. One preacher came on, and with conviction, he said, "What the mind attends to, it considers, and what it considers it eventually acts upon." That quote has resonated with me since then. I think it is a fundamental axiom that directly relates to NLP. It relates to the Law of Attraction. "Where the mind goes is where our energy flows." The reality is the thoughts we have determine the actions that we take and, often, the outcomes of those actions.

Let us look at a basic formula:

Belief + Actions = Outcome

This is the belief I have about myself, my situation, or the future.

The actions that I take based on that belief will equal the outcome or, essentially, my destiny in life. If I have self-doubt and limiting beliefs, I am going to take action congruent with those, and the outcome will be achieving less than my greatest level of potential.

Would you like to rise to your highest level of potential? Then it is important for you to identify the cognitive errors or misbeliefs you have about yourself, your situation, and the future. Often, we create limiting beliefs on a very small scale and, as we create the habit of limiting beliefs, they become bigger.

For example, I might start with a limiting belief about myself, like *I didn't have the breakfast that I wanted today. I did not go to the store and buy bagels and cream cheese. I'm such an idiot.* My belief about myself is I am an idiot. That goes on because one belief leads to another belief about my situation. *Now I am going to work hungry, and to work hungry is awful. I'm going to be grumpy all day because I haven't eaten.* If I believe something to be true, guess what? It is true!

Then I might move toward the future and think, *Gosh, I always screw things up. I cannot even get a grocery list correct. My future sucks.* And if you believe that about yourself, the reality is the future *will* suck.

A bunch of these little examples builds upon each other, creating a pattern of limiting beliefs so we might get to a big misbelief about ourselves. The misbelief is, *I screw everything up.* The belief about the situation is, *Because I screw everything up, I shouldn't even attempt* . . . And the belief about the future is, *Since I haven't even attempted to make a change, my life is over.* In its extreme, these misbeliefs or these cognitive errors, I call stinking thinking, can lead to despair, depression, and self-destructive actions based on those beliefs.

It is really important that we overcome our limiting beliefs.

Limiting Beliefs

Belief + Action = Outcomes

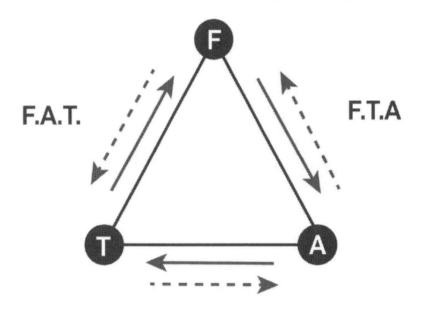

F.A.T.   F.T.A

FAT = Feeling + Action + Think

Whenever we have Action + Feeling (AF), it becomes a cue for the action we take based on that emotion. Then we often Think about this. This is how we react to limiting beliefs. It is a process of being too FAT—every time we feel, we act before we think.

Healthy people reverse that firing order. They reverse the firing order so that when they have a feeling, a sensation, an awareness, or an emotion, they will have a Feeling + Think (FT) before they have an Action (A). And they take an action that reintroduces positive feelings and emotions.

How do we change this firing order? We change it by recognizing our cognitive errors. This is why people go to coaches to help them see their experiences, life, and beliefs from a new vantage point. It is perfectly okay in the coaching process to call out misbeliefs, cognitive errors, stinking thinking, and limiting beliefs.

Our clients can also learn about their limiting beliefs by reading and hearing stories about other people. *Alcoholics Anonymous: The Big Book* has only one hundred and sixty-four pages explaining the 12-step program but over three hundred pages of stories. It is those stories that resonate with many people because they see themself in the stories that are described. And before they relapse, they can realize that they too are on that same path or that same trajectory.

There are many other ways to help clients to recognize their cognitive errors. One thing we can do is have our client reflect. I love switching chairs with the clients, and I play their role while they play the role of me. And they interview me about my beliefs and the things that I hold to be true. That is a very powerful technique that is often a lot of fun.

We can confront. We can reeducate. We can follow things through to their logical extreme, asking questions like, "If you believe [this], what will happen if [this] happens? Well, if [this] happens, what will you believe about [that]? Ask until they recognize that their starting point, their limiting belief, is something they have a new perspective on.

Aaron Beck, back in the mid-1970s, wrote about cognitive errors. He wrote about fifteen types of cognitive errors that are most common in people. These are the things that I am listening for. These are the things I am confronting, reeducating, roleplaying with my clients, and helping them to free themselves from the limits of their beliefs.

Below are the fifteen cognitive errors that Aaron Beck identified:

1. Filtering

This is where we take in all the negative details of an experience and miss all the positive details. You have seen people in a situation experience it only from a perspective where the negative has been retained, and the positive has been let go.

2. Polarized Thinking

This is a mind trap we can find ourselves in where things are either black or white. I'm either rich or I'm poor. I'm either happy or I'm depressed. The reality is we can be more than one thing at any given time, but black or white thinking or polarized thinking can often stop us from achieving our greatest level of potential.

3. Overgeneralization

This is a cognitive distortion where a person comes to a grand conclusion based on one aspect of a situation. For example, "I got a flat tire today. Because I got a flat tire today, my car is crap. And because my car is crap and I cannot afford another car, I'm going to have to quit my job." They have overgeneralized one small thing and turned a molehill into a mountain.

4. Jumping to Conclusions

This is where a person says to themselves, *Because of [this], [this] must be true.* For example, a businessperson might jump to the conclusion, "Well, we had a negative quarter. That means our business is on a downward trend. We're on a down cycle."

5. Catastrophizing

An example is, "If the business is on a down cycle, that

means we'll be out of business soon. We ought to jump ship now."

6.   Personalization

This is another cognitive distortion that people often have. Somebody experiences something, and they believe that it is all about them. It must be because of them. *It rained today, so that must mean that the gods are unhappy with me.*

7.   Control Fallacies

This distortion involves two different levels of belief. First, a person feeling extremely controlled, and then, a person feeling as if they do not have an internal locus of control, that others are the ones who create the experiences for them. I see this often in relationship counseling. "He makes me so mad." Well, he may do jerk things, but I still have the same pants to get glad in that I have to get mad in.

8.   Fallacy of Fairness

I see this a lot in political discussions. People believe that the world should be fair. Years ago, I was driving with my family, and I stopped and bought a pack of Zingers cakes. There are four cakes in a pack. When I got back into the car, I quickly ate two and my daughter, who was sitting next to me, said, "Can I have one?" I handed her one, and she quickly ate that. I started eating the last one, and she asked for another bite, so I gave the rest of it to her. It was at that moment that my son, sitting in the back seat, realized we were eating Zingers, and he said, "Hey, can I have a Zinger?" I said, "No, they're all gone." And he asked, "Why did Rachel get one?" And I said, "Because she's in the front." And he said, "That's not fair." And I said, "What you really mean is that's not equal. It is fair. They're my Zingers, and I can choose who to give them to."

People often believe things should be fair, and the reality is the world is often an unfair place.

9. Blaming

People engage in blaming. They do not see their responsibility in a situation.

10. Shoulds

Albert Ellis used to say you should never "should" on your clients; clients should on themselves. This is where people use the word should to exacerbate the deficits and the failures they have.

11. Emotional Reasoning

These can be summarized like this. *If I feel this way, it must be true.* I have spent a lot of time in therapy sessions explaining to people that feelings simply are not facts.

12. Fallacy of Change

This is where a person expects that other people will change in response to their wants, their needs, or their desires. Sometimes people do, but because the world is not a fair place and many people are narcissistic and self-absorbed, the reality is the only one we can change is ourselves. We should not be disappointed when people do not join us in creating success.

13. Global Labeling

This is a technique called mislabeling, where a person generalizes two qualities into a giant global judgment about themself or another person or another situation. In other words, because a person is slow, or the person is not so verbal, or they don't have any redeeming qualities, they can't function in the workplace.

14. Always Being Right

The reality is, I'm right about what I'm right about, and I'm wrong about what I'm wrong about. When we see our own opinions as facts about life, the feelings wants, and needs of others are often overlooked. This distortion is almost always rooted in self-preservation rather than seeing opportunity on either side of the door.

15. Heaven's Reward Fallacy

This is where a person believes that because they have sacrificed, because they have been denied, then they are entitled to some magical outcome that will make all their problems in the world go away. The reality is sometimes sacrificing is the best thing to do even without a heavenly reward.

I think it is worth studying cognitive-behavioral psychology and the ideas of cognitive distortions related to how clients express their limiting beliefs. Anything they believe to be true, they will act on. It is up to us to find the formula in coaching to challenge, re-coach, reteach and mentor the clients we are working with, so they can transcend their limiting beliefs and step into unlimited abundance.

Chapter 27
The Awareness Wheel

Let us go back to the beginning of NLP to the late 1960s early 1970s and look at some classic books written in the field like *The Structure of Magic* and *The Structure of Magic II* by Richard Bandler and John Grinder, and *Changing with Families* by Virginia Satir, Richard Bandler, and John Grinder. At the same time those books were being written, another book was being written called *Couple Communication 1: Talking and Listening Together* by Sherod Miller, Phyllis Miller, Elam W. Nunnally, and Daniel B. Wackman. *Couple Communication* came about as an evidence-based approach to working with couples.

During the foundations of NLP, Richard Bandler and John Grinder studied Virginia Satir. As far as I know, they were unaware of Miller et al.'s work. But these coexisted at the same time.

Neuro-linguistic programming courses are not typically taught with the Awareness Wheel and many other concepts that I cover in this book. But it is interesting that the parallel ideas of strategies that truly work with couples were born at about the same time. When I look at the model offered by Miller et al., I find many things that integrate well with NLP. If they had preceded their work, they probably would have also become exemplars for NLP and NLP training programs.

The history of psychotherapy is fascinating. In the 1940s and 1950s, we had behavioralism, and through the 1960s, we had the Rogerian and insight-oriented approaches. By the late 1960s and the early 1970s, we had two branches. The Cognitive Behavioral approaches, those of Albert Ellis, and what I think is the more experiential therapy, Gestalt therapy, first developed in the 1940s and 1950s. Fritz Perls was one of the exemplars that Bandler and Grinder studied in the early days. The ideas of *Couple Communication* are also very experiential.

The basic foundation of couple communication is creating enhanced awareness, seeing a problem, not as a problem, but seeing the problem experientially.

THE AWARENESS WHEEL

Miller, S. (1992). Talking and listening together: Couple communication I. Littleton. Col.: Interpersonal Communication Programs.

INCOMING
Deletions
Distortions
Generalizations

OUTGOING

SENSE
(A,V,K,G,O)

DO
Words
Actions
Inactions
Body
Language

THINK
Opinions
Judgement
Thoughts

ISSUE

WANT
Desires
Intention
Need

FEEL
Happy, Glad,
Sad, Mad,
Etc.

In the center of the Awareness Wheel is the issue. In the textbook *Couple Communication*, you will see some illustrations. These illustrations always strike me as being very NLP-ish. In one, you can see a couple literally standing on a model for listening. In an earlier chapter of this book, where the idea of the Awareness Wheel is introduced, they are standing on a representation of this Awareness Wheel.

Think about NLP and the Circle of Excellence, where we put that circle on the floor in front of us, and we step into it. The authors are telling us to envision ourselves in communication with other people, standing on this Awareness Wheel, making sure that we cover each component to have the presupposition of NLP. The message received is that message which was intended by the recipient.

At the center of the Awareness Wheel, the issue could be any issue that a couple wants to explore. Virginia Satir at the Family Therapy Institute of California and the authors of *Couple Communication* were speaking in the context of couple therapy.

As a licensed marriage and family therapist, I am very accustomed to speaking about couples and therapy. But the principles and ideas here apply to *any* couple, whether it is a couple in psychotherapy trying to resolve a problem, a leadership team in a corporate setting, two executives within the C-suite (for example, the CFO and the CEO, working out their relationship and how that is going to create strength within the family of the company), or board members. For any couple, we can be teaching *couple communication* strategies.

We could also be talking about anything related to community development. How does one person in the community relate and communicate and listen to other parts of the community? The idea of couple communication is expressed in this book in the context of couple's counseling.

Psychotherapy usually takes a problem-oriented approach. Let's look at the issues.

"I'm not getting enough support from my spouse in regard to taking care of the dogs." That would be an example of an issue that might arise in conflict couple's counseling.

But the issue does not have to be an issue that is negative. The issue could be something positive. The issue could be, "We just sold our business as a couple and put $17 million in the bank. What is the best way for us to utilize this wealth so that we can create an impact in our community, so that we can now, finally, after spending thirty years of building a business together, enjoy the time that we have left together in a meaningful way? How is it that we can take the wealth and assist our family without destroying our family?" There are lots of issues that could be present here. It does not have to be conflict.

For example, in the corporate setting, the issue might be, "We wildly exceeded our sales expectation with our new product launch. As a company in the early stages, we now have no debt and money in the bank. How do we leverage this so that we can reward the investors and serve the clients?" Again, this model applies itself in several different contexts.

If I was working with somebody in peak performance coaching, a person who was already doing well in most measures of life, and was trying to rise to the highest level, the issue might be, "How can I, at this stage, generate greater levels of insight and awareness so that I can be physically, emotionally, socially, and spiritually, as well as I can possibly be functioning at peak performance?"

The applications here go far beyond Bob and Bertha fighting too much.

The issue is in the center. Whatever the issue is.

Incoming

Anytime we have an issue, we have incoming sensorial awareness, our five senses—auditory, visual, kinesthetic, olfactory, and gustatory. We can put these incoming experiences in the context of NLP. Through our filters, they are deleted, generalized, or distorted. Our filters are of previous experiences, expectations, projection, and self-need. We have these incoming sensorial experiences but recognize something. In the NLP communication model, we find that deletions, generalizations, and distortions are always at work.

The first phase of this Awareness Wheel is the sensorial experience. What is it? What are the kinesthetic experiences? What are the submodalities that describe these sensorial experiences? When we are coaching somebody, we want to work with them to understand the sensory input in the experiences of the world around them.

In the example of "I don't get the support I need," the smell might be, "The house smells bad like a wet dog." The visual experience could be unkempt dogs, "I see dogs walking in my neighborhood that are brushed, and my dogs aren't brushed, and I don't have time. I need support for this." The auditory could be hearing words that have meaning, such as, "I don't have time. You do it."

All these sensorial experiences and inputs relate to an issue, and these create thoughts. Thoughts are a collection of opinions, judgments, ideas, generalizations, distortions, and deletions because our thoughts are almost never four-dimensional. Our thoughts are almost always expressed internally as two-dimensional. They are seen as something rather than from a holistic perspective.

The Awareness Wheel puts this thinking into context with our feelings. Are you mad, glad, sad, scared? Are you excited, exuberant, euphoric? Am I excited, euphoric, exuberant? What emotions accompany these thoughts? Is it anger? Is it joy? It could be any of these emotions coupled with the wants here. Wants are our desires. They are the things that we intend. They are our intentions. They are the needs that we have. This is where assertive communication comes into play.

Something else that is not taught as NLP is the formula sentence for assertive communication, "I feel . . . , want . . . , or need . . ." But this is a very clear way of communicating. If we want to model excellence in communication, modeling assertive communication is certainly a tool that lends itself to effective coaching, influence, helping people make change, and reaching peak states of excellence.

We want to have a person who is presenting with an issue to also explore what it is that they truly want. "I just want you to help me in the morning for ten minutes with the dogs." There is an example of a want. This relates to the fifth element of the Awareness Wheel, which is doing or action. These are the words because words can start a war. Words can end a relationship. Words can start a relationship.

Words can sometimes be considered actions. These are the words that people use, and these are the actions that they take. For example, "I'm washing the dog" or "I'm walking the dog." These are the yin actions that we take. The person might choose to act in a passive-aggressive manner. For example, "I'm not going to walk the dog," or "I'm not going to take the dog outside."

Our body language is a huge filter. It is a considerable way of communicating. We have discussed this already in this book. We want to evaluate.

Outgoing

We have the outgoing result. Notice it is not just a message. It is the result because it comprises all of these things. It comprises our senses, thinking, feeling, wanting, and doing. Then we have a set of experiences or responses that are outgoing because of being attentive to the Awareness Wheel.

What we have is a real tool for us as coaches, working with clients so that we can put ourselves in the center of the Awareness Wheel.

The issue is doing a coaching session where I'm going to be helping somebody today, and I have to evaluate my incoming sensorial experiences, my thoughts about the process, my feelings, wants, actions, and what the outcomes are. My client comes to me with an issue. The issue could be anything. It could be complex. It could be simple. They are going to be going through this exact same process.

But what the writers of *Couple Communication* tell us to do is very NLP. It is literally to take this image of the Awareness Wheel, place it on the floor in front of us, stand in the center of it, and before we create an action, before we make a response, evaluate each segment of it.

One of the elements of this that is really important is, at times, when we help a person to understand all five aspects of the Awareness Wheel, they might not express very much emotion. They might not be able to identify their wants or be paralyzed by inaction, which is actually action. Notice on the wheel there are five equal areas representing healthy experience, understanding the senses, the thinking, the feeling, the wants, and the dos of any particular issue. Since it is called the Awareness *Wheel*, I call it a flat tire, when a person is in one way or another stifled in their emotional awareness, or they have perhaps black and white or rigid thinking and their thought process is limited regarding seeing the issue as it truly is in relation to these other things; the Awareness Wheel lacks awareness in one of these areas. In the textbook, it is illustrated with a smaller slice of the pie. In the Awareness Wheel, the result is a flat tire because the circle is no longer round.

In the book *Couple Communication*, they are advocating the couple to literally stand on this circle, map these things out, and then communicate and explain and share with each other. This is again a couple's activity. What is interesting is I have been aware of the Awareness Wheel for going on probably forty years as my mother and stepfather had the book. Early on in my counselor education training, the Awareness Wheel resonated with me. I began again to study it when I was in graduate school, working in marriage and family therapy.

The ideas of couple's communication that are expressed in this book have been the basis of doctoral dissertations, academic research, and communication. It is an evidence-based approach to helping teams, couples, individuals generating self-awareness and insight-oriented coaching, and businesses to reach a higher level of performance by creating a higher level of awareness using the Awareness Wheel as a map.

In NLP, we take it, put it on the floor, we step onto it. We experience all these things from a holistic or 360-degree perspective. Then we can have outgoing messages that are congruent with the ecology check from NLP, congruent with the communication model of NLP, where we understand generalizations, deletions, distortions, and primary representational systems and how they affect us on a holistic basis. We are able to see the bigger picture.

The fascinating thing about the couple communication model, though, is that it is multifaceted. If I have somebody sharing the insight that they have gained by going through the awareness model surrounding any issue, I can then receive their messages and their outgoing as their partner.

Listening

I can do it with a listening model, a feedback model. The little arrows represent feedback loops. There is no order to this because we could be in any one of these models at any given time.

According to academic researchers, the steps of successful listening are first attending and being present with somebody. In NLP, we call this rapport. It could be body language. Gerard Egan told us that the therapist has S.O.L.E.R., **S**it down, **O**pen body posture, **L**ean forward, make **E**ye contact, and **R**elax. This is a therapeutic posture. Why? Because it lends itself nonverbally to listening and communicating the message that *I am here with you*. The person who is receiving the message, whether it is a therapist or their partner or their coworker, is going to attend first and acknowledge. Acknowledge the issues, the feelings, the emotions, the wants, the needs.

The listener is also going to create both nonverbal and verbal invitations. These are invitations to share more, to go deeper. The Socratic method of questioning is an effective way of doing this in a very non-threatening way that can truly help people to share more so we can listen more. This is what active listening is all about.

As a listener, I am going to be summarizing the things that I hear, reflecting, and repeating back what I heard a person say. The reason we do this is for clarification. I might say something like this, "I've been listening to what you just said. It's very interesting. I'm interested in clarifying, though, does this apply in all situations or only with caring for the dog?" I am summarizing through questioning. "What I heard you say was you're really angry right now." That is a way of summarizing, of acknowledging.

Then, ask questions. All five of these areas of active listening are closely related, but they create a feedback loop for listening. In the book, they express this very NLP-ish. And the way they express this is by drawing this listening strategy schematic diagram on the floor. The listener steps into it and, like a hopscotch board, steps into each one of the segments of the Awareness Wheel as they go through the task of listening. This is done while the person who is sharing their awareness is standing on the Awareness Wheel.

We have these two components, and this is powerful. It's a valuable skill and strategy to teach people. If you deliver seminars or leadership training events or other work with groups, you could break up the participants into smaller groups where one person is on the Awareness Wheel, and one is on the listening schematic. You can use the big paper flip charts and have them draw their Awareness Wheel and literally put that on the floor and put the listening schematic on the floor as well.

Miller et al. tell us something else. They also talk about types of communication and using the right communication in the right setting or situation.

- The first is what is called small talk. This is, in NLP, really what we call rapport, so it is the same idea. Remember, in the history of these, NLP and *Couple Communication* paralleled each other. At no point have they really met. I have never heard anybody talk about couple communication in an NLP class. Yet, the reality is, they mesh together very well. In NLP, we talk about rapport. In couple communication, we are talking about small talk. Small talk must precede deep talk to create rapport, or people will not be willing to share each element of their Awareness Wheel. And they will be reluctant to go through the process of active listening that is reflective of listening that truly engages.

- "How are you today?" "Tell me, what did you accomplish this week?" Small talk. "I see you have a picture of a dog there. I have a dog also." These are nonthreatening, short communications that create a back-and-forth interaction with a person. Now it could be words.

- Rapport also could be matching and mirroring (back to NLP), where I am modeling or matching and mirroring my client's breath rate, their body movements, their body posture. I am becoming in sync, moving with them linguistically as well as nonverbally. Small talk, if we do it long enough, leads to search talk.

- Search talk is where we explore. It is Socratic questions, where we are asking a person to look inside of themself and retrieve the answers and the knowledge and the things that are useful to them.

- We also have straight talk, a type of communication where we have active listening, as well as clear communication.

- Then we have control talk, which is generally viewed in couples counseling as non-resourceful. This is often considered to be reactive listening. This is where a person explodes. Or this is where a person shuts off the communication of others. They are doing this to control a scenario or situation. In the context of crisis management work, control talk might be necessary. "You go there. Come here. Bring this here." There is a place for this type of control talk. As a parent, there may be a need for control talk. Control talk is not necessarily always bad. But in the context of working with couples, teams, in leadership development, or in coaching, we generally want to avoid reactive listening and control talk, preferring instead to remain in attentive listening, straight talk, or search talk, where we are exploring deeper.

All these ideas useful ideas that we can set on top of the concepts of NLP to be effective communicators, effective listeners, and effective life coaches.

Chapter 28
Active Listening

Τhe following skills are hallmarks of active listening. This is a central key to understanding people and creating influence.

Hallmarks of Active Listening

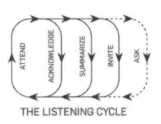

THE LISTENING CYCLE

1.) Know the reason for engagement
2.) Make appropriate eye contact
3.) Pause to think before responding
4.) Lean into conversation (What is S.O.L.E.R.?)
5.) Be interested in the other person
6.) Speak your words
7.) Wait for response
8.) Use search talk to encourage expression
9.) Validate emotions
10.) Pay attention to tone, body language, other factors
11.) Clarify what messages you have received
12.) Use brief affirmations or ego strengthening to encourage more dialogue
13.) Smile
14.) Match and mirror
15.) Avoid attaching judgment or relational frames

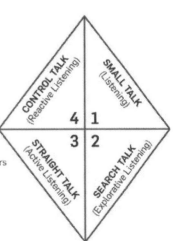

Know the Reason for Engagement

The first thing is to really know the reason why we are communicating with somebody. One of the ways to enhance the quality of your own life is to only enter into communications that are important or have value or may, later on, produce some results or satisfy curiosity.

I talk with strangers, the drive-through attendants, people in public places, and it satisfies a curiosity I have about other people. It does not have to be a deep, lasting relationship in order to enter into communication with somebody.

Know the reason why we are communicating. Are we wishing to share a gift of joy with somebody? Are we hoping to receive affirmation in return? I think all listening begins with understanding. Why am I listening to this person?

Make Appropriate Eye Contact

Eye contact is important. Not the kind of eye contact that penetrates and pierces a person's soul and makes them uncomfortable but the type of eye contact that lets somebody know, "Hey, I'm attending to you. I am here with you. I'm listening to you." Eye contact communicates to the listener that you are fully present.

Pause to Think Before Responding

One of the skills of effective active listening is to pause. I had an interesting experience five years ago when I first met my wife. I did not speak any Chinese, and she did not speak any English. I had just had multiple throat surgeries, so I could not even speak. Now we are at a point where we can communicate clearly about everything. But early on, we would communicate with a translator.

In any relationship, you sometimes have difficulty agreeing on things or understanding ideas. This is where, in my relationship, trust was built; we had to trust because we could not communicate as clearly as other couples could. When we found ourselves in disagreement, we would use the voice translator. She would say, "Richard, I am mad at you. You are a jerk." Then she would have to hand it to me, and I would have to read it. Then I would have to look at the translator and translate, "You are not understanding my perspective on this." Then it would translate it. I would hand it to her, and she would read it.

I attribute this to the strength of our relationship, and the reason why is it is really the first relationship I have ever had where we were forced to literally take turns listening to each other. We were forced to pause before responding in order to translate our messages back and forth. We do not have to do that anymore.

The skill of pausing after hearing is an important active listening skill. It helps people feel validated when they are speaking and helps us clarify how we are going to respond before we make a response.

Lean into the Conversation (S.O.L.E.R.)

Sit down, **O**pen body posture, **L**ean forward, make **E**ye contact, and **R**elax. That acronym really goes a long way in helping us internally ask ourselves, *Am I not only giving words that say I'm communicating to you but am I communicating this nonverbally as well?*

Be Interested in the Other Person

It is also important to express interest in the other person. When we are listening, be genuinely interested in people. I have a massive curiosity about people. It is easy for me to genuinely be curious and interested in them. But for other people, this is a skill that they have to practice. It is okay to have to practice this skill in order to feel like you are truly interested in other people.

Speak Your Words

Speak your words clearly when listening so that the person who is speaking can respond to your questions, your clarifications, your affirmations, and your ego strengthening.

Wait for Response

Wait for a response when you speak because it is their turn to speak. Remember, this is listening.

Use Search Talk to Encourage Expression

In couple's communication, we are going to use search talk to really explore ideas. Search talk asks questions, probes feelings, and gets to know someone at a deeper level. This is where we can facilitate rapport (essential in NLP) and produce influence and change by coming alongside someone as a coach or mentor to help them at the deepest levels. This is the level where we brainstorm ideas with someone, allow them to hear themself reflected back by our words, and engage in deeper levels of questioning. It is the perfect place for the Socratic questions we studied in another chapter.

Validate Emotions

A big part of my job as a therapist is simply letting people know that it is okay to have human emotions even if those human emotions are distressing or difficult.

Pay Attention to Tone, Body Language, and Other Factors

Pay attention and listen not only to words but listen to the body language, listen to the tone, listen to the way that messages are shared from a nonverbal perspective.

Clarify Message You Have Received

It is important when listening to clarify the messages. That's back to summarizing, which is all about clarity. "So, what you've told me is this . . ." It will help in acknowledging whether I have received the message correctly.

Use Brief Affirmations or Ego Strengthening to Encourage More Dialog

It is okay and important to use ego strengthening or affirmations to not only validate but to encourage more sharing. We are going to let people know. "You've done a great job sharing that with me." "I know that it was difficult for you." "Do you feel comfortable sharing more, or is there anything else you'd like to add to my understanding?" These are invitations to have a person continue sharing, and they will.

Smile

Smiling is important as well. I have had people tell me I do not smile enough. Over the years, I have practiced smiling. Smiles communicate nonverbally something important, affirming caring, and listening. When I find myself intently curious and listening to somebody, I will intentionally also smile a little bit.

Match and Mirror

Matching and mirroring is an NLP strategy. If they are sharing, I am listening. When I am doing the opposite, this is mirroring. If they are leaning forward and I am leaning forward, this is matching, doing the same thing. If they have an open body posture, I have an open body posture. If they are sharing with quick words, I might speak quickly as well.

Avoid Attaching Judgment or Relational Frames

I also want to, in my active listening, avoid judgment and relational frames. People are the way they are because of their experiences. They bring those subconsciously to every experience. I must listen, even if it is not words I enjoy hearing or like hearing. I must understand it from my client's frame of reference, or my partner's frame of reference, or the stranger's frame of reference, rather than from my frame of reference. This helps me to be able to cross boundaries in my communication and my listening skills.

As you are listening to people, review this list in your mind and practice introducing these ideas into the skills you already have for active listening. When you do, you will find that you will do an even better job of helping people become fully aware of the world around them and the ideas and solutions that you are offering them as a life coach.

Chapter 29
Intentions and Goals

S.M.A.R.T. You have probably heard about S.M.A.R.T. goals. Specific and Measurable goals that are Attainable, Relevant, and have a Time limit. We are often taught about S.M.A.R.T. goal setting, which in coaching and NLP is often seen as the pathway to creating the highest level of success.

I am a fan of goal setting. Research shows that setting goals is a pathway to achieving more. It is true that when we set goals, we are more likely to achieve those goals than if we do not set those goals.

S.M.A.R.T. goal setting might not be the smartest way to achieve success. What I am about to share is quite controversial.

While I am in favor of setting goals and I do work with my clients to help them set goals, I focus on the objectives, the things they need to do to get there. That is really the pathway for creating success, but there is something even more foundational and more critical than simply setting goals. That is setting intentions.

Intention setting is the key to success. There is research showing this as well. In fact, there's research that shows that goal setting can sometimes be problematic. It is not the panacea everybody thinks that it always is. For example, our natural psychological inclination when we set a goal and get toward that goal, but we have not yet reached that goal, is to revise the goal downward.

Let's put this in the context of sales. If the goal is to sell one unit a day, thirty units a month, and we get near the end of the month, and we have only sold twenty-one units, but there are only two days left, our natural inclination is to say, "Well, I took three days off for an event," or "We had bad weather five days during the month, and that probably decreased sales. So, let's go ahead and revise the goal and make the goal twenty-four." The reason why we do this is because we just cannot stand the cognitive dissonance of not being able to reach our goals. New goals are often set on previous goals, and it can become a downward spiral into mediocrity.

Some of you might remember the case of Sears and their automobile shops setting corporate goals related to the number of auto repairs and the ticket price. Wells Fargo set corporate goals regarding the number of new accounts that would be set up. What was discovered was that while those companies were able to reach their goals and hit their targets, they did so at the expense of both customer experience and consumer protection laws in some cases. They spent a lot of time issuing *mea culpa* and swallowing their pride.

I am a Wells Fargo customer. For the two years following the incident, when account holders had no idea accounts had been set up on their behalf, Wells Fargo contacted me multiple times to assure me they were a good bank. I probably received ten emails from Wells Fargo apologizing profusely and offering other products and services.

Goal setting can sometimes be filled with problems. There is a natural inclination to revise downward, sometimes at the expense of professional ethics. And goal setting can also become extremely frustrating because it is focusing on the future.

I live by the words of the great Master Oogway, who said,

"Yesterday is history. Tomorrow is a mystery. And today is a gift ... that's why they call it present." All we have is the present. Goal setting is about looking into the future. It is about trying to make a change now that impacts something later.

The most powerful changes we can make are changes that we step into at this moment. And that's why intention setting is the key and the foundation to creating success with the objectives, the actions that we take to reach our goals, and the eventual goals we have set.

When I set goals with my clients, the reality is my focus is on the intention. Intentions are focused on the present moment. I cannot achieve a goal today. If the goal is to sell thirty units a month, I cannot sell thirty units a month today. But what *can* I do today? I can set the intention to be honest. That is important in sales. I can set the intention to have follow-through. That is important in sales. I can set the intention to have a rich knowledge of my product and rich knowledge of my customers. I can set an intention right now.

The formula for setting intentions is a lot smarter than the S.M.A.R.T. goal setting. It begins with "I am." "I am" is a powerful statement. The reason why it is a powerful statement is nobody can say "I am" for you. Somebody else can assign me goals. Nobody else can assign me intentions. Being consistent with NLP, intention setting comes from within, not from an external source. "I am" activates action. It activates the steps that I can take today. It literally is abracadabra, which means "I create with my mouth. I create with my words."

An "I am" statement phrased as an intention is really something quite powerful. Let me give you some examples.

I am confident.

I am caring.

I am disciplined.

I am thorough.

I am careful.

I am compassionate.

I am exuberant.

I am excited.

These are all examples of intentions that I could set. And when I set the intention for the day, I can then, with every step I take throughout the rest of the day, step into intention even if I have not yet achieved my goals. It is my belief that if we set an intention each day for the new day, that by the end of thirty days, even if we never set any goals, when we look back, we will have seen that we will have wildly exceeded our expectations in any goals, we would have set by setting intentions.

I engage in a ritual for intention setting. This ritual is simple. When you get in the shower in the morning, you probably use shampoo and wash your hair. The shampoo has directions on the back. It says to apply the shampoo to your hair, foam it up, wait two minutes, rinse and repeat. Every morning, when I wash my hair, I put the shampoo in my hair, and I set an intention. I think to myself for a moment before I rinse my hair, *Richard, what is your intention for the day? What is it that you can step into? Richard, if you could create any resource state, what would that look like?* I formulate an "I am" intention.

And as I rinse the shampoo off my hair, I say to myself, *I am confident, I am exuberant, I am energetic, I am compassionate,* or whatever intentions I have set for myself. Sometimes I set one, and sometimes I set more. As I go through the day, I reflect on the intention or intentions that I have set for myself. And I recall the intention, and I ask myself this question, *Today, am I acting in congruence with the intention that I set for myself?* This is a guide to moving forward. It is a guide to achieving success because it keeps us focused on the present moment—the power of now. It keeps us focused on the internal resources that I have rather than the external constructs somebody else has decided for me.

I do work with my clients to help them set goals and ask them what the objectives are. These are the tasks they need to do. It helps them create order out of the tasks that are needed to accomplish things in life. But the foundation of my work with clients is not goal setting. It really is intention setting. My clients might have a multitude of problems they want to solve, but by setting intentions, I set them on a pathway right now, today, this moment, to achieving success.

Chapter 30
First Session Template

Now that we have a toolbox filled with some NLP strategies and tools, how could you conceptualize it? What would an actual coaching session look like? I will give you the structure for a coaching session, utilizing some of the tools that we have already talked about.

Something that is important to recognize is that each one of us will have our own style, our own personality, and we are also going to have our own type of scheduling.

Over the years, I have done a wide variety of different types of sessions. Almost all my first sessions with a new client are typically between an hour and a half and an hour and forty-five minutes. I make sure that I have plenty of time. That is if it is in my office. I long ago got out of the therapy model of fifty-minute hours.

Online, I spend less time with people. The reason why is that while I find the online format a great and very effective format, people have a little bit of attention deficit sitting in a chair without the same interaction we have in the office. They are focusing on the screen. In my online sessions, I am probably spending an hour to an hour and fifteen minutes with a new client.

Sometimes when I am working with individuals in the context of corporate coaching, I am typically spending all morning with a new client. I might meet with them at nine o'clock in the morning and continue until noon. I have three hours with a new client when I am delivering on-premises corporate coaching.

We can adapt the different strategies.

There are a few differences between my first session online and my first session in the office. The most significant differences are paperwork and payment. Online, they pay me before they ever meet with me. I never meet with anybody who has not already paid me for coaching. They pay me when they schedule the session.

In my in-person sessions, rarely have they paid me in advance. I prefer to make it part of the therapeutic process where I spend some time talking with them, and then I collect the payment at the end of what would in hypnosis be called the pre-talk. It is the point where I have decided I am going to work with them, and they have decided that they are going to work with me. By collecting that payment in person, it becomes a commitment point.

When people are seeing me in my office, I generally do not provide paperwork in advance. Again, I do this as part of the rapport-building process, my assessment of primary representational systems, the classic intake form, a personal questionnaire, the coaching contract, and the coaching agreement. If they are doing this with me online after they book and pay for the session, it takes them to a page, and that page has forms for them to complete right there online. I am getting those forms before I am meeting with a person online.

Both systems work. It is really a matter of personal preference. I am going to describe this process for you that conceptualizes a session in three parts. I call it Act One, Act Two, and Act Three— a beginning, a middle, and an end.

The beginning is very important. I have never met this person before. I probably have not talked to them too much, if at all. Most of my appointments are booked through my office. Stephanie, my business manager, may have talked to them, but I probably have not talked to them at all. The first time we meet, the first time we talk is often our very first session. If you are answering your own phone and somebody else is not doing your scheduling, you may have done an introductory call with them, built some rapport, answered some questions, found out some things, but it has probably been a few days or even a few weeks. And so, it is really important to refresh at this point.

Let's go through the checklist, and this is completely adaptable and flexible. You do not have to do all the things I am doing. You can do things in a different order if you want to. But that concept of a first act, a second act, and a third act is important.

FIRST SESSION SAMPLE STRUCTURE

Act One:

- ☑ Welcome and positive suggestion
- ☑ Rapport building
- ☑ Matching and mirroring

Questions:

1.) Tell me about yourself
2.) Tell me your greatest strength
3.) How did you hear about my services?
4.) How would you know if the time we spent today was valuable to you?

- ☑ Explain services
- ☑ Do you have questions for me?
- ☑ Calibration
- ☑ Identify desired outcomes from coaching:

1.)
2.)
3.)

- ☑ Assessment of primary representational systems
- ☑ Strength and resources assessment
- ☑ Coaching contract
- ☑ Positive suggestion and ego strengthening

Act Two:

- ☑ Teaching skills
- ☑ S.C.O.R.E.
- ☑ Hypnosis/mindfulness
- ☑ NLP Patterns
- ☑ Ecology check
- ☑ Commitment

Act Three:

- ☑ Set intentions
- ☑ Set goal
- ☑ Define action steps
- ☑ Affirmations
- ☑ Homework assignment

ACT ONE

In this first act, what I want to do above all is create rapport and elicit commitment. Those are the two primary goals of Act One.

Welcome and Positive Suggestion

As soon as a client comes into my office, I greet my client with a smile on my face and ready to work with that client. When I greet that client, I shake their hand, and I ask them to sit in the chair in front of my desk. This is my first hypnotic suggestion. I'll say to them, "I'm really glad that you're here. A lot of other people have sat in that same chair and gone through a coaching process with me. They found it beneficial. I'm sure that you will too." Whether you are a hypnotist or not, begin with a hypnotic suggestion. A hypnotic suggestion that future paces that they will be successful because they have come to see you. It starts the session off correctly.

Rapport Building

I immediately go into rapport building. The easiest way to build rapport with other people is to ask other people about themselves. It is human nature that people love to talk about themselves.

Matching and Mirroring

I typically use the technique of matching and mirroring. This is a technique where I mirror their body posture. If they are slouching, I might slouch a little bit. If they are sitting very formally, I might move to the edge of my chair and be a little more formal. I match their body language because this creates comfort with the client.

Questions

When I am speaking to them, I usually ask them my traditional opening question, which is, "So tell me a little bit about yourself." Notice I did not say, "What about the problem?" or anything like that. I said, "Tell me a little bit about yourself." What is interesting here is they are leading with probably on a subconscious level what is most important to them about themself. This is an excellent place to begin the calibration process. I ask a few questions about them and about what it is that they have told me. And then I almost always ask them, "Those things that you just hold me are interesting. I am curious. What is your strongest asset? What's your greatest strength that's helped you with life or business to this point?" This almost always causes that transderivational search where they must look inside of themself and really identify one thing that has been a real strong point for them.

I am starting the session off on a positive note. I am asking what is right with them, not what is wrong with them. Then I follow up. I ask them another question. This is a great rapport-building question. "I'm curious. How is it that you heard about my services?" Most people hear about me because they have either read my books, taken my courses, know somebody who has read my books and taken my courses, or found my social media channel. But a lot of times, people find me because they had been referred by somebody else. And they will say something like why that person came to see me and that they found tremendous success and they are looking for that same kind of success that their friend had.

What I almost always discover is that the client has some connection to me already, which is probably a positive experience. They either liked my book, or somebody had success working with me, or somebody recommended me. I am really interested in the answer to the question, "How was it that you heard about my services?" It gives me another opportunity to suggest they are going to do well because their friend did well, or the many people who have read my book have found success.

Do You Have Any Questions for Me?

I think rapport building also requires that I be open. I think self-disclosure is very important in the coaching process, but I am not going to start telling my client about me. They are not interested in everything about me. They are only interested in some things about me. Rather than me guessing what they are interested in, I will say to them, "I'd like to know if you have any questions for me. Did you come to this session with some questions either about coaching or about my services or even about me personally and the work that I do?" This is a great opportunity for them to ask me what is important to them about me. What are they curious about? I am almost always happy to answer the questions that they have.

I have been sober now for thirty-two years, since March 31st, 1988. I got sober through the 12-step program with Alcoholics Anonymous and have continued to maintain my sobriety. My recovery process is a personal process. It is something that I have spoken openly about. I did a TEDx Talk about it. I started out in this field as a substance abuse counselor. Unfortunately, many substance abuse counselors think that because they got sober after abusing drugs and alcohol, that experience somehow is valuable to the client. For some clients, it is valuable. They want to feel a sense of camaraderie or know that their coach has gone through that process as well.

But I do not disclose that to most of my clients. Sometimes they have seen my TEDx Talk, or they might have read one of my books where I mentioned it. But generally, when a person asks me if I have been in a recovery program or used drugs and alcohol, it is at that point that I will tell them that I have been sober ever since James Brady was Ronald Reagan's Press Secretary back in the 1980s. And so, I will self-disclose, but I self-disclose when my clients ask me about me.

I will sometimes make small talk. "Do you have a dog? What kind of dog do you have? "Are you a cat person, or are you a dog person?" I ask some questions that just generally build rapport and help me to utilize that tool of calibration to find out how they answer questions. Are they open? Are they closed? I remember my favorite quote from Guiguzi, "Listen as if you are a tongue seeking the marrow from the center of a bone." In other words, it is really important to employ our listening skills here.

Explain Services

I then go on and explain the services I offer and the coaching contract.

Calibration

I will be spending all this time calibrating with my client.

Identify Desired Outcomes from Coaching

I ask this question, "At the end of our time today, how would you know that that time, the time that we spent together today, was beneficial to you, was useful to you?" In other words, I want them to identify the desired outcome of this particular session. Now it is probably not going to be all the answers to all of their problems. It probably is something along the lines of they would like to feel hope or like to know that there's a plan that they can engage in to take them to the next level, but I would like them to identify the specific outcomes that they would like for this particular session. I want two or three specific outcomes for them. I am usually taking some notes, and I usually write those down.

Assessment of Primary Representational Systems

I am probably going to move into a short explanation with them of primary representational systems. And I will use the assessment Primary Representational System Quiz. As you know, it only takes about one minute. I simply take the sheet and explain that it is a great tool to help me understand their primary learning style. People are either auditory, visual, or kinesthetic, and this is really going to help me to be able to connect with them and teach them the strategies and skills that are going to help them achieve that outcome by creating alignment. I further explain that it will help them in some of the areas that they might not yet have strength. I explain in layman's language, auditory, visual, kinesthetic, and let them take that quiz. Then, I review it and share with them a little bit about what it means. You can get a prainable copy of this document at SubliminalScience.com/NLPbook.

NSRI - Nongard
Strengths and Resources Inventory
Copyright © 2014, Richard Nongard.

Name: _____
Date: _____
ID #: _____

1/PUT Make a mark next to any and all of the following that you possess or have access to:

- Close friend
- Reliable transportation
- Pet
- Internet access
- Stable living environment
- Uniforms and clothing
- Healthy food sources
- Primary care physician
- Source of income

2/ISO Make a mark next to any and all of the following that apply to you:

- Can solve problems
- Can follow directions
- Can give clear directions
- Can work well in team
- Can work well independently
- Can listen well
- Can express thoughts or feelings
- Can create plans
- Can develop creative options

3/EJS Make a mark next to any and all of the following items that you have or can do:

- High school diploma or G.E.D.
- Military training
- Vocational or technical certificate
- College degree or higher
- Resume
- Management or supervisory experience
- Volunteer or charity work
- Job history more than 6 months
- Job history more than 2 years
- Can pass alcohol or drug screenings
- Able to use typical business communication skills
- Appropriate attire
- Able to learn new skills easily

4/PAA Read this list of 24 items before marking any spot. Then mark the 6 items that you think best describe you:

- Creative
- Curious
- Open-minded
- Inquisitive
- Wise
- Brave
- Persistent
- Honest
- High energy
- Loving
- Kind
- Aware
- Team player
- Fair
- Leader
- Forgiving
- Humility
- Careful
- Impulse control
- Appreciative
- Grateful
- Optimistic
- Humor
- Spiritual

5/PIA Read the list first. Then mark 4 of the following which best describe your interests or abilities:

- Cooking
- Playing sports
- Exercise
- Building things
- Music
- Arts and crafts
- Games and puzzles
- Singing
- Reading
- Writing stories or poems
- Dancing
- Travel
- Family time
- Community involvement
- Religious services

6/SSS Make a mark next to any and all of the following who you think are willing to help you at this time:

- Mother
- Father
- Sister
- Brother
- Step-parent
- Grandparent
- Other relative
- Best friend
- Close friend
- New friends
- Boss or supervisor
- Co-worker
- Religious leader
- Neighbor
- Support group
- Mentor
- Coach
- Counselor or therapist
- Spouse
- Medical professional

Strength and Resources Assessment (I have included the assessment in previous chapter number fourteen.)

I almost always then go into the strengths and resources inventory. "As we go about helping you create goals and intentions and success in the coaching process, I'm going to be drawing on the strengths and the resources that you already possess." I explain to people that we can almost always find the solutions inside of us. We just do not yet know how to implement them. That is what I am here to coach them on. A tool like the assessment of strengths and resources will help me to help them identify some of those things that can be helpful.

Coaching Contract

This is where I generally get payment. I explain, "Stephanie told you that the four sessions would be $1,295, correct?" Nobody gets to my office without knowing how much it is. They will say yes, and I continue, "I have a couple of forms here. One is called a Coaching Contract. That simply describes the services that I offer and gives me permission to work with you. And another form here is called an Intake Form or a New Client Questionnaire, and it just asks some questions about you. While you do that, I will get you a receipt." It is at this point that I collect the payment. "Are you using cash, check, or a credit card?" I step out of the room and get them a receipt and give them time to fill out both the Coaching Contract and the Intake Form.

This gives me five to ten minutes in the other room to reflect on some of the things we talked about and develop a plan for Act Two, the middle of our sessions.

Positive Suggestion and Ego Strengthening

I return to the office where the client is and cover any questions they have. Usually, I do two things. I give them another positive suggestion and ego strengthening. A positive suggestion is, "Now that we've completed the paperwork, we're ready to make the changes. Sounds fantastic, doesn't it?" For ego strengthening, I say to them, "I know you're going to do well. I'm really looking forward to being able to tap into the resources you have to help you live your best life."

In an in-person session, I have probably spent forty minutes with somebody doing all that. In an online coaching session, I have probably spent about thirty minutes. They have probably done the paperwork. Twenty minutes on the short end and forty to forty-five minutes on the long end for Act One is absolutely fine because I have set aside and budgeted the time for my client.

ACT TWO

Teaching Skills

In Act Two, I focus on teaching skills. I use a markerboard to teach clients things that they need to know. I teach them a skill that would be valuable to them. If I have a client who is dealing with fear·and anxiety, maybe I teach them the skill of mindfulness. If I have a client who is dealing with conflict at work, maybe I teach them assertiveness. Every client is going to have different skills that we need to teach, but I am probably going to focus on one, or two at the most, skill that would be useful to them to help them begin making change right away.

S.C.O.R.E.

After that, I go into the S.C.O.R.E. model of coaching. The cool thing about the S.C.O.R.E. model of coaching is that I could do a complete session on each one of those letters in the acronym in a weekly session, or I could go through the symptoms, the cause, the outcome, the resources, and the effects at a basic level with somebody in probably ten or fifteen minutes. I can do a short S.C.O.R.E-focused session now and then expand on each of these in successive or future sessions if I want to.

Hypnosis/Mindfulness

I am a professional hypnotist, and most people who see me know that I am a hypnotist. A lot of my clients expect that they will do hypnosis with me. I might do a formal hypnosis session with my client. I might say, "I've taught you some of these skills. We have talked about the S.C.O.R.E. model. Let's go ahead and use hypnosis as a resource to tap into the strategies that I've taught you today that can be helpful to you." I might do a seven, eight, or ten-minute hypnosis session as part of my coaching. Depending on the client, I might do a longer hypnosis session with them, but generally, I find short hypnosis sessions are extremely effective. If you are not a professional hypnotist, doing the formal process of hypnosis is not required. We can utilize conversational hypnosis, the language patterns that are hypnotic of NLP, to help encourage, motivate, direct, and focus our client's desires.

NLP Patterns

I am probably going to use a couple of NLP patterns with them in Act Two as well. I might introduce an idea. "Let me show you something really cool. We have been talking about how to make this change. Let me share with you the Swish Pattern." Maybe it is confidence or the Circle of Excellence. Maybe it is an answer in creativity, the Disney pattern, and I will guide my client through one of the patterns, always ending with an Ecology Check.

Ecology Check

The Ecology Check Pattern in NLP is a simple technique where we're ratifying if the change that the client has committed to making a change that's actually beneficial to them? Is it actually something they want to make changes with? This is important because if our client, say a smoker, is incongruent in their desire to make changes, they know they need to quit smoking, but they do not want to, then they will not. And so, I want to use an Ecology Check Pattern to determine if this something that they really want to make changes to.

Commitment

When the client arrives at the positive conclusion, that is when I am going to get that commitment from them, and I am going to ask them questions. "Are you ready to make the change?" "Yes." "Are you ready to step into it now?" "Can you set an intention?"

ACT THREE

Set Intentions

Now I set intentions. What can they do now to activate the change that is important to them?

Set Goals

I will have the client write specific behaviorally oriented goals so that we know what it is we want to accomplish in our successive sessions.

Affirmations

I give all of my clients a dry-erase marker and say, "The reason I've given you a dry-erase marker is so you can write on your bathroom mirror, and you can see it as you blow-dry your hair and brush your teeth. I want you to see in your own handwriting the solutions that are important to you." I have them create an affirmation such as "I am good enough. I am smart enough. I think I can. I think I can. I think I can." If the affirmation is wanting to focus on their comfort, not their pain, I'll have them write on the bathroom mirror, "I am comfortable." If they want to be a better golfer, I will have them write, "I can reduce my handicap this season." Whatever it is that is important to them.

Homework Assignment

I will have them identify those affirmations and then give them the homework assignment to write those affirmations on the bathroom mirror.

I am probably also going to end by giving my clients specific homework assignments based on the work that we have done and the goals.

My coaching session homework is kept very simple. I ask them to maybe practice mindfulness daily using an MP3 I give them, or I ask them to keep a journal four or five times this week. Not daily. And the reason why is I want to give people a chance to not be perfect because if I expect them to be perfect and they are not, they will say to themselves, "Well, I didn't do it right, so I must not be able to make the change." I give them real, doable homework, something that really reinforces the things that we have talked about.

This could easily take nine minutes or two hours to cover all these things one-on-one in my office. The online format lends itself to being a little bit speedier, a little more streamlined, especially when doing processes like the Swish Pattern or a hypnosis session. That is okay. Both are highly effective. Both are equally good at meeting our client's needs. Have flexibility. Adapt this to your personality, your style, and the things that you think are important.

And another of my favorite NLP patterns or acronyms is A.B.C.—Always Be Calibrating. From start to finish, I am assessing their language, submodalities, congruency, and ecology. For a first session, this format is powerful and has served me well now for many decades.

Chapter 31
Decision Destroyer

One of the cornerstones of the NLP presuppositions is it is better to have choices than not to have choices. Often, we engage in repetitive behavior because we are really not sure what choices we make.

Often, people who have made a decision, and that decision has become a habit for them, do not really know how to revisit their prior decisions and destroy them.

This is what is called the Decision Destroyer in NLP. It is a strategy for working with somebody to help them to make different decisions when the decisions they have made to this point have been non-resourceful to them. An example of this might be the decision to start smoking again. As a hypnotist, I have worked with a lot of clients who have stopped smoking, and, now and then, a client comes back eight months later or a year or two years later because they have started smoking again. If they started smoking again, they made that decision. Sometimes, I have clients who I have never worked with before, who quit smoking ten years earlier and suddenly started smoking again a few months ago, wanting hypnosis because they want to be a nonsmoker again.

We see that people often want to revisit the decisions they have made in the past.

Maybe the decision was to day-trade options without any actual knowledge of how the market works, and they incur huge losses as a result of not day trading with knowledge. Sometimes, people want to revisit the decisions that they repetitively make in their dating life. Sometimes, businesses want to revisit the decisions that they have made that have cost them customers, cost them customer satisfaction or cost them money in the end.

The Decision Destroyer can be utilized in several different situations. I will walk you through this process, using smoking as an example, somebody who made the decision to start smoking again after a period of time.

Revisit Problem

It all begins when we revisit the problem. I have a new client in my office who says they have been smoke-free for a number of years and started smoking again. Maybe they were at the bowling alley, and their friends were all bowling and drinking beer, and they were smoking cigarettes. They thought one wouldn't hurt them, and so they had one, and every day they promise themself they will not smoke another cigarette, but every day they get up and buy another pack of cigarettes. They are right back to where they started. I have heard this time after time. You can think about the decisions that you have made in your life which have been non-resourceful and ask yourself, "Is this a decision that I am continuing to make, despite the knowledge that it has adverse consequences or that it's a non-resourceful state for me?"

When I am working with somebody, I have them revisit the scenario or situation.

Get Person Focused on the Moment of Decision

The first thing I do is have them focus on that moment of decision. I might say, "What I'm hearing you tell me is that you made a decision to engage in smoking again, even though your goal or your intention wasn't to become a smoker again, that night you made that decision. Go ahead and close your eyes down now, just for a moment and revisit that moment that you made that decision. Revisit that moment when you had a feeling, a want, a need. Describe for me what that feeling, what that need was, that moment that you made that decision." And I will have them go ahead and open their eyes again. I have them close their eyes because it helps them really to revivify that experience, that exact moment of making the choice.

What Was Going on at That Time?

Then I am simply going to ask them, "Tell me what was going on at that time? Who were you with? What were you doing? What were you sensing? What were you feeling?" You can see how the elements of the Awareness Wheel can be brought into this discussion where we have them really paint the picture of what was going on in their life at that exact moment.

Just Before That You Were . . . ?

The second aspect of this is to have them rewind and back up to a point before they made that decision. The question I'm going to ask is this, "Immediately before you were at the bowling alley and smoking the cigarette, what were you doing? What was happening immediately preceding that decision that you made?" Now, I might hear something earth-shattering. "Well, I was at home, and I got bad news. My cat had been run over by a car." It could be something dramatic, or it could be something nondramatic. It could simply be, "I was in my car. I was relaxed. I was listening to the radio. I really wasn't even thinking about smoking, but I walked in that bowling alley, and that's when I made that decision."

What I am trying to get them to do is rewind in their mind, again experientially, to the moment that preceded the decision that they made. The immediate moment. The five minutes before, the ten minutes before, maybe the hour before. But I really want to know what they were doing right before they made that decision?

As You Think about the Present, Notice the Options You Have

It is at this point that I have them think about the present and notice the options that they have.

I have them close their eyes down again and explore with them. "Now that you're here with me, I want you to think about the different options you have. You spent many years as a nonsmoker. I wonder, aside from smoking a cigarette, what could you do to meet your need for socialization or to help you make the choice to choose fresh air rather than carbon monoxide air? I wonder in this exact moment if you were faced with the challenge of making that decision over again, what options you have. Could you get up and leave? Could you simply use a sort of communication? 'Oh, no, thank you. I don't want a cigarette.' Is there some other choice or option that you have when you think about this decision that you've made?" I am probably going to have them take a minute or two and really identify some of those decisions.

The Next Time You Think About X, With What You Know Now, I Wonder If You Will Pick a Different Option. Will You?

"Go ahead and open your eyes up again. Now that your eyes are open, I'm going to ask you a really important question. "The next time you think about, in this case, smoking a cigarette, with what you know now, I wonder if you would pick a different option? Would you?" The answer to that leading question is almost always going to be an affirmative; they are going to choose a different option. Then, my question is going to be, "What option would you choose if faced with that decision again?"

Let's put this in the context of business. The problem, or the issue if we want to use the Awareness Wheel model, is we have made the decision to stop tracking customer satisfaction on a scale of one to five. Instead, we have simply given them a frowny face and a smiley face on the customer satisfaction survey. The result is because we are measuring it differently, that perceived customer satisfaction is lower now than it was before.

The conversation might go like this:

"Let's revisit the problem. The way you've been measuring customer satisfaction, has it been really a resource for you?" "It hasn't." "Has it yielded the information you need?" "No, it hasn't." "Well, think about the moment you made that decision." "Well, the moment that we made that decision, it was that moment when we realized that people weren't completing their customer satisfaction survey. So, we wanted to make it as easy for them as possible." "What was going on at that time?" "I was sitting in the room with the CEO, the head of customer service, the customer experience officer, and one of our sales representatives. And we were all really talking about these things because customer feedback is important to us, and somebody drew on the board and said, 'Look, we need to have our customers smiling,' and they put up a smiley face. They thought that by having that option for a smiley face, people would be drawn to it, and it would up our customer experience scores. But, in fact, it has actually decreased the customer experience scores. We're getting forty-five percent frowny faces, and only fifty-five percent smiley faces."

"See yourself in that room with those people, making that decision, the smiley face being drawn on the board. Just before that, what were you doing?" "Well, just before that, I was actually making customer calls. I was asking customers a question. I was asking them, 'What's one thing that we're doing right? How is it that we are actually helping you?' We were focusing on the positive." "Wow, that's incredible. That's awesome. That's great. You were in your office, and you were making those phone calls." "Yes, I was."

"Now, I want you to close your eyes, and I want you to think about the present moment. When you think about this present moment, notice how many options you have in measuring customer experience. Tell me, other than a frowny face or a smiley face or a scale of one to five, is there any other way to measure customer outcomes or customer satisfaction?"

It is in this moment, in this exact moment, that the ideas will probably come forth, and they will come up with two, three, or four ideas. The conversation may continue in this way:

"Next time you have a meeting with those individuals regarding customer satisfaction, and you think about the tendency to simplify things in a way that isn't actually beneficial to measuring accurate outcomes, with what you know now, I wonder if as an executive you can make a recommendation that would look different? Wouldn't you do that? And if so, what do you think that recommendation would look like?"

Maybe they will come up with a recommendation that creates a word sphere, a word cloud. Maybe they will come up with a different way to measure customer satisfaction.

This is a way of changing previous decisions, whether they are individual behaviors, whether it's in the boardroom and even within the family.

I can do this with a teen child. Here is the problem presented to the teen. "The problem is you've made the decision to return the car without gas. Let's focus on that moment that you decided not to return the car with gas." I have a teenager who has done this before.

"What was going on at that time?" "I was with friends. I was having fun. I looked at the clock. It was 11:59." "Just before that, you were doing what?" "I was sitting in the McDonald's drive-through window." "Well, when you think about the present and how many options you have, I wonder what they are?" "Well, not go to McDonald's. Ask my friends to chip in for gas money. Any of these options I have." "Great. So, the next time it's quarter to twelve, and almost time to come home, and you think about not returning the car with gas, with what you know now, I wonder if you'll pick a different option? Will you?" And the reality is the answer to that is going to be yes, and they'll tell you what that new option is.

The Decision Destroyer is a way of revisiting prior non-resourceful decisions and helping people to make lasting change.

Decision Destroyer

 1 Get person focused on moment of decision.

2 What was going on at that time?

3 "Just before that you were..."

4 "As you think about the present, notice how many options you have..."

5 "The next time you think about _____ with what you know now...I wonder if you will pick a different option. Will you?

Chapter 32
Neurological Levels

One of my favorite ideas in contemporary NLP is the Neurological Level idea of Robert Dilts. This is the idea of what is sometimes referred to as neurological levels or sometimes just simply logical levels. It has been expressed as a pyramid with six levels.

Neurological Levels
(Robert Diltz)

SIGNIFICANCE
"What am I a part of?"

MEANING
"Who am I?"

SECURITY
"What is important?"

HOW
"How can I create
/do/experience this?"

WHAT
"What are my actions?"

WHEN AND WHERE

Each one of these, because it is a pyramid, is becoming a little bit smaller. The reason why they are smaller is not that they are less important, but because at the deepest level or the lowest level, the environment is the biggest area in size. It consumes much of our attention, our focus, our awareness.

That is why it is important to be able to conceptualize these neurological levels as a pyramid. We recognize that sometimes the important things are the small things, and we can still pay attention to those in order to have a complete pyramid.

- The first level is environment, and that is the biggest because the world where we are, where our problem is, where our solution is, where we exist, is the largest component of this model.

- On top of that are the behaviors, the things that we do, the actions that we take.

- Built on top of that are the capabilities that we have. Sometimes I like to phrase this as the strengths and the resources that we have.

- Then the values and beliefs are on top of that.

- Built on top of values and beliefs is what is called identity.

- Built on top are the spiritual or metaphysical aspects of how we achieve the greatest satisfaction levels in life.

This is one of the reasons why I love coaching. Rather than helping people who have a problem move to an adequate level of functioning, I am often working with people who already have an adequate level of functioning or an exceptional level of functioning, and I am helping them rise to be congruent with their highest level of performance.

The neurological levels model can be utilized in several different ways in coaching.

The way that I use it is to simply take clients through a process of decision-making—first looking at the biggest area, their world, and the environment that they are in. Then the behaviors, capabilities, values, beliefs, identity, and spirit.

Let's use this hypothetical situation: Should Richard buy a new Tesla? The Tesla Y is $49,900. Or should he purchase something different?

Environment

Let's take a look at the when and the where of the environment. The environment is I have a three-car garage. The environment is I live in an area that's just about five minutes away from a Tesla supercharging station. My wife and I only have one car. Having a second car would be useful.

Still looking at the environment here, I also own this house, so I could install an electric vehicle (EV) charger in my garage. I could charge up my car whenever I wanted to. How often do I drive? How often does my wife drive? Currently, we are not spending very much time driving, but occasionally I need to go to the university in Dallas, where I sometimes do some work with them, or sometimes I need to visit family in another part of the state. Let's look at the environment and the scenario and the situation of how this decision to buy a Tesla Y would fit into my world.

Behavior

Behavior is the *what*. The what is I'm tired of buying gas. The what is it's cool to have a Tesla. The what is we need a second car. The what is I can afford it. These are the what types of questions in regards to this decision and the behavior. What is driving this behavior? A couple of weeks ago, I drove to Dallas, and I was away for almost eighteen hours, and my wife was stuck at home. She could not go anywhere because we only have one car right now.

Capabilities

The capabilities are the *how*. Well, I'm pretty tech-inclined. So, I can drive a Tesla if I want to because I understand how to work a car on an app. Even though I have never done it before, I have these capabilities, and I could do it, I would be interested in that.

Values and Beliefs

What is really important? So far, it sounds like I am getting a Tesla. What is most important at this point in my life, now that I really think about it, is actually financial security. I am getting older; I'm not getting younger. I am interested in preparing for my future in a way that is far different than before. So how can I achieve security? What is my value and my belief?

Tesla has an amazing appreciation rate. After three years, it retains ninety percent of its residual value. That is incredible. Many cars lose thirty, even forty percent in a three-year period. If I bought one for $49,000, at the end of three years, it would still be worth, at least according to current projections, $40,000. So it costs me $10,000 a year, and I'm not buying any gas, and that's pretty congruent with what my desire is.

What would be super handy would be to not have to bother my neighbor when I need to move something. And so, I could actually buy a decent six or seven-year-old pickup truck with, probably, 75,000 miles on it for about $13,000. That would be a wise use of money. Or maybe, since I already have an SUV, my wife just needs a runaround. I could buy a 2015 very nice BMW with 60–70,000 miles on it. It is still a very good reliable car, a 328 for probably $16,000–$17,000. Really what is most important here? So far, it looked like I was getting a Tesla, but security is really the most important thing.

Identity

I want to now look at identity, the meaning, who am I? There was a point in my life when the kind of car I drove was important to me. The reality is, I derived my meaning from being a good dad, a good friend, a hard worker. And while the pickup truck that keeps me from bothering the neighbor or the BMW would save me a little bit of money, there is absolutely nothing wrong with an Altima. I could buy a recent model Altima for, probably, $12,000 or a Honda Accord for $13,000, being consistent with developing financial security and who I am. I am still a hard worker. I am still a good dad. I am still a good friend. Even if I drive an Altima. And, those are two nice cars.

Spirit

Significance. What am I a part of? I am a part of my bigger world, my family, my community, my child's life, a fellowship of other people who I care about.

What is the spiritual aspect of should I buy a Tesla or not? Maybe it is that I want to go green and contribute to the environment. Or maybe the significance here is that I want to be part of being financially responsible so that we can stay in this community where we currently live for a long, long time.

We can see here how guiding somebody through these neurological levels can help them in the decision-making process. We can also bring this into the corporate world. We can bring this into family coaching and into couple's coaching. We can bring this into dealing with emotional aspects. Let's say somebody is wondering about whether they should see a psychiatrist and start taking antidepressants. They could go through this whole thing here.

When and where? — *I'm depressed more often than not for a period of thirty days or longer.*

What is my behavior? — *I am not getting out of bed. I am not going to work.*

What are my capabilities? — *My capabilities are to actually go to the gym. And cardiovascular exercise has been shown to be more effective than psychotropics for the treatment of major depression, so that is a capability. Maybe I'm going to change my track here.*

What is really most important about my values and beliefs? — *Caring for myself. Who am I? I am Richard. I am a guy who actually cares about other people.*

What is the spiritual significance? — *Getting out of myself and into the lives of others. That might help me with my depression.*

We can take this understanding of the neurological levels or the logical levels that Dilts identified, and we can use this as a roadmap for problem-solving and helping clients who are in our office or online that we are coaching to truly rise to their highest level of peak performance. This creates stability. It creates a congruence, and it creates, at the deepest levels, security, significance, and meaning.

Chapter 33
Perceptual Position

Perceptual position is, perhaps, to be one of the most useful concepts in NLP. The reason why is simple. When I am coaching individuals, it is often useful for me to have them move their position so that they can see things from a new perspective. This helps in the decision-making process, and this helps with empathy. It can truly be a useful tool, a useful strategy.

The perceptual position is about me in proximity to other people and their experience. It can also be about me and how I perceive myself. Let me share with you the five key perceptual positions that NLP talks about.

- The first one is simple. This is you as you in any situation. For example, if I am describing an issue, I am describing it from my viewpoint, the way I see the issue, what it is that I am experiencing. That is the first perceptual position.

  If I am using NLP in a hypnosis session, I am imagining a scene on a movie screen that is a movie of my experiences. It is me who is in the movie playing the part of me. The first perceptual position is me as me.

- The second perceptual position is me in the shoes of another person. It is me being able to say, "I wonder what

Susie's vantage point of that is?" or "I wonder what Bill's vantage point of that is?" It is me leading with empathy, moving into their perspective or their situation, and observing a situation as if I were them. In a movie, I am doing self-study; if I step back and watch the movie of me in the movie, that second perceptual position is from a singular perspective.

- The third perceptual position is me as an observer of the other person who is observing the situation. This can be a useful tool for getting a large bird's-eye view. We talked about the Awareness Wheel as a tool for understanding all the elements surrounding a particular issue. This third perceptual position, imagining that you are an observer of one and two together of Suzie and myself or Suzie and Bob, allows me to see things from a perspective that is once removed. When I have worked with individuals who have experienced trauma, intense grief, or other very intense emotions, there is a need to step back from the emotion of an experience or a situation to create a new vantage point.

The third perceptual position can come in handy in self-reflection. The idea here is that there is a me playing in the movie, and that is me as me experiencing the scenario or situation. This is what a flashback really is. The second perceptual position is me observing me, and for some people who've experienced trauma or grief or other intense emotions, this might still be too close. This third perceptual position is another me who is floated out of myself to observe me observing me.

The language of this in NLP usually is something along the lines of the following example.

Go ahead and close your eyes and imagine you're watching

a movie, a movie of the situation, or the scenario that's distressing to you. Do you see the *you* in the movie? Do you feel as if that's you on the screen?

This is your first perceptual position. You being you acting out the movie on the screen.

Imagine that that movie continues to play, but a you floats out of you and into a seat in the movie theater to observe what's happening on the screen.

This is you observing yourself on the screen. This is the second perceptual position. If we need to get an even bigger view, we can continue.

Imagine that another me floats out of me all the way to the back of the movie theater, up to the projection booth where it can see, it can observe the me observing second perceptual position; the me in first perceptual position.

What it does is it puts some space between a client and intensity. It can put some space that can help provide clarity and promote problem-solving and give new perspectives because the me as me in the middle of the screen cannot see anything that is not directly in front of me or in my peripheral vision.

The me who is observing me can now see that while there might be other elements or other players, if I move to a third perceptual position, this Awareness Wheel might be big, and I might see how it is connected to other Awareness Wheels.

NLP Perceptual Positions

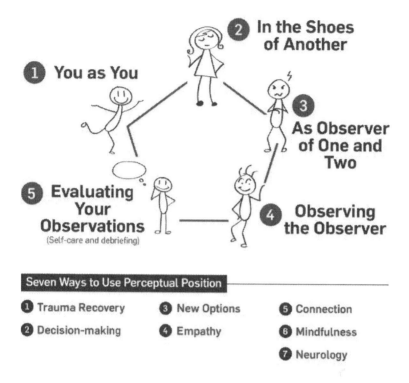

2 In the Shoes of Another

1 You as You

3 As Observer of One and Two

5 Evaluating Your Observations
(Self-care and debriefing)

4 Observing the Observer

Seven Ways to Use Perceptual Position

1 Trauma Recovery   **3** New Options   **5** Connection

2 Decision-making   **4** Empathy   **6** Mindfulness

                                 7 Neurology

The three perceptual positions that we primarily talk about are you as you in the shoes of another and as the observer, but there are two more perceptual positions that are not talked about as often in NLP, and I find them fascinating.

- One of these is the fourth perceptual position—observing the observer. Now, why would we want to observe the observer?

  Years ago, I was at the Rembrandt Museum in Amsterdam. I do not know a whole lot about art, but I went just like all the other tourists and I thought the art was fascinating and interesting. I walked around, and I looked at the pictures, and I looked at the display tags, and

I read what they said, and I tried to understand the art a little bit more.

After perhaps an hour or two, I noticed that I was no longer watching the art. Instead, I was sitting on a bench inside the museum, and I noticed that I was watching people who were watching art. To me, that was even more fascinating. It gave me a new vantage point of the art itself by watching those who are watching art. There was a fascinating array of different people ranging from students who were seriously studying art theory to tourists who were as lost as I was, observing the art. There were locals and international visitors. A lot can be learned by observing the observer.

Ask yourself, "What is it that I am noticing about the observer's viewpoint?" This fourth perceptual position is one more level removed, but it can provide a fascinating vantage point.

- The fifth perceptual position, which is rarely ever talked about, is me as me evaluating the observations, looking at the observations that I have made. We are noticing the auditory, visual, kinesthetic, olfactory, gustatory observations that I have made and then asking myself, *Are the observations and the conclusions that I'm drawing congruent with the Ecology Check, congruent with the presuppositions that I have made, or congruent with the decisions that I have made?*

This first, second, and third perceptual position coupled with the fourth and the fifth perceptual position can really be of utility in any type of coaching session.

I often say to clients, "Go ahead and step back from the decision you're trying to make. View it as an observer. What would that be like? And if somebody were watching you watch the decision being made, what would they say about the decision being made? Let's get an even bigger viewpoint here." The result of this is that these five perceptual positions are particularly useful in trauma recovery. They are useful in decision-making. They can help a person to discover new options. They can help a person to generate empathy. They can help a person see the connection they have with other people and other Awareness Wheels. They can help a person become more mindful, put some space between them and their emotions, and be present as an observer.

Mindfulness training teaches us to observe the breath, be in this moment. Sometimes the trauma of the moment or the difficulty of the moment can be too much for me to stay mindful. By moving my perceptual position, I can increase my acuity level in the area of mindfulness.

One of the other primary uses for the perceptual position is as a coaching activity to engage the neurology of the client. Remember, it's *neuro*-linguistic programming. This is an exercise where I do not simply talk to people. I ask them, "Stand in this spot and be in the first perceptual position. In first perceptual position, what's your state?" "Stand in this spot and be the observer or the other person in this situation. In second perceptual position, what's the state?" "Stand over here, be the observer of the person who's observing the situation. In third perceptual position, what's the state?"

By doing this, by moving clients around and having them engage neurologically in the process, I can help my clients gain a perspective that goes far beyond simply thoughts and engages the mind and body together to create valued experiences.

Chapter 34
The Milton Model

A lot of people associate NLP with what is known as the Milton model or, in other words, the hypnotic language patterns of Milton Erickson. I have written another book, *Speak Ericksonian: Mastering the Hypnotic Methods of Milton Erickson*, a practical guide and instructional manual on his language patterns.

In NLP, an observation of the way that Milton Erickson worked was made. John Grinder, who was the co-founder of NLP, was a linguistics professor. Language is what he studied. In observing Milton Erickson, he noted that the language he used was artfully vague.

There are two models to specify information in NLP. There is the meta-model, which is based on Virginia Satir's work, that chunks down and tries to get very specific. "How did you feel? When you felt that feeling, what did that feeling feel like? Tell me about feeling that feeling that you felt." In other words, we are getting into the minutiae, the tiny details here. This is the Virginia Satir model or the meta-model.

The second is the Milton model, the hypnotic language patterns of Milton Erickson, which are predicated on certain types of language choices that he would use in his sessions with clients. The reason why is Milton Erickson believed that the client had the resources within them necessary to solve any problem. They might solve it in a nontraditional way. They might solve it in a unique way, but those resources are in there. It was his goal to bring those resources out. By using certain linguistic phrases, hypnotic language patterns, the client would attach the meaning to the process of hypnosis that the client believed was so important.

What is the Milton Model?

Hypnosis training programs often make outrageous claims: "Get anybody to do whatever you want using these fantastic language techniques and language patterns handed down in secret by Milton H. Erickson to his most trusted students!"

Of course, those claims are greatly exaggerated, but Milton Erickson did pioneer a form of hypnosis that uses particular language patterns rather than relying exclusively on formal inductions. Because this form of hypnosis seems more like a conversation than a formal trance process, these techniques are often called Conversational Hypnosis. Because people don't always recognize what's going on in these language patterns, it's sometimes called Covert Hypnosis.

When Richard Bandler and John Grinder, the founders of NLP, studied Erickson and analyzed his use of language, the name they gave to these techniques was the "Milton Model." Essentially, the Milton Model consists of language patterns that focus a person's point of attention and create an internal experience or internal dialogue that lets them tap into their unconscious resources.

The purpose of the Milton Model language patterns is to invite a person to respond. This invitation can call for an internal or experiential response, a verbal response, or even a behavioral response.

The Milton Model is associated with using artfully vague language patterns to avoid unconscious objections or the imposition of the therapist's bias into the process.

These are the core foundations of persuasion techniques, whether we're talking about sales or whether we're talking about romance and seduction. It's certainly one of the core aspects of effective communication during the manipulative process of therapy.

The Ethics of Manipulation

By the way, did I, as a licensed therapist, just call therapy *manipulative*?

Certainly therapy has elements of persuasion and manipulation. When used by the ethical therapist, persuasion and manipulation are part of helping a client ultimately achieve their goals.

Therapy is a form of manipulation. Really, so are most human interactions. And this is why, of course, therapist ethics are important. Manipulation can be powerfully helpful or harmful, depending on the operator and also the ego-strength of the client.

I'm going to deviate here for a minute and answer the question: "When using the techniques or the language patterns of the Milton Model, can we really get anybody in Covert or Conversational Hypnosis to do anything we want?"

The reality is, there are seven billion on the planet earth, and some of them have what I would call a greater "ego strength" than others, and some people have a very weak sense of self-identity. They really don't know where they stop and somebody else begins. In psychotherapy or psychiatry, this might even have the diagnosis of Borderline Personality. It is quite possible for an unethical authority figure to take advantage of these people, with or without hypnosis of any form.

The world is full of people who have used persuasion to manipulate people into doing things that they otherwise would not have done. I mean, you can look at history and see examples like Adolph Hitler. You can look at examples from crime like Patty Hearst. You can look at other criminal examples. There was the Washington, DC, shooter case a few years ago, in which an older man (an authority figure) manipulated a teenaged boy to lie in the back of his car and shoot people with a sniper rifle. The world is filled with examples of one person manipulating another person.

It is my belief that with or without studying Milton Erickson, the extreme personality who is an abusive individual has the capacity to take advantage of what might be called in pop psychology "weaker-willed people" or those with lesser ego strength. When I hear stories like that that are attributed to the power of hypnosis, it really isn't the power of hypnosis—although hypnotic methods may be employed—it really attests to the skill of the truly abusive or maybe even evil person for choosing the right victim to perpetrate their evil deeds on.

I thought I would go ahead and address that because anytime you talk about language patterns and Covert or Conversational Hypnosis, those sorts of things come up. But this is not really a book about manipulating people to do things against their will. The purpose of this book is to bring therapists to help other people experience success. And so that is how we are going to use the information in this book.

The Art of Being Vague

Let me share with you a generalization about the Milton Model. Most Milton Model patterns are designed to avoid specificity because the more specific we are, the more likely there is to be opposition from the client's subconscious mind rather than the development of rapport. Let me give you an example using visual imagery:

> "Imagine a heavenly flight of stairs. The stairs are tall and narrow. Imagine standing up the top of these stairs. They are majestic stairs and covered with red carpet. Your hand is holding onto a polished brass rail. You make your step from the top stair to the next stair and down to the next stair. With each step, allow yourself to become more relaxed, stepping into that red carpet feeling your feet step into the deep red carpeting, but safely holding onto that descent down to the sixth stair, and the fifth stair, and the fourth stair. All the way down now. Three, two, one. Stepping off the stairs into a heavenly feather bed."

Now, that was very specific. I called the stairs "tall and narrow." I called them "majestic." I told you there was a "polished brass rail." I told you there was a "red carpet." But chances are, as you were going through that brief process, you said to yourself, *Wait a minute, my stairs don't have red carpet.* You may have thin carpet instead of thick carpet. When I said thick carpet, you had to change the carpet on your staircase. As I counted up the specific number of stairs you were on, said, *Wait a minute, I'm still up higher; I have to try to catch up.* You see, because I was specific, there were all kinds of conscious suggestions that were probably interrupting your process.

Let me give you an example of how you can use what is often referred to as a Staircase Deepener, using different language choices that make it completely different for the client's experience:

> "Close your eyes. Breathe in and breathe out. As you descend into an even deeper state of trance, imagine an elevator, an escalator, or even a staircase. Imagine that you're at the top; you're heading towards the bottom,

where there is comfort and relaxation. As I count backward from ten to one, descend down each step, descend down each floor, down to a point or a state, a resource state we call hypnosis. Ten, nine, eight, seven, six, five, four, three, two, one, zero. Perfect. Completely relaxed."

Notice I didn't specify it had to be a staircase or what the stairs looked like. It could be an elevator, escalator, or staircase. Instead of giving them colors, what floor they were on, instead of telling them the details of what I think they should be visualizing, I let the readers bring their own visualization to the process.

Let me give you another example. I generally avoid the use of the word *hypnosis* or *trance*. I typically, in my own personal style, prefer to call it a *resource state*. I certainly don't use the word *sleep* during my sessions, but Milton Erickson did. We must remember that word definitions and usages of words change over time. Milton Erickson used the word *sleep* or the phrase *deep sleep*. Those are not words that I use in my hypnosis sessions at all. Not because it is wrong to do so but because there are better words. *Resource state* is what I usually say because I teach my client that is what hypnosis is all about.

Let me give you a couple of examples here:

"As you go deeper into trance, achieving hypnosis easily . . ."

vs.

"You should set aside the day, focusing on your experience here in my office, as you access that resource state which is going to be most helpful to you today."

In the first example, I was very specific. They must go into hypnosis. They must go into trance. In the second example, I was much more ambiguous: "Let yourself access that resource state which you would find most helpful today." Everybody can find that. The art of vagueness is one of the hallmarks of Ericksonian hypnotherapy.

Key Concepts of the Milton Model

How do we go about using artfully vague communication and suggestion with our clients? There are many key concepts to understand and principles to practice. As you read these ideas, I encourage you to come up with your own examples, even to take time to write them down.

For reference, here is a list of the key concepts in the order we will discuss them:

- Nominalizations
- Unspecified Nouns and Verbs
- Unspecified Referential Indices
- Presupposition with Adjectives and Adverbs
- Presupposition by Comparisons using As
- Mind Reading
- Linkages
- Lost Performatives
- Modal Operators
- Presuppositions
- Embedded Suggestions
- Negative Commands
- Double Meaning Words

Nominalizations

Concept number one in the Milton Model is the idea of nominalization. In NLP we refer to nominalizations as "any noun you can't put into a wheelbarrow." For example, I could put my little brother into a wheelbarrow. I could put a dog / refrigerator/ TV remote control into a wheelbarrow. But when we take a verb and turn it into a noun, more specifically when we make a noun out of something intangible, we can't really put it into a wheelbarrow. Let me give you some examples.

*"During this training course, these **learnings** you have acquired are useful in almost every situation in life."*

The word "learnings" is a nominalization. It is a verb that's been turned into a noun. "Learning" becomes "learnings." "Learnings" isn't a tangible. It is a nominalization. You can't put "learnings" into a wheelbarrow.

*"The **joys** you can count are present in many ways."*

"Joy" (an emotion) becomes "joys" (a plural noun). Again, you can't put "joys" into a wheelbarrow; they are intangible.

But why would you want to use nominalization? The reason why is that, oddly enough, it makes an intangible into something concrete. It makes an intangible obtainable. I hear people say all the time, "I just can't learn." But when I tell them to metaphorically "hold on to these learnings," that's something they can do. So a goal becomes attainable when we use a nominalization.

Similarly, a nominalization can change the relationship with something. For example, "owning joy" is probably more powerful than "feeling joy." "How many joys do you have today?" What a great question to ask a client. Joys have become something that they possess, and that changes the relationship. It's not something they hope for or long for. It's something that's very real today.

It's important to recognize when our clients may have nominalized in unhealthy or unhelpful ways. For example, many of our clients say they "have depression" instead of saying they "are depressed."

One of the things that we can do in hypnosis is we can un-nominalize their nominalizations. We can take away ownership. For instance, we can change "having depression" to "being depressed." We can also change a relationship with a nominalization. For example, rather than "being anxious," we might say that a client "feels some anxiety," the way one might feel a draft. Either approach can lessen the sense of ownership and provides distance between our client and the issue.

Unspecified Nouns and Verbs

The next key concept is unspecified nouns and verbs. What these actually do is they force the listener to "fill in the blanks" with ideas from their subconscious mind. The interesting thing is that the natural state of people is that we're probably a little self-absorbed, a little bit narcissistic, and so they often fill in the blank with themselves. This is very powerful because if I say in a hypnosis session, "People find it easy to go into trance." I have not specified which people, or how they're going to do that. And so, what's the subconscious mind's response to these unspecified nouns, "Who are the people?" The subconscious response is, "Wow! I am a people! And if I'm a people, then I find it easy to go into trance!"

We take action on whatever we believe. For example, you believe that if you pay your electric bill, you will continue to have power. So you pay it. If a client believes "People find it easy to go into deep trance" and the subconscious mind believes they are a people, what will they do? Well, they will actually go into trance.

I use this often in my suggestions as well as my inductions. In my office I have recliners, and I will often say to my clients, "People find that when they sit on a hypnotic chair that it's easy to go into a deep trance state quickly." They recognize that they are people and they are sitting in a chair, and so the response to that indirect suggestion is to go into trance deeply and quickly. I use this approach all the time in my Suggestive Therapy:

"Many people have found that by learning self-hypnosis and practicing the techniques that I've shared with you they find it easy to lose weight, quit smoking, stop chasing cars, or whatever it is that brought them to my office."

Unspecified nouns and verbs really are a powerful linguistic tool that you can use in your hypnosis sessions.

Unspecified Referential Indices

The third category is unspecified referential indices. They are actually nouns that do not refer to anything with a capital letter. For example, "Richard" vs. "person". Richard has a capital R; person doesn't. They refer to something non-specific. "This is so beneficial, isn't it?" What is *this*? *This* is whatever the client attaches meaning to. It could be the session, the process, this time, these words, whatever. And when we couple *this* with a suggestion that this is beneficial, the subconscious minds come to agreement. So I could use this sentence in my induction:

"As you continue to breathe in and breathe out, it's so beneficial, isn't it? Feeling good, taking a moment out of your busy day to set aside stress and deeply relax here in my office."

In my pre-talk, I often use unspecified referential indices. For example, I might say as I lean over the desk, "This is one of the greatest things you have done." What have they done? The subconscious mind will find meaning, and the subconscious mind will say, "I did it!"

If I have a client in a deep trance state and I'm offering suggestions, I could say, "Everybody finds something of value in this experience." *Who is everybody? I'm a body, so I must be everybody. What is 'something'? What is 'experience'?* Milton Erickson's idea was that our subconscious mind is infinitely wise. What these patterns do is engage the mind with what Erickson found were internal resources and internal dialogues for problem-solving.

Presupposition with Adjectives and Adverbs

The fourth pattern in the Milton Model is adjectives and adverbs that presuppose. This approach tends to gain agreement from the subconscious mind. They get "buy-in" and the acceptance of our pre-suppositions that are made in the therapeutic process. For example I could say, ""People are *pleasantly* surprised by the *incredible* capacity to change." *Pleasantly* modifies the word *surprised. Incredible* describes the word *capacity.* I could say to the client, "As you relax, you will find a **pleasant** surprise in your ability to **easily** recall all the information in this book."

To make this book truly useful to you and for you to become hypnotic, which is ultimately the goal of this book, pay attention to the adjectives and adverbs that you're using in your daily conversations with people. Become essentially a more colorful speaker by adding these adjectives and adverbs that presuppose the meaning you want.

Presupposition by Comparisons using As

The fifth language pattern is a comparison with the word *as. As* is a two-letter word but extremely powerful. *As* increases connection and reduces conscious opposition. Sometimes in hypnosis you're going to hear about "bypassing the critical faculty." How do we bypass the critical faculty? We do that by reducing opposition. The word *as* is a very effective way for structuring a direct suggestion within an indirect suggestion. So it lets my clients subconsciously feel that they are the one who has a choice and they're in control.

Let me give you some examples of comparison with the word *as:*

*"Just **as** you can relax here, you can relax and access this state anywhere—at home, at work, or even in traffic in your car."*

I use that a lot as a post-hypnotic suggestion with my client. At the end of my session I'll often say to them:

"And just as you were able to reach a deep resource state here in my office, if at any time anywhere over the next day or two or three, you have a need to access this deep state of relaxation or confidence that you've created here, you'll be able to do it just as you were able to accomplish this in my office; you will be able to accomplish this everywhere."

Another example of using *as:*

*"If anyone is **as** easily able to relax as you are, they will find it easy to experience deep trance at just about any time."*

Or here's another one:

*"Just **as** you can create confidence here, you can create confidence anywhere, even in front of a group where you are speaking."*

Mind Reading

Now, despite how we're portrayed in movies, hypnotists are not psychics, but our clients sometimes feel as though we can read their minds. Really, it's just projecting what the client needs to know through a language pattern that predicts the future or predicts my knowledge of their state.

So here are some examples:

"As you continue to relax in that chair, I know you are learning as you experience something new today."

That's mind reading. How do I know that? I don't really know it. The only way I could know it is if I were a mind reader. But I'm projecting what I want them to do and learn as they experience something new today,

Here is another example:

"You may wonder if it is ok to have thought while you practice hypnosis. It is of course normal for the mind to wander: after all that is what minds do, they wander and think. But instead of following those thoughts, just let them exist without judgment and without following them, returning your attention to the breath."

By the way, that sentence is really one that would be identified from the field of Contextual Psychology, and you can find that even in Contextual Psychology, we can use Ericksonian language patterns to enhance our effectiveness.

Here's another example of mind reading sentence:

"You are curious to discover how relaxed you can become."

Now, how do you use that sentence? Well, I might use it in a pre-talk before we ever get to the hypnotic chair. I might say to my client who's sitting at the desk:

"I know that you've been looking at the hypnotic chairs. Don't worry, in a few minutes we're going to move over there for our session, and I know that you're curious to discover how relaxed you really can become."

When I activate their curiosity, now they want to accomplish that, and so it makes trance induction even easier.

Linkages

Linkages presuppose a link between two things, even when linking them truly is completely arbitrary, a mental exercise, what may be called a "relational frame" by contextual psychologists. Students of Steven Hayes and those who have taken my courses in Contextual Hypnotherapy recognize Relational Frame Theory. Linkages suggest the mental process for creating those frames. In Ericksonian hypnosis we are still creating these frames to facilitate change.

In addition to using Linkages to create new relational frames, the therapist should also be aware of the Linkages that clients have created that might actually need to be "unhypnotized" from their subconscious mind. So what we are doing here really is two things: We are learning these language patterns so that we can create arbitrary relational frames (relationships between two things are really probably are completely unrelated) while at the same time, we're looking for the arbitrary relational frames that our clients have created because part of our work can actually be unhypnotizing.

Relational frames are important to understand because they are what separate humans from the other animal species. The reasons why humans are at the top to the food chain rather than giraffes ruling the world is that humans have the ability to create arbitrary relational frames.

Engage in this exercise to understand relational frames:

Think of something, anything that is a noun. It can be car, a microphone, a cup, anything you want to. It doesn't matter—any person, place, or thing. Think of an object, something you can hold in a wheelbarrow. Actually write that down on a piece of paper or type it out on that notepad note to yourself. That's Object Number One.

Now that you thought of one thing, think of another thing— another noun, another something. Again, it can be a DVD, a computer, a TV, a bug. It doesn't really matter what it is, just think of anything. That's Object Number Two. So now you have two unrelated things listed on your piece of paper.

But humans have the ability to create relationships that are really completely arbitrary even when no relationships actually exist. And so, I have three questions for you to answer regarding these two objects:

1. How is Object Number One like Object Number Two?

Think about that for a moment. You can write down your answer. I picked a cup and a TV remote control. How are they like each other? Both sit on a desk. It's really completely arbitrary, but our minds have the ability to create this relationship frame and see how two things that really are random are related to one another least in our own minds.

2. How is Object Number One better than Object Number Two?

Maybe a little more difficult than the first question, but your mind has ability to come up with an answer, even though that answer truly is arbitrary. And so think about how the first one is a better than the second one. My answer is the cup is better than the remote control because I can drink from it, and water is necessary for life. That's really completely arbitrary, but in my own mind I've created this relationship—just like you did with your two objects.

3. How is Object Number One the parent of Object Number Two?

This may take a little more creativity, but our minds have the ability to create relationships that are arbitrary and abstract. In my own mind, I came up with something really completely arbitrary, but I was still able to answer the question. A cup holds ice. A remote control is made out of plastic. In order to mold it, plastic must be cooled with ice. Therefore, the cup gives birth to the remote control. It is the parent of the remote control.

No matter how arbitrary, we're still able to come up with some way to answer the question. This is really important though, because the question is absurd. Not all things can be the parent of all things, and yet we're always able to answer the question. That is an adaptable evolutionary trait in our psychology that put us up the top of the food chain. It shows our cognitive abilities that even exceed smart animals like elephant and dolphins. They cannot create relational frames; we can.

Although Milton Erickson did not call this Relational Frame Theory, he certainly understood the concept and employed Linkages to imply new relational frames.

Erickson used three types of linkages:

- Conjunctions: *And, But*

- Connections in Time: *As, When, During, While*

- Cause and Effect: *Makes, Causes, Forces, Because, Requires*

Linkage using Conjunctions

Remember that old Schoolhouse Rock song? *"Conjunction junction, what's your function?"* Conjunctions are words that connect; that is, they imply a relational frame.

English has seven coordinating conjunctions, but we're going to focus on the words *and* and *but*. Here are some examples:

*"You are deeply relaxed **and** that means you are able to easily set aside anything known or unknown that has kept you from success. You can release those things now **and** move into this new chapter of life."*

That nest example is actually adapted from a line that my colleague John Cerbone uses frequently. It actuates the creative capacity of the subconscious mind to have somebody release that which is either known or unknown keeping them from success. But when we combine that with conjunctions, we create linkages;

we create relational frames that are truly beneficial to our clients.

"You are deeply relaxed. I can see that your breath is smooth and rhythmic, and that means you are able to easily set aside anything known or unknown."

You see, those two things "being deeply relaxed" and "being able to set aside anything known or unknown" are like the cup and the remote control—not actually related. But because I used a conjunction I forced a relationship.

"You can release these things now and move into this new chapter of life."

"Releasing things" and "moving into the new chapter of life" are totally unrelated until I use that conjunction.

Presupposition is at the heart of using Linkages. They imply or presuppose the connection we want the client to adopt.

Linkage using Connections in Time

Words that presuppose a time-based relationship between two actions include the following:

- As
- When
- During
- While (or Whilst in British English)

Here are some examples:

*"**As** you relax, you can feel any stress melting from your muscles."*

So "feeling stress melting from my muscles" is linked to the present with word *as*.

*"**When** you breathe in, it is as if you are breathing in energy, confidence, and power."*

I use that often with my clients who need to feel unstoppable confidence in any situation.

*"**During** this time, you will feel relaxed to know that your time has been well spent learning something new that will serve you, not just during this transition in life, but in every aspect of life."*

Note the connection between what's happening now and what will happen in the future.

Linkage using Cause and Effect

Implying a cause/effect relationship is a powerful way to create a beneficial relational frame. These are several of the words that can presuppose such a relationship:

- Makes
- Causes
- Forces
- Because
- Requires

Here are some examples:

*"**Because** you've come here today and set aside time to learn something new, we know that you will be successful at weight release / smoking cessation / fear of flying / fill in the blank."*

This is a great one to use during a pre-talk or during a session.

*"You have lost ten pounds in the past four weeks and this **makes** achieving your goal even easier over the next few weeks. Your devotion to this **requires** you to be successful, and this **makes** it even easier to stop smoking without discomfort."*

Lost Performatives

Lost Performatives are words or phrases that indicate the

performance of an action without stating who performed the action. Again, the subconscious mind attaches meaning internally, so when a therapist uses a Lost Performative, the client tends to think it's about them.

These words are often used in Lost Performatives:

- Important
- Essential
- Good
- Necessary
- Right
- Promise

Here are some examples:

*"The great **promise** you will experience because you came here today."*

What promise? your client wonders. Was does the promise entail? I must have made a promise to myself or maybe somebody made a promise to me.

This sentence also involves Mind Reading, by the way, plus a causative conjunction, so that's actually a fairly complex suggestion.

*"It is **important** to learn language patterns."*

Important, why? Why is this important? Important to whom? This statement forces the subconscious mind to create a connection and meaning out of these words.

*"It is **good** that you came to my office and its **benefit** is multi-faceted."*

What is good? What is the benefit? That's not specified. It's lost because it's not attached to anything. Your clients will attach it to themselves: Therefore, I am good, and I am going to benefit. Boy, that makes me feel hopeful.

Modal Operators

Language patterns that direct the subject's experience to a certain direction are known as Modal Operators.

"**It is great** *that you are able to learn so easily, applying what you have done here today to new experiences over the next day or two.*"

"It is great" is the modal operator. That what's pushing your client forward.

"**This foundation** *is one that you can build from and quickly achieve your goals.*"

Whether I teach a pain control client Progressive Muscle Relaxation or I teach Mindfulness-Based Stress Reduction to a client who may be quitting smoking and worried about withdrawal, this is a great suggestion.

Presuppositions

Presuppositions are a powerful tool in persuasion; in certain ways, they underlie most of the other language patterns. Presuppositions gain agreement from the subject by implying that an idea is true rather than putting it up for discussion.

Presuppositions about Time

Words used to presuppose relationships about time include the following:

- Before
- After
- During
- Continue
- Yet
- Already

- Begin

- Stop

- Start

- Still

- While

- Since

- As

- When

Here are some examples:

*"You **begin** each session with increased ease at going into deep hypnosis."*

*"As you **continue** to breathe, you will **start** to notice it is easy to experience only each moment measured by each breath."*

Ordinal Presuppositions

These presuppositions give a client the appearance of choice, but really they create a faked alternative (also known as a false dilemma or double bind) since an outcome is actually presumed.

So may I ask a client a question this question:

"Do you want to give up smoking now or do you want to have a last cigarette before we begin the session?"

It has the appearance of choice—"Do you want to give up smoking now or have the last cigarette?"—but the outcome is the same: quit smoking.

The word *or* is another presupposition. *Or* provides a choice which, by the way, is again often faked. Let's say your client has a fear of flying. You might ask:

"Would you prefer to be able to fly in a hypnotic sleep or simply fly without fear but remain awake?"

It doesn't matter what their choice is, they're going to get on the airplane and see grandma, which is what they couldn't do before the therapy session.

When doing demonstrations, one of my colleagues will ask volunteers whether they want to go into hypnosis slow or fast. While the question helps him pick which induction to use, it also presupposes that the volunteer will go into trance.

So *or* implies two choices, but both choices ultimately have the same outcome.

Presuppositions of Awareness

A third type of presupposition involves awareness:

"Are you aware that you have already become a non-smoker, simply by coming here today?"

I use this one with my clients all the time. It brings their awareness to something. Because my clients are tied up with the question of whether or not they are aware—and let's face it, no one wants to admit to being clueless—they accept the idea that they have already become non-smokers.

During my sessions with my smoking cessation clients, it is my belief that when they sit in the chair and close their eyes, they've already become a non-smoker. They've committed to that by calling me, by taking the time off work, by driving to my office, by paying me, by having their last cigarette either before the session or before we go on to the formal hypnotic trance. By the time we finally get to the hypnotic furniture, my client is actually a non-smoker. So I use that question all the time.

"And as you relax, become aware that the issue here today is not 'how do I quit smoking?' In fact, you've already become a non-smoker simply by coming here today."

I might even draw their awareness to that by adding to it.

"Become aware of what it feels like to be a nonsmoker, to breathe in your first breaths of fresh air."

Presuppositions can be powerful tools for change during pre-talk, trance induction, suggestion, and even after the formal trance work.

Embedded Suggestions

Throughout the scripts that I often write, and in any of Milton Erickson's writings, you can find many Embedded Suggestions. As pointed out earlier, this was one of Milton Erickson's favorite strategies. Here are some ways to embed a suggestion:

*"I don't know if **you will go into trance** quickly today or if it will take you a little bit of time."*

Your Embedded Suggestions here is: "You will go into trance."

Another way is to simply use the word *now*. That is an Embedded Suggestions related to action at this moment, so we could say:

*"Well, **now**.... There will come a point when it is just more comfortable to close the eyes."*

The implied suggestion is that now is the time to close the eyes.

A Word about Analog Marking

This concept, sometimes called "Analog Striking," comes from Neuro-Linguistic Programming. It builds on the idea of embedded suggestion. The idea is that by saying certain words in a certain tone, or making the same gesture when you say each word, you can string together an embedded suggestion even if the words are separated by some distance in your statement.

I really don't put much stock in Analog Marking, but it's a popular concept in the seduction community, which has borrowed a lot of ideas from NLP and therefore from Ericksonian Hypnosis, so I want to address it here.

Here's the kind of example seductionists will often use:

*"The rock band **KISS** owns a football team in LA. It makes **me** wonder if I should start being a football fan **now**."*

Of course, the embedded command here is "kiss me now."

Yes, I know this is an absurd example—yet those claiming the validity of Analog Marking try to make it sound like a reasonable thing. There are probably 101 more effective ways to get the suggestion acted upon, and there is no evidence that I am aware of showing its utility in producing a response or an action. Sure, you can find stories of the power of Analog Striking in the "super-secret mystical Ericksonian training courses" that are often sold online. But the reality is, those are anecdotal and probably made up by the people who are selling the course. Unfortunately, those looking for a magic formula to help them score with women will buy into this nonsense.

So I do use Embedded Suggestion. It's logical that the embedded suggestion would be understood by the subconscious mind. It is completely illogical to me that there's any real value in Analog Striking.

Negative Commands

Negative Commands, as we are discussing them here, mean suggestions that use logical negation, that is, the use of the word *not* to reverse the meaning of the sentence.

This is a topic that is somewhat controversial and confuses many students of hypnosis. So let's spell this out clearly:

First, by "negative command," we don't mean a suggestion that is harmful, toxic, or damaging. For instance, "You will always be a failure," while dripping with negativity, does not use logical negation.

Second, while the subconscious mind *can* process negation, it does not seem to do so consistently. Sadly, many hypnosis courses miss this subtle nuance, instead teaching an absolute idea that is nonsense: the idea that the subconscious can NEVER process negative.

Nonetheless, because the subconscious has trouble with negation, there is a way we can exploit that weakness to embed suggestions.

To *not* think of something actually requires that you *do* think of something in order to rule out thinking about it. For example, as you are reading this, do not think of a pink elephant. Whatever you're doing right now, do not think of a pink elephant. And of course, what are you thinking of? You're thinking of a pink elephant. The reason why—this is really paradoxical therapy at its finest—is that you have to process the negative into a positive in order to understand it. And so, negative commands can actually be effective.

Milton Erickson is famous for using this one:

"You will not want to go into trance too quickly, enjoying the process of going deeper."

That's really a pretty complex sentence. It has an embedded command ("go into trance"). It also employs reverse psychology: Anytime somebody tells me what I shouldn't do, I always want to do it. If you tell a child, "Don't touch the stove; you will burn yourself," there's a great chance the child will get burned. Every little kid burns himself because we have to think about touching the stove in order to think about *not* touching the stove.

Here's another example of a negative command:

"It is important that you don't buy that now, but rather, wait until you know that buying it is the right choice for you."

A salesman may use this in a hypnotic language pattern. It tells somebody not to buy something but at the same time tells them to buy. In order for them to process not buying it, they have to create a mental construct of them buying it now in order to refuse to do it.

In the seduction courses, they actually used to sell tee-shirts that say: "Stop falling in love with me." The idea was that somebody who read the tee-shirt had to actually think of falling in love with somebody in order to understand what *not* falling in love with somebody was. And of course once a thought is created, that thought is the germination for all reality.

A colleague of mine once observed an organization that chanted at each of its meetings:

"We're building a group with no gossip, no back-stabbing, and no in-fighting—no kidding!"

The organization collapsed within a year, due to gossip, back-stabbing, and in-fighting.

As you can see these negative commands can include embedded suggestions, and negative commands can actually be employed quite effectively in almost all forms of hypnosis.

Double Meaning Words

Words that sound alike but have different meanings are called homonyms; using these words to embed suggestions is often called phonological ambiguity.

Some common homonyms in English include:

- your / you're
- too / two / to
- hear / here

Many words and phrases can have double meanings in English:

- down
- back
- mind now
- your unconscious / you're unconscious

Here is an example:

*"As you focus **your unconscious** [pause] **mind now** how you relax more."*

The subconscious suggestion here is "you're unconscious"— as in experiencing trance. "Mind now" becomes an embedded command to pay attention.

Chapter 35
Association and Dissociation

A key concept in NLP related to our primary representational system and to the modalities is the concept of associated or dissociated. This is an important aspect of NLP. Often, we view dissociation as something that is negative or bad. The DSM-IV and the DSM-V have a dissociative personality disorder. We often view that it is wrong to dissociate from things, but there is a time and a place for the art of dissociation. And either one of these vantage points is a correct vantage point. There really is not a right or wrong.

When we are coaching, and when we are working with individuals, we are looking for signals from them that they are associated into an experience or that they are dissociated from an experience. Associated means they are into that experience. They are experiencing that experience as themselves. Dissociated means they are viewing it from an observer viewpoint.

We are going to refine this using hypnotic language, and we can call it revivification versus reflection.

Associated & Dissociated
(Revification vs. Reflection)

You as you V̶s Being in the picture

Make it real V̶s Make it compelling

Re-experience V̶s Learn a lesson

Toward V̶s Away

You as You

Revivification is the idea that I am me experiencing a previous me as if it is happening right now. This is, in trauma counseling, something that we sometimes view as a negative experience. In hypnosis, we might view this as abreaction, but the reality is revivification can be a process that is beneficial to individuals. It can help a person to relive experiences that have been meaningful or of value to them. There is a place for revivification and for being fully associated into an experience.

When my grandmother died, who I was very close to, the memorial service was held in the chapel at the facility where she passed away. Right after the end of the service, when all the relatives were hanging around talking with each other, I decided I would just go for a walk. I walked down the hallway to my grandmother's room. I just looked, and I observed, and then I went back toward the dining area where there was a sitting area and an aviary. My grandmother and I used to sit there, and she would talk about the birds. My grandmother was a birder. She loved birdhouses and watching birds.

I remembered that just a few weeks before this, I had sat in this place with my grandmother, and I was listening to her tell me stories about the birds that she had been observing here in the aviary. I am not sure exactly when that recollection of the previous experience with my grandmother turned inside of me, but I was no longer forty-some years old, remembering my grandmother a few weeks before. I was now eight years old again at my grandmother's house, watching her watch the birds and showing me her bird books and the pictures of the birds. I do not know if I was standing there for five seconds or five minutes, but suddenly I felt a tap on my shoulder. I jumped, and it was Carissa, one of the nurse assistants who had taken care of my grandmother. She said, "Richard, are you okay?" and I jumped because I was no longer me in this place. I was fully associated into a revivification, and I was eight years old again, on my grandmother's back porch. And for me, that is one of the precious memories that I was able to reassociate into some forty years later.

Association and dissociation can be both positive and negative experiences, but it's just about being a person.

The revivification is me as me reexperiencing the reflection as me, as part of the picture, being able to see me and reflect on my feelings, thoughts, and actions in any given situation. We could look at associated and dissociated, as you simply being in the picture, being an observer of you holding that recollection or that image of you in your hand.

Our clients are going to reveal whether they are associated or dissociated with their language. They are going to tell us things like "I feel" versus "I am." That is what we are listening for. They will talk to me about their experiences, and they will tell me whether they are fully associated into a mind, body, and spirit or whether they are observing and evaluating those things. From a dissociated perspective, they might say, "It's as if I see." From an associated perspective, they might say, "I feel." We are listening for their language, the differences in their submodality expressions, as well as their primary representational systems.

Make It Real

The associated position might be viewed as making something real versus dissociated, making it compelling. I am telling a story, so I am compelling. I just told you the story of me after my grandmother's funeral. I did not revivify and make the experience real again as I told the story as an observer, hopefully sharing with you a compelling story that not only taught a point but was interesting to read.

Re-experience

Associated might be about trying to re-experience something, and this could be valuable. Go back to that point before you made the decision. In other words, associate into it. If I am working with a person who wants to have confidence in any situation, I ask them to associate into an experience where they had confidence before. "Make it real right there in the office. Be as if you were in that peak level of performance previously, right here and now, so we can associate into a resource state." A dissociated position might be one that allows me to learn a lesson. And from that experience, what lessons were learned?

Toward versus Away

The associated position really moves toward something. The dissociated position moves away from something.

In NLP, we often talk about motivation. We are only motivated by two things. We are either motivated toward something. *I'd like to have a happy, joyous, and free experience.* Or away from something. *I'm sick and tired of being sick and tired. I don't want to experience that anymore.*

Our associated and dissociated components of the coaching process can really help me to connect. It can help me to build rapport. It can help me to assist clients in understanding their experiences from a deeper level. This can be integrated within any of the concepts from neurological levels to the Awareness Wheel, to our traditional coaching model, to the perceptual positions that we also talk about in NLP.

Content Reframing

Content reframing is not simply looking at the bright side of a bad situation. Content reframing is a skill that goes far beyond that. In its simplest terms, we are going to take a non-resourceful state and transform it into a resourceful state. This is the art of content reframing. If somebody has, for example, a fear that is not resourceful to them, is there a way to reframe the situation where they find themself so that that fear becomes a resourceful state to them?

We know that fear can be either non-resourceful or something that is resourceful. Fear is not something we are trying to banish. It is the non-resourcefulness of the fear we want to work on. I am going to give you a couple of examples here so you know exactly how this works. I will share with you some applications that are effective in life coaching and NLP in therapy and in mentoring people in business and leadership. This is a skill that is very important, and I want you to practice the principles that I am sharing with you.

Content Reframing

Non-Resourceful ⟶
⤷ Resourceful Viewpoint

❶ Your Suggested Reframe

❷ Client Generated Reframe

How to Generate Content Reframe ⤵

   ① **Perceptional Position + Socratic Questions**

   ② **List 5 Potential Positive Outcomes**

   ③ **Model Other**

     "Do you know anyone with this experience? What were the eventual positive outcomes?"

How to Generate Content Reframes

Content reframing during a session with a client is going to come in one of two forms.

1. Your Suggested Reframe

You reframing a situation for the client so that they can see the resourceful state amid the non-resourceful states is perfectly okay. It is acceptable for us to have ideas, listen to our clients, and share with them potential reframes that could be of value to them. If it resonates with them, if they look inside themself, do a transderivational search, and see that what we have suggested could benefit them, it is often the case that they will adopt our ideas then as their own ideas.

2. **Client Generated Reframe**

    There is another powerful strategy in NLP, and that is having the client suggest, create, discover, and step into their own content reframes.

    This is a strategy that I use with clients in several different ways. I want my clients to elicit their own reframes, to have that "aha" experience that insight-oriented therapy talks about, that Carl Rogers talks about. There are several different ways we can do that.

Perceptual Positions and Socratic Questions

In this book, we have already discussed the idea of perceptual position. Most people who are experiencing crisis, difficulty, or overwhelm are in the first perceptual position. They are them as them experiencing the distress that surrounds them. But working with them to uncover the second perceptual position, them as an observer observing them in a situation, gives them a new vantage point.

We can then combine that with Socratic questions. "When you see yourself in this position, do you get a sense that things are different?"

We could combine this with the Awareness Wheel as an exercise to help a person in second or even third perceptual position to be able to discover a new content reframe.

List Five Potential Positive Outcomes

There are other ways we can use a content reframe to have a client generate that experience from within. We can simply give them a piece of paper and a marker and ask them to write on the markerboard. I'll say, "I want you to think of five things that you can discover in the situation that have the potential to be positive." That is really important. We do not want to ask them to discover five positive things in this lousy situation. That can come across as nonempathetic. It is perfectly okay to say to a client, "Wow, the situation you've described is really difficult. I can understand why negative feelings and non-resourceful states have emerged. I wonder if by stepping back from this situation, it's possible to think of five potential outcomes or experiences that could make this valuable or useful."

Alcoholics Anonymous: The Big Book, the 12-step program, referred directly to this. They say that no matter how far down we have gone, we can see how our experiences benefit other people. A lot of people come into the 12-step program feeling a sense of negativity, a sense of depression, a sense of regret, a sense of despair, with maybe legal problems, health problems, and/or vocational problems. They come into the program, and they are confronted with the idea that no matter how far down the scale they have gone, they will be able to see how their experiences can benefit other people. That is a positive reframe that is taught early on, really to the newcomers of Alcoholics Anonymous and other 12-step programs. The idea of having them list five, seven, or ten potential positive outcomes that could be found in this situation is a strategy that can be effective.

I like to push the envelope here. If I ask the client for five potential positive outcomes or resourceful states that could come about, I want them to really come up with five or seven or ten or whatever the magic number is. The reason why is that they will be more convinced of one or two of those than all of those. When they stretch their mind and try to come up with five, seven, or ten things, I find that the answer that resonates most with them is usually number four or five or number eight or nine. When you have clients do assignments like this, really push.

Modeling Others

Neuro-linguistic programming is all about modeling others. If you have found yourself in a different situation and in this situation you are accessing non-resourceful states, let me ask you a question. The question really is simple. "Do you know anyone else who has experienced something similar to this, and they surprised themself by discovering meaning or value in this difficult situation?" I must look inside. *Do I know anybody like that? Have I heard of anybody like that?*

"Yes, there was this person, and they experienced something like this, although I could never have the outcome they had." "Let's talk about this because what you're saying is there's the potential for a positive experience here." "There's the potential, but I don't have the money or the resources [or whatever else somebody else had]." I am into strengths and resources. You can see how this all begins to tie together. I can tap into those strengths and resources as tools that they do possess to help them move toward a positive state.

Content reframing is about moving from these non-resourceful states to resourceful states. I am going to give you an example of how that can be seen in several different situations.

The first is a book I wrote a few years ago, *The Couples Treasure Chest: The Seven Most Effective Ways to Move Your Relationship from Misery to Joy*. The entire premise of the book is reframing in couples counseling. This is an excellent strategy that you can use even if you're not a couple's therapist. You can use it with people in relationships. You can use this in your own life.

One of the biggest problems in marriages is that people save, what I call, marital green stamps. "On July 3rd, 1972, you failed to take the trash out." That is a green stamp in the book. "We were walking through the mall, and you noticed somebody else that was attractive, and you stared at them, and that was embarrassing to me." That is another green stamp. "On August 11th, 1983, you said something hurtful toward my mother, my father, my sister [or whomever else]." That is another green stamp. What happens is people always look at what is wrong. The husband, or the wife, doesn't do [whatever it is], and so those are green stamps to put in the book.

And when people focus on non-resourceful states long enough, over a long enough period, what happens is they cash in the green stamp book. In life, the green stamp book is taken to the supermarket, and they cash it in for a blender, a toaster, or some plates. In marriage, they cash it in for justifying their adultery. They cash it in with the big divorce. They cash it in by justifying violent behavior or passive-aggressive behavior. I see that time after time after time.

I give an assignment to every couple I work with. It is a content reframing homework assignment. The assignment is to take a spiral notebook home and use the one book for both of them.

I tell them that what I want them to do is put it in a room where they both pass through every day. It could be the bathroom, garage, or kitchen. Each day, whether it is one word or one sentence, or one short paragraph, I want to teach them to think of and write down in the book one thing they value about their partner that day. I tell them never more than a paragraph. Do that again the next day, and the next day, and the next day. I do not necessarily want them to do this together.

This is often the first time that they have looked at what's right with their partner. That is why it is called *The Couples Treasure Chest* because instead of saving up those marital green stamps, they are saving up their couple's treasure. If you save up resourceful states, kind words, appreciation, and gratitude for a long enough period, you can cash in that treasure chest for a pirate's bounty later. This is a simple but profound technique for reframing content that can change the entire dynamic of a dysfunctional relationship and turn it into a healthy relationship.

Even if we did nothing else in couples counseling, the reality is the couple's treasure chest is a powerful experience. I have had couples who have done this day after day, week after week, year after year. They have gotten through many notebooks, and it has become something that they cherish and value, as their relationship has become much stronger as a result of this content reframe.

Just last week, I was coaching somebody in my twelveweekbook.com writing class. (I teach other people how to write books, typically having anywhere from seventy to one hundred students per class.) Recently, someone had written to chapter five, but they had not written any more of Their book. They were afraid to continue, and the reason why they were afraid to continue with their work was that they were afraid that what they were sharing about their own spiritual experiences was not okay. They were raised in a home that was nonreligious. It was a home hostile toward religion. Although their parents had long been deceased, this individual held on to these ideas that it is not appropriate or okay to talk about religious or spiritual ideas. But they really wanted to, in the self-help book they were writing, share how their spiritual faith had helped them to solve the problems outlined in the first part of the book.

This person said to me, "But I just can't go on. I know my parents are deceased, and I am not going to disappoint them because they are not here to read it, but I'm just really afraid to continue. What if other people don't like my work?"

I said to them that so far, what they had articulated in the book was great content, so the worst thing that could happen would be that somebody would come along to this chapter where they were vulnerable, and perhaps, they might say, "This is not something that resonates with me. This isn't something I value." But they could also say to themself that the first part of the book was amazing, and continuing to the next part of the book, they would probably find something of value.

I asked them if they had ever read a book and thought to themself, they really liked one specific part but didn't really like another part? They replied in the affirmative. I continued explaining that every single book is like that. And because every book is like that, their book would be like that too. Although somebody might say they didn't relate to a chapter, it is very possible, based on what this person had shared with me, that another person who grew up in a nonspiritual home might say to themself that the chapter really resonated with them and that they had never thought about it in that way and they will find this chapter is the best part of the book.

Or maybe somebody who came from the opposite, a very religious home but a dogmatic home, a home filled with ritual that was not resourceful to them in their adult life, might consider that what they had shared gave them a sense of freedom. It might even be useful to those who are still on a spiritual quest or those who might not even know they are on a spiritual quest. Perhaps it will help them open their mind to their deepest level of need. But the reality is the very worst thing that could happen is somebody might conclude that it was not their favorite chapter of the book. And here is the content reframe: If they got to chapter six, they would have already found another chapter that was of value to them, or they wouldn't have read the book that far.

I asked if they had ever bought a book and read a chapter or two and then put it down and never came back to it? It was because it didn't resonate with them. By the time someone is on chapter six, they already think something is awesome because nobody reads half a book unless they find something valuable. They simply move on.

We can reframe in our coaching as I did with that individual or a client who lost their job not too long ago. They had worked seven years for one company. They had made a change to another company to take a higher salary. They only worked there for three years, and then the company laid them off. The reason why the company laid them off was that the company was not doing very well.

This individual finally found another job. It took them almost nine months. And so, they remembered the nine months of difficulty and stayed with this job that they didn't particularly like. But again, the economy changed, a result of COVID-19, and they were paid for a short period of time after the lockdown but eventually let go. Feeling distressed, they were unsure of what else they could do.

I met with him, and I talked about the skills that he had developed in those years working for those companies. And I talked to him about the opportunity to share those skills not as an employee but as an expert. And he said, "As an expert?" I said, "Absolutely." I said, "You've been doing this type of work now in this industry for fourteen years."

I continued to explain that after all those years, he had developed some expertise other people didn't have. As a consultant, he has the opportunity to have flexible time, potentially make more money, at least on an hourly basis, and move from an expert level to a sage level in the industry, which means that after a period of time, he could develop a consulting business and the great news was that he could be doing that online with companies right now who are gearing up for reopening.

Astonished, he replied, "Wow. I never even thought about that. I had always been told you have to have a job."

I shared my experience that the last time I got a paycheck from somebody else was in 1994 and that entrepreneurship is a pathway to success; those who create wealth are often those who have created businesses. One of the primary businesses people create that creates wealth is consultancy services.

The whole idea of content reframing also occurs in business coaching. The entire concept of Appreciative Inquiry is predicated on looking at what's right rather than what's wrong. In a nutshell, Appreciative Inquiry takes an organization or a community, and it enlists all the stakeholders. That could be the employees, the C-suite, the executive team. It could include members of the community that perhaps surround a geographic location, customers, vendors. It gets everybody together. Then it asks the question of all these people what the company is doing correctly and how it can do more of what it's doing correctly?

Rather than looking at what is wrong and trying to fix what is broken, let's look at what actually works.

A company that has a six percent complaint rate might be looking at "How do we eliminate the six percent of our dissatisfied customers?" But really, the question is, "How can we do more of what the ninety-four percent are satisfied with?" By focusing on what is right rather than what is wrong, by focusing on what is resourceful rather than non-resourceful, we can elicit a powerful change. In the Law of Attraction, we say, "Where energy goes, prosperity flows." We want to put our thought into positive energy. So, where the energy flows is where the mind goes.

We want to be able to use content reframes as a strategy in personal development like the Law of Attraction. The Law of Attraction is all about content reframes or evidence-based approaches to consultancy like Appreciative Inquiry.

During the COVID-19 era, much of our business coaching and hypnosis therapy over the last year has moved online. Some people have said this limits their ability to provide the services that they did and to do the things that they enjoy. Let me ask you, what opportunities come about as a result of moving your business online? Can you serve a larger geographic area? Are you now not competing with your rate on a local basis but on a national stage? And of course, COVID-19 has been tragic for many people. My uncle passed away as a result of the virus in later 2020.

This pandemic has had some dramatic losses for people and caused pain for people. But in this pain and in this difficulty, the question is what content reframe can you create so that despite the difficulties, we step into resourceful states in our own lives and with our business as well?

Chapter 36
Motivational Strategy

Part of our job as a coach is to motivate people and help people move toward that which will be beneficial to them. In my coaching processes, I am always going to be looking at motivation as one of the essential tools for success.

Neuro-linguistic programming has long taught that there are only two ways to motivate people. We can either motivate people away from something, as in not wanting to touch that stove because it will burn and it's hot, or moving toward something as in wanting to move toward creating wealth because then one can buy a Bentley, for example.

We can either be motivated by the desire to stay away from something or be motivated by the desire to go toward something. We might be motivated to stay away from a relationship because of negative emotions. We might be motivated toward a relationship because of positive emotions. This really applies across the board, and it is really pretty simple. To help people change their behaviors, we need to look at the motivations they have. Is it an away from motivation, or is it a toward motivation? And guess which one of these two is more powerful? The toward motivation is more powerful, generally, than the away from motivation.

AWAY ←→ TOWARD

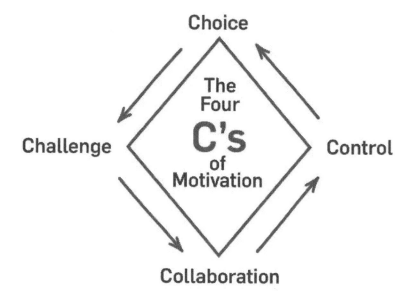

Let's take a look at what the research says about motivating people.

If I am coaching and I want to motivate people, there are four Cs of motivation.

Choice

Neuro-linguistic programming says it is better to have a choice than not have a choice. People are only going to be motivated when they have choices, and when they choose the choice, it becomes their own choice rather than one imposed on them. This is why intentions are more powerful than goals. Intentions come from within. Goals often come from the expectations of others. We want to work with our clients who need the motivation to accomplish something or do something or change something, make a choice, and feel that they have a choice, and that choice is not simply to move away from something but to step into something awesome.

Choice is the first component, and in our coaching, we always brainstorm and elicit options. Ask your client what else could they do? What have other people done? What choices could they make? All of these are important questions.

Challenge

The next element of motivation is people are not motivated unless there is a challenge. This is why competition is very popular. We set up competitions between students. We set up competitions between sales teams. In couples counseling, we might even set up competitions between spouses sometimes. A challenge is something that creates an internal motivation, usually toward a reward.

Collaboration

The next element of motivating people is collaboration. People are more motivated when they do not do things in isolation. Isolation brings about weirdness and problems. Most people do not do well independently, or most people do not do well with the absence of other people, whether they are participants, helpers, or observers. We want to figure out when we are trying to motivate somebody, whether it is a student in a classroom, an executive in the boardroom, a spouse in a marriage to collaborate with their partner, with other people, with mentors, with us as a life coach, to stay motivated and to move toward that which is most important to them.

Control

People want to feel a sense of autonomy, a sense of freedom. One of our deepest spiritual needs is the ability to feel a sense of freedom, to feel like they have control over the outcomes and the decisions and the experiences as well as their emotions and their physical state. Is there anything we can do in our coaching to foster a sense of control that is going to be super important as well?

Chapter 37
Motivational Interviewing

Motivational interviewing is rarely ever taught in NLP training. As a strategy, it has been around for a couple of decades, but it is proven to be an effective strategy in moving people toward that which is most important to them. The people who have taken the course have found it extremely effective and extremely helpful. They found it to be one of the most helpful components in helping people make change related to stopping smoking. You will be able to take these same strategies and apply those to the type of clients you are working with, even if it is a different type of client.

In this section of the book, I am going to focus on the ideas of motivational interviewing. I want you to see how it is delivered in a variety of different healthcare settings.

Motivational interviewing is a particular strategy for eliciting motivation from an individual, particularly when there's ambivalence present.

I have worked with substance abuse clients for many years, and it seems as if the nicotine users have the highest level of ambivalence of all. They know there are health consequences, but they derive a sense of pleasure from the behavior that they are engaged in.

Nobody smokes cigarettes because they want lung cancer, heart disease, emphysema, COPD, strokes, complications of pregnancy or impotence, or any of the other warnings that are on the side of a package of cigarette. They smoke cigarettes because it meets a legitimate need, maybe at first in the context of teen peer groups, acceptance, or maybe for socialization. Maybe it is a stress reliever. In fact, the cigarette smoker is an expert at deep breathing.

Teaching them deep breathing can replace the habitual behavior of cigarette smoking because the reward for them comes from the deep breaths. I teach every one of my cigarette smokers breathing techniques. It is one of the reasons why hypnosis is so effective for cigarette smokers. When we do progressive muscle relaxation therapy, or we do other forms of hypnotic induction that incorporate breathing, particularly techniques related to mindfulness, we find that it often is a way for them to meet their legitimate needs without the harmful behavior.

But because cigarette smoking, dipping tobacco, or vaping meets a legitimate need, there is often a lot of ambivalence. They know that there are dangers to it. Maybe they have even experienced some already, but they are not ready to give up the rewards yet because of the pleasure or because of the immediate gratification or the other needs that are met. And so, motivational interviewing is a specific strategy designed to move people toward a motivation that is consistent with their core values.

Here is the thing about motivational interviewing in healthcare settings. It has been adopted as a strategy in nursing and respiratory therapy, counseling, and physician training. Almost all medical residents are now trained, particularly in family practice and internal medicine, in motivational interviewing because the evidence shows that when we use this approach to communication, we are more likely to elicit a motivation that gives up the ambivalence and steps into those core values.

Those familiar with NLP are very familiar with the core concept that rapport building is essential. These strategies from motivational interviewing are literally the strategies that are the foundation of effective rapport building. If you have ever had any NLP training or any training in eliciting rapport with individuals, these can build on your skills and really take them up to the next level.

O.A.R.S.

The O.A.R.S. model of essential communication has four basic skills.

Open Questions

O stands for **O**pen questions. Instead of asking questions that have a yes/no answer or even a numerical answer, they are open-ended questions. This is important because open-ended questions lead a person to create what, in NLP or hypnosis, we call a transderivational search. It causes them to create an internal dialogue, essentially to look within themself for the answer. A closed question, yes/ no answer, or a numerical number, causes a person to look outside of themself for an answer.

Anything we do that causes a person to look inside is something that causes in communication what we call search talk, and in NLP, a transderivational search. In acceptance and commitment therapy, we might call this eliciting an individual's core values. Each of these different disciplines is looking ultimately for the same results, and open-ended questions do that.

Affirmations

The second letter in our acronym stands for **A**ffirmations. I use affirmations from the very beginning to the end in all my sessions with my clients.

Every time I have a new client who comes to my office, I stand up, and I greet them with a handshake. And I say to them, for example, "Hi, I'm Richard. Stephanie (my receptionist) told me you were going to be here. I am really glad that you're here today. I know that you're going to be able to accomplish great things." I begin with positive suggestions and affirmations.

Reflective Listening

Reflective listening is a strategy where, rather than telling our clients what they should think or do or feel, we reflect what they think or feel. We become a mirror to a person so they can see a bigger picture. Reflective listening is a well-known basic counseling strategy.

When I was in graduate school learning Rogerian therapy, I learned how to say "uh-huh" (affirmative) and reflect back to a person what I thought I heard them say. I have kind of mocked Rogerian therapy for its simplistic approach earlier, but the reality is that training was very, very valuable to me. When we do not interject our biases, beliefs, values, and experiences, and reflect, we provide an opportunity again for that transderivational search, for clarification of values, and for our client to step into a new level of experience and understanding, so they actually see the bigger picture.

Summarizing

Summarizing is recapping what it is that we have had presented by the client through the assessment process, decision-making process, and action process. Our clients go through this process on a meta-level and micro-level. On a meta-level or macro-level, they have thought about quitting smoking, and they have made a call to our office. Now they have taken action, and they have stepped into our office. Once they are in my office, I might ask them if they still have cigarettes or tobacco in their car or their purse. They must make a decision to give it up. And they must take action and choose to bring those in. By summarizing, we can help our clients to go through that process and emerge victoriously.

O.A.R.S. is an acronym that helps us to remember those key communication strategies. They are effective strategies that we should seek every opportunity to utilize, whether we are counseling a client, or doing a hypnosis session, or whether as a respiratory therapist, a nurse, another medical professional, a teacher, or a minister coaching or consulting.

D.E.A.R.S.

What are the five principles of motivational interviewing? Another acronym helps us out here.

Develop Discrepancy

The first letter is to **D**evelop **d**iscrepancy. In our interview with a client, we want to help the client begin seeing that what they say and what they do are different. This is certainly an easy thing to do with smokers. They have a conscious action that they take, but it is not reconciled with their subconscious habits, and this is where the frustration over quitting often comes about. One of the goals of effective intervention is to magnify or develop these discrepancies so that it causes pain because one of the ways we motivate clients is not only to pleasure. We can say that by becoming a nonsmoker, the client will be happy, joyous, and free, but also by avoiding pain. This is something that we can do by developing discrepancy.

I worked with a grandmother who wanted to quit smoking. She had a diagnosis of leukemia. She knew that her ability to recover and enjoy the time that she had left with her only grandson, a two-year-old, was going to be predicated on quitting smoking, and yet she did not do that. I magnified the discrepancy between her action of giving in and smoking those cigarettes, continual relapse, and what it was that she valued most about her time with her grandson. Through developing those discrepancies between what a person says and what a person does, I was able to help her step into a successful new chapter of life.

Express Empathy

Expressing empathy is exceedingly important in any type of human service—counseling, nursing, etcetera—and is sometimes referred to as bedside manner.

I have done thousands of smoking cessation sessions with people over the years, and it would be effortless for me just to fall into the routine, the habit of what it is that I always do. Genuineness and empathy are essential. When I was in graduate school, my professor came into my very first class, and he drew many things on the board about counseling and the counseling process. And then, at the bottom, he wrote empathy.

This really tied in with some of the hypnosis training that I received in the mid-2000s. I have had hypnosis training long before that, but I went to a course sponsored by the American Counseling Association in Germany. The title of the course was Advanced Accurate Empathy. Really, it was a hypnotherapy course. Ernest Rossi was a contemporary of Milton Erickson's who wrote many books with him, used a metaphor for hypnosis that it is really belly button to belly button communication. In other words, empathy is, at the core, the foundation of our ability to build rapport. We find in counseling and psychotherapy that no matter what approach we use, no matter how clinically sound it is—and some are more evidence-based than others—clients are more likely to respond positively than if we use no therapy. The reason why is simple. King Solomon said it best: As iron sharpens iron, so one man sharpens another. The reality is that people respond to other people.

Let me give you an example of smoking cessation. Years ago,

there was a product on the market that was a homeopathic medicine. Without getting into a debate here, there is no science behind homeopathy. The whole idea of homeopathy is that we will create antibodies to those things that are dangerous or bad for us, unhealthy for us, but we create stronger antibodies with the smallest level of exposure. This is why homeopathic medicines are measured in 10X, 100X, or 1000X, etcetera. And so 1000X of nicotine or tobacco is a minute amount.

I have a friend who was a Walgreens manager at the time. I asked him what their best smoking cessation product was. He looked at me and said that, hands down, they sold more of the cigarette-giver-upper product than anything else. It was a homeopathic medicine, and people swore by it. They said they used the cigarette-giver-upper product and quit smoking. Here is why: It was not because of the science behind homeopathy; it was because a person made a decision that they were going to quit smoking. They took an action. They drove to Walgreens. They invested in the product, $50 for the box of magic pills. They followed the instructions. There was a ritual. Every seven days, take this, this, and this, and they would be smoke-free. And so, often, the exact method that we use to help a person quit smoking is really a ritual to ratify a change that has already taken place with our clients.

Amplify Ambivalence

The third element is to **A**mplify their **a**mbivalence. We want to do this so that we are following things through to their logical absurdity. A communication technique must have a personal look at two sides of an issue. What are the benefits of quitting smoking? What are the benefits of remaining a smoker? This amplifies their ambivalence and brings it to the point of absurdity where people are often willing to give that up and commit to a valued path.

Roll with Resistance

The R stands for **R**oll with **r**esistance. This is what I really appreciate about being an Ericksonian hypnotherapist. I do not see anything as being resistant. In motivational interviewing training, we usually say that if you meet resistance, it is a telltale sign that you need to respond differently. Everybody comes to me not the way they could be, should be, or ought to be, but just the way they are. The effective counselor, the effective hypnotherapist, the effective coach, the effective minister, community leader, teacher, whoever is working with an individual, is going to recognize that the client's experience may not be the same as ours or other people's that we have worked with. That rolling with resistance, letting our clients become the best them that they can be, rather than the best me that they could be, is highly effective.

This may include even sometimes alternating our goals. I had a schizophrenia client who I worked with, and he was in remission. His schizophrenia was well-managed by a psychiatrist and medication. He came to see me. Most schizophrenics are cigarette smokers. Why? Because nicotine as a drug affects the way that we think. It is a cognitive stimulant that helps people focus. This is why students use it; it clears minds and helps someone think a little bit better. A lot of people won't work with a schizophrenic and smoking cessation because the statistic is that ninety-eight percent of all schizophrenics smoke.

I worked with him, and he stayed off cigarettes for about eight months. And then I worked with him again. The next time it was about three months. Then I worked with him again, and he stayed off cigarettes for about a year. I continually worked with him, and I did not berate him for failure. There was no failure. This is what I love about NLP. The first predicate in NLP is there is no such thing as failure, only feedback. And for a schizophrenic, who has other mental cognitive disorders going on, it is very important to recognize that they are not failing, that relapse is often a part of both conditions. We can create strategies to help them so that we can mitigate the severity of the relapse or avoid relapse.

I had no problem continuing to work with him over a period of ten years. I think with many other clients, a therapist might have said since the client had relapsed five times, it was time for the client to find a new approach, deciding they could not work with that client because they were not willing to do what was offered. Maybe that works in traditional chemical dependency treatment, but not with a schizophrenic client.

We need to recognize that rolling with resistance rather than trying to break through the power struggle is a strategy that works.

Support Self-Efficacy

The S stands for **S**upport **s**elf-efficacy. We want our clients to bring to the table the solutions that work for them. The suggestions that we make in hypnotherapy come from the client. The interventions we use in nursing are the things that our clients bring to the table—in counseling the internal resources, the psychological coping strategies, the methods of relapse prevention that have helped them in prior attempts to experience success.

I ask every one of my clients is, "Have you ever quit smoking before?" and they'll say, for example, "Well, yeah, I quit for thirty days." "Yes, I even quit for a year." "See, that's fantastic." "Yeah, but I blew it. I relapsed," and I validate that. I say, "No, that's a year you spent not smoking. It was a year of your body being healthy." I will often let my client know that they did not lose that year by beginning to smoke.

That is really powerful for them. They did not lose the benefits of that year. They still have all those benefits. I let them know that if they had the ability to quit for a year, our question then today is not can you quit smoking, but how do we extend beyond a year because we know already the client can do it for at least a year.

The D.E.A.R.S. acronym is a principle of motivational interviewing that you will find very effective as you develop your skills in creating rapport and working with individuals.

Motivational Ruler

In motivational interviewing, one of the key concepts is the idea of a motivational ruler. This really is a Likert scale. A Likert scale is anything we rate on equal intervals. For example, rate on a scale of one to five, not ready to change, thinking about changing, undecided, probably want to change, to ready to change.

I generally use a Likert scale on a scale of one to ten. The reason why the Likert scale, or what motivational interviewing calls "the readiness to change ruler," is important is because it lets a person know that it is not all or nothing and that there's room for small movement.

I work with a lot of pain control clients, and it is not about getting rid of all their pain. If you have a chronic pain client or patient who can get rid of twenty percent of their pain or forty percent of the pain, will that make a difference in their life? It would make a huge difference in their life. It is the same thing with ambivalence about smoking. It is the same thing about readiness to change. If I can increase it just by twenty percent, I can step into a commitment for lasting change. The readiness to change ruler is a very useful concept.

Active Listening

This is one of the key components in motivational interviewing as well. For us, in working with individuals, these are often some of the roadblocks to success: giving advice, moralizing, making suggestions, or telling them what they should do or ought to do.

People do not want us to "should" on them. They want us to help them elicit the suggestions that are going to be most effective for them.

Persuading somebody to become a nonsmoker never works. Let them know you are available when they are ready. I only work with people who are highly motivated. This is one of the reasons why I do not do smoking cessation for free. All my smokers must pay me my full fee. The reason why is simple. Unless they are willing to do that, they are not willing to make change. You cannot buy a gift certificate from my office for somebody else to see me for smoking cessation. The reason why is because they will not be persuaded with logic and lecturing and arguing.

Another roadblock for success is disagreeing, criticizing, or blaming a person. There may be some therapeutic value in this from a provocative therapy perspective, but only after we already have rapport.

These roadblocks to listening are general principles, but there may be a therapeutic purpose to use them with some of our clients some of the time. Shaming, ridiculing, labeling does not work. Even sympathizing with them can backfire.

Visiting my doctor, the nurse just kept asking me endless, pointless questions, and it was clear to me the reason why. She had to complete her written assessment to meet her requirements for documentation. If your clients ever feel you are merely asking questions to meet a need for documentation, you have probably ended rapport with that client.

All these things can be roadblocks to listening, as can any other unhealthy communication pattern. It is important to recognize that motivational interviewing is about helping a client achieve their very best. We want to support them by helping them move to and elicit their highest level of functioning.

Am I Doing This Right?

This comes from an informational guide on Motivational Interviewing from Case Western Reserve University. Case Western Reserve University is also known for asset-based community development and studying this as a tool for changing communities.

This guide, though, is about encouraging Motivational Change. The eleven points are either/ors or the two sides to help us understand if our communication really is fitting within the context of a motivational model.

We can spend the rest of our life building the skills of effective motivational interviewing, but this single guide from Case Western Reserve University is particularly useful.

1. Do I listen more than I talk? Or am I talking more than I listen?

2. Do I keep myself sensitive and open to this person's issues, whatever they might be? Or am I talking about what I think the problem is?

3. Do I invite this person to talk about and explore his/her own ideas for change? Or am I jumping to conclusions and possible solutions? Sometimes we do this, not because we are a careless communicator, but because we are trying to shorten the time. We need to recognize that in scheduling clients, we need to give them ample time.

   I typically spend between an hour and an hour and a half with a new client in a first session. I never schedule new clients in blocks of time that are less than two hours. I want to make sure that I have ample time. If I have time between clients, that is fine with me. I can do something productive. But it helps me to avoid jumping to conclusions to shorten the process because I am pressed for time.

4. Do I encourage the person to talk about his or her reasons for not changing? We can learn as much about a client by asking them what benefit they would get from not changing, where we only force them to talk about change.

5. Do I ask permission to give my feedback? Or do I just presume that the ideas that I have are what they need to hear or want to hear?

6. Do I reassure this person that ambivalence to change is normal? Or am I telling them, pushing them to take an action or a solution that may be ahead of time for them? Working through the ambivalence is a big part of that pre-talk in our initial interview and assessment with a new client.

7. Do I help a person to identify successes and challenges from his or her past and relate them to present change efforts? Or am I encouraging him or her to ignore or get stuck on old stories? I am not much of a Freudian. I am not interested in doing regression work with clients. I have them talk to me about their previous experiences so that we can move forward and avoid being stuck on old stories, or we talk about prior events only so they can learn what worked for them.

8. Do I seek to understand this person? I really enjoy my clients. I love working with them. Or do I spend a lot of time trying to get them to understand me and my ideas? How would you know that? Look at your brochure or your website. Is it about you and your

credentials and how awesome you are? Or is it about the solutions that they can find when they come to see you? Your clients really do not care about you. What they care about is them. I can tell you how good a therapist is by what content they have on their website.

9. Do I summarize for this person what I am hearing? Or am I just summarizing what I think? They are two different things.

10. Do I value this person's opinion more than my own? Or am I giving more value to my viewpoint?

11. Do I remind myself that this person is capable of making his or her own choices? Or am I assuming that he or she is not capable of making good choices? I see this a lot with individuals who are considering nicotine replacement therapy or other alternative approaches from laser therapy to homeopathic medicine. Although I questioned homeopathic medicine earlier, if I had a client who came to my office who said they were going to use the quit smoking homeopathic medicine, it is not going to hurt them. I am probably not going to decide that that is an issue for me to prove my rightness.

Hopefully, this can help you to understand how to encourage motivation by change.

Chapter 38
Anchoring

The idea of hypnotic anchoring comes from the metaphor of a boat's anchor. If a boat sits in the harbor, it casts an anchor, and that anchor holds the boat in that place.

In NLP, we use the term for doing something, setting an anchor that usually elicits a positive resource state or a set of strategies. It is important to know that most of what we do in coaching and NLP comes from real-world experiences. I have always said that hypnosis and hypnotic living is not about doing anything to clients. It is about eliciting from within that is the NLP strategy—eliciting the resources that already exist. You and every one of the clients you have ever worked or ever will work with are already the anchoring expert. What do I mean by that? You probably have a treasured item at home, and when you come across that treasured item, whether it is put away in a closet or whether displayed on a shelf, it instantly elicits a positive resource state, or else you probably would not be holding onto it all of these years.

For me, it is my shrimp boat. When I was around ten years old, my dad sent me a wooden shrimp boat. He died shortly after that, and it is one of the few things I have from him. Every time I run across that shrimp boat, it instantly brings back a positive resource state or a feeling or sensation. I immediately associate it with the joy of getting that shrimp boat when I was a kid because back then, it was awesome to get packages in the mail.

A mother's kiss is another example of anchoring. The kid hurts themself, and we offer to kiss the hurt—the mother's healing kiss. We have that anchoring strategy that we learned when we were little kids.

In sales, we anchor product satisfaction. Every slogan that a company has is the desire to associate a resource state, something positive, with the company's name or with the product or service that they offer. This is what branding and advertising are all about. It is all about anchoring: the color, the look, the sound. Your T-Mobile telephone rings a certain way. Your AT&T telephone rings a certain way. Your Sprint telephone rings a certain way. Your Cellular One cell phone rings a certain way.

We are anchored to these things. The "You've Got Mail" message that we used to get on America Online to the "like" that we get on Facebook are all anchors. Facebook has a billion-plus people with an account, largely because of positive reinforcement, because of anchoring. It has been proven that we love the like.

When a boy meets a girl, decisions are going to be made as to whether this relationship is going to make any progress. Whether or not they decide to stay in a relationship with this person might revolve around what they have anchored in their beliefs about finances, or their job, or their physical health and wellness. More attractive people do not necessarily look prettier but often carry the anchors of what we associate with in evolutionary biology, the ability to procreate, to make more people. It is hardwired into us to have anchored those beliefs or judgments.

We have negative anchors as well. Post-traumatic stress disorder may have anchored a non-resourceful state to a sound or anchored a non-resourceful state to a physical sensation or anchored a non-resourceful state to an emotion. Somebody who grew up in an abusive home with an abusive parent yelling at them has likely anchored conflict with a non-resourceful state. Even though the parents are dead and gone, maybe it has been fifty years since this occurred, when somebody, or their spouse, starts yelling at them in a public place or in the place of employment, the individual is anchored to the fear that they have, and they over-respond in the context of this situation. Over-response might have kept them safe in the previous situation, but then mapped out across, it becomes non-resourceful to them.

Anchoring is something that we all do naturally.

In NLP, we will be working with folks to help them create positive, resourceful anchors. These can be anchors of a physical feeling such as relaxation or confidence. It could be a physical feeling related to comfort rather than pain, such as a sound. Maybe we want to anchor something to a sound. Maybe for somebody who is distressed by the busyness of life, we suggest, "Every time over the next couple of weeks when you hear that phone ring, it will be a recognition to you that opportunity lies on the other end." We can start anchoring positive resources to the things that have been distracting to them in the past.

We can anchor to a sight, something they see. John Cerbone is famous in stage hypnosis for his red pen. "And when you open your eyes, you're going to see my red pen. A smile is going to come on your face, and you're going to laugh like an eight-year-old kid." And so, he gives that person that anchor. When the show is over, he shows them the red pen. A smile comes on their face, and they laugh.

When I was a kid, my youth pastor at church used to say, "Every time you see a UPS truck, remember that Jesus loves you." Even now, when I still see a UPS truck, a smile comes on my face because I had positive experiences in youth group, and it brings that to mind.

We can anchor something to a sight, to a sound, to a sensation, to an emotion, to a belief. These occur naturally in life, but we can also elicit them in NLP.

ANCHORING

1 **Physical Feeling**   → **STEPS**

2 **Sound**

3 **Sight**

1 Fully access desired state

2 Amplify state

3 Fire anchor

4 Neutral state

5 Fire anchor (T.O.T.E.) Test, Operate, Test, Exit

Here are the steps we would use to elicit a resource state and anchor it:

1. Fully Access Desired State

    Let's say I am coaching a client, and I want to elicit happiness. I have the client fully access the state that they would like to experience.

    Take a moment. Close your eyes down for just a

minute and bring yourself to a state of happiness. I do not know if you have had a happy day or if you have had a bad day, but you have experienced happiness. You know what happiness is.

Allow yourself, at least at this moment, to set aside any regrets of the past or fears of the future and let yourself at this moment just breathe in and breathe out and sense the feeling of happiness.

Notice what that feeling of happiness is like. What does that feel like in your body, in your mind, in your spirit? What does happiness sound like? What does happiness look like? What are the submodalities of happiness when you are happy? If you were to move to a second perceptual position and watch you becoming happy, what would you be seeing?

2. Amplify State

Now go ahead and amplify that. Move your happiness up the scale of happiness. Move it to a level 5, 6, 7, all the way up to an 8, 9, or 10. Imagine you have a dial that controls happiness in front of you, and you can turn that dial up. Go ahead and reach out. Put your hand out in the air and turn that dial up. Crank it up to a 10. Notice the smile on your face, the sensation, and the feeling of being happy.

3. Fire Anchor

And now, I will snap my fingers. And with each snap of my fingers, allow yourself to notice what it is like to be as happy as you possibly can.

4. Neutral State

Now go ahead and open your eyes. Take in a breath. Allow yourself to return to what I referred to earlier as a saltine state or a neutral state. Get your neutral state back.

5. Fire Anchor (T.O.T.E.)

And now check. Notice. Close your eyes down. [Snap fingers.] Notice. Did it bring you back to the happiness that you just created just a moment ago? Is there a smile on your face? Open your eyes if your eyes aren't open yet.

In hypnosis, we often use a simple anchor with a thumb and index finger. My client will fully access the state, the joy of being a nonsmoker. They will amplify that state. Imagine what that is like to finally have achieved their goal. Ask them to notice what that commitment level is. Before we start, I ask my client to touch their index finger and thumb together. They can just let it lay on their lap.

Go ahead. Touch that thumb and index finger together now, having made that decision to put cigarettes behind you forever. Now our session is over. Go ahead and open your eyes.

I usually give this as a post-hypnotic suggestion, but after the session is over as well.

Anytime in the next day or two or three, or a week or two or three, or even the next year or two or three, if a thought crosses your mind or the sensation of withdrawal crosses your mind, touch that thumb and index finger together. Just squeeze it together for a moment and bring yourself back to this resource state that you have created here. And notice the craving disappears.

I have had a lot of my smoking clients come back to me in session number two and say to me, with a big smile on their face, telling me they have been touching their thumb and index finger together. The reason why is because anchoring is a strategy we learn when we are kids, one way or another, that we take into our adult worlds. Neuro-linguistic programming and life coaching use this as a strategy to elicit positive responses, to help people increase their acuity in auditory, visual, and kinesthetic responses creating new associations and new patterns that can really support any change they are trying to make.

SECTION THREE

Classic NLP Patterns

Neuro-linguistic programming patterns are the distilled processes for making change. These can be used as tools in personal growth or problem solving, and professional coaches can use these patterns to guide a client into change.

One: The Swish Pattern

The NLP Swish Pattern is my starting point, not because it is the most important pattern but because it is the pattern that almost everybody has heard of. I rarely meet any counselors or professional hypnotists who, no matter how little NLP they have studied, do not know about the Swish Pattern. They may not know what it is or how to apply it, but they have heard of the Swish Pattern.

It is recognized by seeing somebody pointing to something and saying swish. What they are doing is they are *swishing* one visual image into another visual image. The pattern is fun because, in addition to just thinking, there is the action of pointing, swishing, and visualizing. Although this does not have to be a visual image, it could be altering one sound into another sound or one feeling—either physical or emotional—into another physical or emotional state.

In working with a lot of individuals who deal with post-traumatic stress disorder, a Swish Pattern is something I have used with a number of clients who have reported intrusive and distressing images at recollections. We can use the Swish Pattern not only with clients who have a diagnosis of a psychiatric disorder like PTSD but with anyone who struggles with excessive thoughts. For example, people who are pathological gamblers have excessive thoughts.

I also work with a lot of people who are unhappy in their personal relationships. They do not feel like they are getting what they want or what they are owed out of a personal relationship. Then they have catastrophic images about that other person with whom they are in a relationship. Distressing images can paralyze us emotionally and even at a physical level. It can even be situational images. For example, let's say that I have a boss who I just can't stand, and as a result of the abuse that I seem to have to take at the office or the factory or wherever I work, I feel defeated, depressed, and miserable. Driving to work, I experience mental images of how awful it is going to be when I walk in the door of the workplace.

I am a big believer that wherever we put our attention is what we end up creating. Nothing ever existed without being a thought first.

The mental images that people create in their minds are the mental images they step into every day in life. To a large extent, we program ourselves through our visual images, but the subconscious automatic visual images that we reinforce through negative experiences often become the predominant forces in our life.

The Swish Pattern is a technique that can help us take those intrusive mental pictures, those distressing mental pictures, those self-defeating mental pictures you are going to defeat, and develop a process that can alter that mental imagery. I call this *changing our mental channel.*

I have often offered to a client who tells me that they are depressed to take an index card, and some markers, or some colored pencils, and, over five minutes, simply draw an image or picture of what happiness looks like to them. They may tell me that they don't ever feel happy. And I will ask them, "When you did feel happy, or if you did feel happy, what would it look like?" I have never had a client yet say that they couldn't do it.

Some of them create simple drawings. They draw a picture with the sun sticking out in the corner with some rays sticking out. Or they draw a stick figure of themself with somebody else or with a stick dog or something very basic.

The reason why I have them do it on an index card is simple. What I tell them to do is to take that index card and put it in their shirt pocket or tape it to a computer monitor or the dashboard in their car or carry it around in their side pocket or their purse or tape it to the bathroom mirror, wherever they think would be valuable to them. And whenever they find themself being aware of intrusive, distressing, depressing mental pictures, use that index card almost like the remote control of their TV to change their mental imagery, and pull out that card and look at it. That is really the same assignment that I have done in therapy as the Swish Pattern.

Here is the way the Swish Pattern works:

The Swish Pattern is a simple and effective technique for helping clients instantly replace a negative visual image with a positive image. The goal is to reduce anxiety, put some space between them and their thoughts, create emotional stability, and help achieve a sense of calm because these distressing images can often be anxiety-producing and powerful to them.

There are five stages to the process that I guide my clients through when I demonstrate or utilize the Swish Pattern with them.

Here are the five steps:

- **Step 1** — Think of the distressing mental image which has been bothersome—a place, a state, an experience—that keeps haunting them or that they are afraid that they might have. Ask them to think of it and have them describe the submodalities. "What does that picture look like? Is it near or far? Is it colorful? Is it black and white? Is it focused or unfocused?" Have them describe in detail the mental image that distresses them.

- **Step 2** — Create the opposite of that image and describe it in as much detail as possible and again using those submodalities. "Is it near or far, is it colorful, or not colorful, is it hazy, fuzzy, is it crystal clear, is it painted, is it drawn?" "What do you hear when you look at that picture?" "Do you hear others talking?" "Do you hear yourself talking?" We can bring kinesthetics into it if we want to. For example, "When you look at that picture, how do you feel?" "Do you feel light?" "Do you feel heavy?" "Is it harsh or soft?" "Is it violent?" "Is it calm?" "Is it ugly?" "Is it pretty?"

- We create two mental images: the mental image that is easy for them to create as to what they have either experienced or what they fear they are going to experience or what they are currently experiencing. Next, I have them create a mental descriptor—a picture that is in their own mind the antithesis of that. Most of the time, I ask them to do this with the eyes closed. The reason is it is easier to create mental pictures when our eyes are closed, and we are not looking at things in the room.

- **Step 3** — Have them open their eyes and ask them questions. "What triggers that negative image?" They may respond, for example, "Every time I get in my car and head to work, as soon as I'm around the corner and I have a half a mile before I get to the factory entrance, my doubts and pictures come into place." "Or is it an emotion?" "Every time I feel sad, I have this mental image of me being lonely on the beach without my girlfriend or boyfriend" (whomever it is that the person is relating to experiencing an absence of). Maybe it is a song. Every time you hear the Eric Clapton song *Tears in Heaven*, does that instantly produce a response? A lot of our life experiences are a result of natural reoccurring hypnotic phenomena. We associate that with something, and as soon as we hear the first note or two, we dissociate from the real world around us and are transported to our own mental images. I ask, "What triggers that distressing image, the one that bothers you?"

- **Step 4** —I ask them to close their eyes again. And imagine that the negative image is on a big screen in front of them. They are looking at it, and they are able to see it. I have them imagine that off in the lower left-hand corner a postage stamp size image of the positive picture or the preferred scene.

- With their eyes closed, I have them imagine that position, the tiny image that is positive or the preferred scene with giant visual imagery of the distressing image, and then I have them point and put their finger on that tiny postage stamp. Like a tablet or a computer touch screen, I have the client simply *swish* and *swish* across the mental screen of that postage stamp size image, expanding it and completely obliterating the negative mental image.

- **Step 5** — Next, I ask my client to make a swish sound when they go across the touchpad of their own life. It can sometimes feel silly, but it is kind of fun doing that, and it brings a little bit of levity to what is usually a very serious situation for some. I have them swish one image into another and do that a couple of times, and each time make a swish sound. The reason why is so they can see how simple, how easy it would be to instantly replace one mental image with another image. There is a positive image hiding right at their fingers in the lower left-hand corner that they can swish into and over the larger distressing mental image.

- When my clients do that, they are instantly switching a set of submodalities and representational systems for another set of representational systems and submodalities. It instantly alters their physiology. I can see their skin change—a sign of trance. I can see the eyes sometimes move quickly, or I can sometimes see a smile come across their face. It is interesting and powerful to see how effective this is. Then I have the client open their eyes but continue to think about that positive image, which has replaced the negative image for a couple of moments. And usually, without saying anything, I will just simply sit with them for a moment and let them experience that positive image.

Two: Ecology Check Pattern

We will focus on what I think is an essential NLP pattern that every NLP practitioner needs to know. That is the Ecology Check Pattern.

It can be utilized as a stand-alone intervention, but it can also be used at the end of another pattern to make sure that things are congruent for the client. If a client comes into your office, decided to make a change, and leave with the belief that they have made that change, but there is an incongruency within them, that is where our client ends up smoking between sessions or eating a giant box of chocolates or not getting on a plane. The Ecology Check Pattern is one of the most useful but often overlooked NLP patterns, and I utilize it with almost all the clients I work with. It is also something we can use before a client goes into a process of change.

The reason why we would do this before a client goes into a process of change rather than after a process of change is to make sure that what we are changing is actually broken. In other words, *If it ain't broke, don't fix it.* A lot of therapy, particularly traditional counseling and traditional psychotherapy, is just about fixing. We are looking for problems that are not problems with the client, but we think need fixing.

Suppose I have a client that is going through a very big change like becoming sober or getting divorced or some other big life change like going back to graduate school. In that case, it can be a very useful strategy to help a person to achieve their greatest level of potential and find out whether or not the proposed change would be beneficial to them.

Steps in the Ecology Check Pattern:

- **Step 1** — Allow the client to associate fully into the present, having a mindful experience, mindfully experiencing life as it is at this moment. In almost all our therapeutic coaching and hypnosis work, staying in the present as much as possible is advantageous to the client. I almost always want to begin every process with a mindful awareness of the present—a non-judgmental, non-shaming awareness and experience of being present.

- I often do an informal trance with their eyes closed after an induction or progressive muscle relaxation induction, or some other form of induction. Or I can do an Ecology Check Pattern without a formal induction. I just ask my clients in the second step to close their eyes and identify the proposed change. "What change is it that you would like to make?" For example, they may respond they would like to go back to graduate school, get divorced, quit smoking, whatever change it is. The second step is simple: Identify and describe that proposed change.

- **Step 2** — In this step, I want to move the client into a second or a third perceptual position so the client can observe themself from outside of themself as if they have already made the changes. It is one of the valuable things about the perceptual position process.

- **Step 3** — In this step, I interact with my clients by exploring the proposed change, asking questions. A lot of new hypnotists wonder what happens if I talk to my client when they are in a trance. They will talk to you. Everybody is always in trance.

• What we do is utilize naturally occurring trance states, and these can occur while we are talking. You can speak to a client anytime you want to. "What are your limitations on making this change?" "How do you feel when you think about making the change?" "Do you like or dislike that change?"

• Here is a recognized question that comes from Solution-Focused Brief Therapy: How will you know if you're successful in making the change? It is a really important question. "What will it feel like to you?" "What will it look like?" "How would you represent that?"

• That is one of the ways we can actually set goals in therapy in coaching, counseling, and hypnosis by knowing how a client would define success if there were to experience it.

• **Step 4** — And then, in the classic NLP pattern, Ecology Check, we go into what is called Cartesian Coordinates. There are four Cartesian questions: What will happen if you do [fill in the blank]? What won't happen if you do [fill in the blank]? What will happen if you don't do [fill in the blank]? What won't happen if you don't [fill in the blank]?

• Consider whether it will help the client explore from several different perspectives the meaning of the change that they are about to undertake.

• **Step 5** — This step in the process is to then make a decision— to pursue change or to stay the same. This is the Ecology Check. We can add, "Are you congruent with this?" "You have made that decision, or you are ready to take action on it and move into another process?" "Do you feel comfortable with that?" "Are you accepting of that?" Sometimes, we are not happy about the decision we are ready to make. Sometimes we can only feel accepting about the decision we have to make.

Three: Creating a Resource State

As a clinical hypnotherapist and as a counselor, the resource state is the most frequently used pattern in my work.

It is the most frequently used pattern because people often come to see me for emotional issues—issues related to anxiety, depression, or anger. Those states are uncomfortable. In many cases, these are not resourceful to a person, and instead, they would like to feel or create the antithesis of that. For angry clients, it is often calm. For anxious clients, it is often a state of being able to accomplish something—channeling that anxiety into a resource state of stick-to-it-iveness where they get things done, or a state where they can excel, a state of acceleration. For depressed clients, it is often obvious, coming feeling depressed, but they would like to feel happy.

As a public speaker who does training and consulting with individuals to help them achieve their highest level of potential, I often work with those who have a fear of public speaking. They say that it is one of the most prevalent phobias or fears that people have, and that resource state that I try to help them elicit when they step up to the podium to give that speech or presentation is a resource state of confidence.

I also do a lot of sports performance hypnosis. When I do sports performance work, I am trying to help athletes to achieve a resource state that is sometimes described as *the zone.* A professional golfer, a professional baseball player, or any top athlete will be using some conscious resource state to achieve their greatest level of potential.

A professional baseball player does not grab the bat and say, "Okay, I need to be three degrees to the left, and my vision needs to be over here." Yes, those things are important, but those things are done subconsciously; they are done automatically. That is being in *the zone.*

The resource state for that top-performing athlete where every action that needs to take place both physically as well as posture and power comes automatically from within through repetitive practice and commitment to not only muscle memory but also to subconscious memory. That resource state that they are describing is often *the zone.*

There is a particular platitude or saying that is pretty valuable: "You have the same pants to get glad in that you have to get mad in." In other words, we always have total control over how we feel and the resource states that are available to us.

If we need to access a resource state, whether it is competency, confidence, happiness, or stick-to-itiveness, or any other resource state, we have the ability right now and right here at all times to create that resource state.

Neuro-linguistic programming really focuses on helping people to develop the skills or the patterns necessary to elicit a resource state at any time, any place, anywhere. This is really a nine-step process that we can guide a client through. These nine steps can take place in mere seconds once a client has rehearsed the process.

Here are the nine steps that we would utilize to guide a client:

- **Step 1** — First, we have them sit next to us or across from us and elicit a neutral state. Bring them to a place where they are not feeling the depth of depression or the highs of happiness—just a neutral state. I refer to this often with my clients as a mental saltine. It is not really feeling anything, not even feeling ambivalent. It is being present without really having any thought or concern about whether we are achieving goals or not achieving goals—just be there. It is a state of being present or maybe even waiting. This is a state that in NLP we often hear referred to as "break the state." Have a mental saltine, return to normal, whatever that baseline is, but we have our client elicit a neutral state, just being present and with us. No pressure, no judgment. This is something we can borrow from mindfulness and bring into our NLP: The idea of just having thoughts, having feelings, and having sensations without judgment and without determining what those mean and what actions we should take.

- **Step 2** — Now that our client has elicited a neutral state, we have the client identify a preferred state—for example, confidence, stick-to-itiveness, or happiness. A lot of clients know what they would like to elicit or create because, in the past, they have experienced that. Even though in this situation they do not have confidence, they recognize they have experienced confidence in other situations or scenarios.

- **Step 3** — If our client has experienced this resource state before, what I will try to do is revivify it and bring them in the present back to that state that they experienced in the past.

- If the client cannot revivify or go back to creating a state that they have experienced in the past, then have them elicit a similar state that they have experienced before. Or bring them to an almost second perceptual point position to a vantage point of an observer where they can see themself experiencing what it is that they would like to experience as this resource state.

- **Step 4** — Have the client fully associate into that resource state they summoned. Bring them to a physical experience of that resource state. If confidence has erect posture, bring them to that state. Use submodalities to describe the aspects of each of the senses as they are experiencing this resource state. For example, if confidence has an emotion of power, bring them to that emotion of power. Ask them what they are feeling, hearing, seeing, and sensing. Even spiritual needs are felt through a sense of security or significance, two of our very most basic spiritual needs. When the client feels a state of confidence, have them really identify that and fully associate into that state feeling and not only feeling but being that resource state that they would like to develop.

- **Step 5** — This step is for verifying with them, checking with them. You might ask, "Are you able to attain, at least at some level, a basic level, an experience of that resource state?" Ninety-nine percent of clients will say yes by the time we have gotten to this step. Because we are talking and working with the client, we are going to get to this point if they have actually been able to, at some level or not, experience it. If not, then go back to step three and revivify if they were not able to attain the state. Have the client move to that outside observer perspective or borrow from other people.

- Neuro-linguistic programming is about exemplars. It is perfectly okay and is the heart of NLP to tell the client that other people are experiencing this. They may respond, "That's what I wish that I could experience also." "Well, really, what is that? Describe that." And that is the heart of this step.

- **Step 7** — Now that we have verified with the client that they are able to, at least on some level, attain the resource state, then in this step, we go through a process of amplifying it. You have seen a Likert scale where, for example, you rate on a scale of one to five how much you enjoyed the food served. 1 — It was awful, 2 — It was just a little bit awful, 3 — It was average, 4 — It was decent, and 5 — It was totally awesome.

- With my clients, I usually use a scale of one to ten. I want to amplify from one, just the experience, or a two or three for their starting point, all the way up to the highest level of experiencing a resource state. Amplify it to a level eight or nine or all the way to the top to a level ten.

- When the client is in this state (a level ten), they are feeling fantastic. It is a resource state that is available to them, not only in this session but one that they can take with them. It is a to-go order, if you will, in NLP. We are going to make it possible to take this resource state to go so that they do not have to come back into our office every time they need to experience it. This is what I think really separates the NLP practitioner, life coach, and clinical hypnotherapist from many modalities of counseling and psychotherapy. Often in counseling and psychotherapy, we help clients to attain these states in the office, but we do not teach them how to take it to go.

- **Step 8** — Coaching, NLP, and hypnotherapy really are all about equipping the clients to no longer need us. We know we are doing our job well when our clients no longer come back. The way you do that in this step is to create an anchor or to simply create a post-hypnotic suggestion. A post-hypnotic suggestion might be, "And when you step up to the podium where you're going to be giving your speech, bring yourself back to this resource state that you've created here today." We could anchor it. Let's just take classic anchoring. "Touch your thumb and index finger together. Before it is your turn to speak, right before the last speaker is done, touch your thumb and index finger together, press them together, feel that tension there and then release that tension. Notice a wave of calm come over you, replacing any anxiety with a sense of confidence."

- We can use any variety of anchoring or post-hypnotic suggestions to give our clients the ability to take the resource state they have created in the office with them. In my hypnosis patter, what I often say to my clients is this, "This state is not one that I've created for you but one rather you have created here. And because it is one that you have created from within you, you will always have this resource state with you, and you can take it with you anytime, anywhere and access it anytime that it's needed."

- **Step 9** — This step is a form of an Ecology Check. You can do this with the eyes open or with the eyes closed after the work is done or during the work—either way is fine. The Ecology Check can be the complete process that we went through before, or it can be an abbreviated format. "Is this good for you?" "Is this going to be useful to you?" "Is there something else that we need to accomplish?" "Is there something we need to add to it?"

- This is really an NLP pattern that is very similar to something that I have always done in counseling. My clients come to me often and say, "But I can't be happy. I'm not happy." And then I ask them, "Have you ever been happy before?" And they say, "Well, I was a long time ago." I tell my clients to bring in pictures or a family photo album. They bring them in, and I look through the pictures and pointing to specific photos, I ask if they were happy here? Or indicate, "Here's one where you look happy." "Yeah, well, I was happy then." Then I say, "Great! If you had the capacity to be happy then, there is the capacity within you to be happy in the present time."

- Being able to create a resource state by using revivification, creating a resource state by looking at others, and coveting what they possess as far as emotional or spiritual, or physical resources is something that we can do with our clients.

Four: Six-Step Reframe

This is based on the process of the Six-Step Reframe that Richard Bandler and John Grinder wrote about in their NLP text *Frogs into Princes*. Since this was one of the earlier publications in the field of NLP, it has been one of the most widely taught and most widely used patterns in NLP. It is one of my favorites, and you will find it to be very valuable. The idea of reframing things is not an idea that is unique to NLP. Many different therapeutic modalities have certainly used that. This is certainly not exclusive to therapy or coaching. We gain new understandings and new perspectives on things and see things from a different vantage point and come to new conclusions all the time.

R.D. Laing was a famed psychiatrist. One of his famous quotes was, "All madness has meaning." In other words, no matter how crazy somebody's behavior is, there is always something valuable in that behavior for them.

Bandler and Grinder recognized this early on. If a client smokes cigarettes, for example, there is a part of them that finds smoking cigarettes valuable even though we all know that cigarette smoking is unhealthy.

We all know that cigarette smoking is incredibly unhealthy from a number of different perspectives. Everybody knows that cigarette smoke is unhealthy for them. There is not really anybody who does not have that knowledge, but people smoke anyway.

People do this with all kinds of things in life. They know that yelling in their relationship causes them more grief, or more problems, or more stress than if they did not yell. And yet, every time they get angry, they yell. There is a part of the unconscious mind and probably part of the conscious mind that finds value in what R.D. Laing referred to as madness. There is meaning in *all* of the unhealthy behaviors that we do.

If you talk to any cigarette smoker about why they smoke cigarettes and ask them what it does for them, they will come up with a wide variety of different answers. For some, it physically helps them feel a sense of control. For some, it is an appetite suppressant; they believe it helps them control their weight. For other clients, it is a break, a break from the stress of the day, five minutes of really experiencing serenity, even enjoying outside, out in the smoke hole, rather than the stress of the cubicle or wherever they are.

When I ask clients to focus on the reasons why they smoke, there are almost always some very valid reasons. The Six-Step Reframe recognizes that there is a part of us that finds value in our unhealthy behaviors. And it asks the subconscious mind to identify the alternative ways of meeting those very same legitimate needs.

For example, is there an alternative way to experience calm and serenity and commune with nature, other than to go outside to the smoke hole to smoke a cigarette? Is there a different way to feel a sense of control in this relationship other than to yell and rage at somebody? Is there a different way to feel physically full rather than eat an entire box of chocolates? The answer is yes.

This is a behaviorally focused NLP process because so much of our behavior is automatic. When we go through life, we do not think to ourselves, *Do I put the right foot or the left foot in the pants first?*

We don't think to ourselves, *How do you drive a car? Do you turn the key, then use the steering wheel and back up, or do you back up a little bit, then turn the steering wheel?* We do all these things automatically, subconsciously. There are many things you need to know how to do, a lot of tasks in safely driving a car. We do not drive a car with a conscious mind. It was Milton Erickson who said he would not want a New York taxi driver who was not in a state of trance. Why? Because the conscious mind cannot possibly put all these things in order, but the subconscious mind can do that.

The flip side of that is that our subconscious mind, to meet legitimate needs, often goes to the unhealthy behaviors we have established in many different areas of life. The Six-Step Reframe helps us identify alternatives to these automatic coping strategies and choose to elicit those instead in the same situations. It is a reframe of the behavioral strategies that we have to live life.

I have broken it up into these six steps:

- **Step 1** — Select a behavior to change. For example, to stop raging, stop eating boxes of chocolates, stop smoking, stop shaking, or feeling a sense of physical anxiety when clients must talk to people, or whatever it is.

- **Step 2** — Have the client close their eyes. Establish communication with that part of the subconscious mind that creates the unwanted behavior. You can simply say to the person as their eyes are closed to access that part of the mind that creates that unwanted behavior; that part of the mind that reaches for a cigarette or eats too many chocolates, or that part of the mind that begins to rage when you're talking to somebody you love. Almost all my clients are able to identify that part of the mind.

- **Step 3** — Elicit from them a positive intention that is coming from that behavior. In other words, "What value is there in this negative behavior?" "What is it doing for you?" Then ask the client to access that part of the subconscious mind and to identify three alternatives for meeting all those always very legitimate needs. We have a need to alleviate boredom. We have a need to feel physically full. We have a need to feel a sense of control. These are all legitimate needs.

Bandler and Grinder, in the book, *Frogs into Princes,* come up with three alternatives. For some of my clients, that can be overwhelming. It can be too much choice, so I might have them identify one or two. It is perfectly okay to deviate from the script to adapt things to your client or your own style.

The ideas must come from them. If you sit with a client in silence for five minutes while that subconscious part of the mind is eliciting a new response, that is okay. It is very important to recognize that ideas must come from the client, or else they are the practitioner's ideas. If I suggest things to them, they are my ideas, and they are probably never going to do them. This is one of those times where sitting in silence while they really think is okay.

- **Step 4** — We have the client evaluate their new choices. "Would that be wise?" "Would that helpful?" "Is that possible?" "Can you do it?"

- **Step 5** — Have them check for objections from the other parts of the subconscious mind by future pacing. "Bring yourself out two months from now, three months from now, six months from now. If you had been eliciting that new response, would that be helpful to you? Will you find that it continued to meet your needs?"

If there are any objections that continue to exist, then just go back and run through steps two to five.

- **Step 6** —In this step, I create an anchor or post-hypnotic suggestion for the adaption of the alternative behavior because most of the work that I do is in the context of hypnosis. Almost all my clients leave with post-hypnotic suggestions, which I have given them.

Five: Fast Phobia Cure

The Fast Phobia Cure is something that I regularly use in my office. I must confess, I used to be fairly phobic. I used to be afraid of elevators. Once, I walked away from a job interview because it was in a secure medical facility where I could not take the stairs. I used to be afraid to drive in traffic. There were times when I would not get on an interstate - it just would not happen. And there was a time when I refused to get on an airplane. I was afraid to fly for many years. Now one of my most prized possessions is my top-tier frequent flyer card. It represents to me that I have overcome my fear of flying. I have flown all over the world in the last twenty years or so, and I have really enjoyed those experiences.

To overcome my own phobias, I used a combination of different techniques, including hypnotherapy, mindfulness training, and confronting those fears.

I also utilized the strategies of the NLP Fast Phobia Cure. Let me outline for you how this process works. It uses what is a classic NLP script or pattern or imagery of the movie theater. You can utilize this without that script, without that pattern; simply adapt it any way you would like. I am going to share with you again the classic version utilizing the script of the movie theatre. This is a very popular script that Bandler popularized that many people have utilized.

The steps are simple:

- **Step 1** — First, we want our client to identify a phobic response that they have. We want them to elicit that phobic response when they are in our office. We do not want them to go into full-blown abreaction, but we want them to feel that. And that is an important part of this process because we want to work with them while they are associated into the ability to experience the phobia because if you can experience the phobia, you can un-experience the phobia.

- **Step 2** — Have the client remember that even though they experienced a phobia, they are always safe afterward. We know our clients are always safe after they have a phobic response because they are still here; they are not dead. Whatever they were afraid of hasn't killed them yet. It may have been traumatic, it may have been difficult, but there came the point when they were safe. After we elicit the response, then we have the client assure us that there was a point when they were safe after the fear.

- **Step 3** — We are going to have the client imagine that they are sitting in a movie theater, and they are going to watch themself on a screen. Make it a black and white image. Make it a small image on a big movie screen. We do that because we don't want to add too much depth to this movie, this visual imagery because we don't want to produce abreaction.

I know that there are some people who want to produce abreaction in hypnosis. I do not. Producing abreaction in hypnosis is not particularly valuable. Success should be measured in change, not by the quantity of tears produced in a session.

Have the client dissociate by having them float out of their body and all the way back to the projection booth. This gives them a level of dissociation and a level of control.

From the projection booth, they can watch themself sitting in the movie theater seat watching themself on the screen. This is a very safe vantage point; it is the third perceptual position. Have them, from this safe place, way back in the projection booth and third perceptual position, watch that movie. Watch a movie of them being phobic, being in the situation, and being fearful. You can amplify it. At this point, you can bring some color to it. You can make it larger. You can bring them almost to the point where they are experiencing phobia again, but when they get to that point, when they watch the movie to that point where the phobia is over, and now they are safe, have them freeze it. I say to my clients, "Freeze." I say that to clients all the time. "Freeze that image; let it be frozen on the screen."

• **Step 4** — The next step in this process is to have the client float back out of the projection booth, out of the seat, and into the film. Now we're in that first perceptual position where *me is me* in this film.

"We are at the end of the film; remember the end of the film where we're safe. And now, from that vantage point, play the film backward. Play it backward with full color. Play it twice as fast, three times as fast, four times as fast. Rewind it, playing it backward, seeing yourself going from safe to unsafe rather than the way the mind normally thinks about things, which is *I'm safe*, and now *I'm unsafe*.

"Play it backward and be a part of that film on that screen, moving yourself from where you know you are safe backward through the process to that point where you start the phobia."

Now the amazing thing here is that when we do that, when we experience from a different vantage point from safe to unsafe rather than unsafe to safe, we reverse the neurology of our experience, if you will, and by doing that, our clients experience a complete perceptual shift of all the representational systems. The emotions, spiritual, and metaphysical needs they have and overcome, report overwhelmingly that their interpretation of the response is completely different.

- **Step 5** — The next step is to continue to repeat the previous steps until the client is comfortable with the experience and then perform an Ecology Check to find out if this worked. I say to my clients, "Now think about what it was that you were afraid of. You were afraid of snakes. When you think about that, is your response at any level different now than it was even fifteen minutes ago?" The answer is almost always yes.

Six: NLP Spelling Pattern

The NLP Spelling Pattern is probably not considered by many people to be one of the most important NLP patterns of all time. But for me and my work, it has been particularly valuable. I teach a how-to-write a book class at TwelveWeekBook.com, so I spend a lot of time working with individuals helping them achieve their greatest level of potential when it comes to writing.

I also spend a fair amount of time delivering leadership training courses for the business industry and others. Part of effective communication is being able to spell correctly. Not only that, but I have also carved out in private practice a very decent niche in academic performance, helping students achieve their highest level of potential.

Other than mathematics, where people seem to have a lot of difficulty, the number two area where people come to me for achieving academic excellence is in improving their spelling. A lot of people find that spelling is difficult to do and something that they wished they could do better. The awesome thing about NLP is that it recognizes that we can recode or rewire our relationship or experience to words.

When I teach speed reading courses, I often talk about is subvocalization. One of the reasons why people do not read to their greatest level of potential is because when they are reading a book, they are actually sounding out the words in their head, hearing the words in their head, and we can actually read a lot faster than we can talk.

One of the other reasons people tend to slow down their reading is because they write the words in their mind, visually for the visual learner; they are seeing the words. It is almost as if they were doing two tasks at the same time: seeing the word, reading the word, but taking the time in their mind as if they were writing or typing out the word.

Subvocalization is an auditory component, and the subwriting is the visual component here. These not only slow us down in our reading and in our academic performance, but they can also contribute to misspelling words. We know that much of life occurs on a subconscious level. If early in one's academic career we are subvocalizing and subwriting, what will happen is we are going to commit misspellings to error. They can see how subvisualization can contribute to a spelling error—writing the wrong letters in the wrong places or adding a lot of extra visual, whatever it is that people do. But I am often asked how subvocalization contributes to a spelling error.

Subvocalization contributes to spelling errors because when we are first learning to read, write, and spell, we are also learning how to speak and pronounce words correctly. For that reason, a lot of people spell words the way they pronounce words. A lot of people pronounce words incorrectly. We have a variety of different dialects in the English language, and some of them are contributing to incorrect spelling because they are, in fact, wrong pronunciations of the words. And so, the subvocalization and the subwriting or the subvisualization can create a life-long pattern of misspelling words.

Neuro-linguistic programming gives us an effective technique, an NLP pattern. It is swift, efficient, and from this point forward, it can change our subconscious association with these words.

I applied the NLP Spelling Pattern to my own work and to the words that I find particularly difficult. Because of that, my spelling has greatly improved.

- **Step 1** — Have the client identify a word that they misspell. It is amazing how we often misspell the same words repeatedly and have particular difficulty with certain words. We can usually identify those words if we are not a good speller. Have them identify the word.

- **Step 2** — Have the client take pen to paper and write down the word that they cannot spell correctly.

- **Step 3** — Have the client look at what they have written. Then ask them to close their eyes, and in their mind's eye, look up to the left and visualize that word spelled correctly. This should be easy for them to do because your client just wrote it down, so they are probably looking at a visualization of their own handwriting in the upper left-hand side of their mind's eye field of vision.

- **Step 4** — Now, you can have them change that to their favorite color. You can ask them to even change it to their favorite font and make it a little bit bigger. You can play with the submodalities to help them create a visual image that is very realistic to them.

- **Step 5** — Have the client open their eyes. And on a new piece of paper, have them write the word correctly. If they need help in the process, they can look up to the left in their field of vision, and they can recall that word that is in their upper left-hand field of vision, and they can write down the word correctly.

- **Step 6** — After they have written it again correctly, have the client close their eyes again and look up into that left-hand side of that field of vision within their mind's eye.

- **Step 7** — Ask the client to spell the word in their own mind, but instead of spelling it left to right, they spell the word backward, starting with the last letter and spelling right to left. And so, our client would do that in their mind's eye.

- **Step 8** — If they did not spell it correctly, then we return to step two, which is to go back and go through the same process again, starting with the second step. In my experience, going through it again usually resolves any difficulties, but I have had a few incidents where I have even gone back a third time. Interestingly, I have never experienced failure after the rare occasion I have gone through this three times.

This is the NLP Spelling Pattern and what it does is rewires our mental association. It changes or rewrites over our subconscious learnings, which have been errant, to the correct way of spelling a word.

Seven: The Well-formed Outcomes Pattern

I first had the experience of working with Well-formed Outcomes back when I had my first job in this field. I was a psych tech in an inpatient psychiatric ward.

I also had the opportunity to do some teaching with these folks. It was my first experience really trying to help people in a professional context to make change. For the year and a half that I worked on this unit, something interesting happened. The clients kept coming back in repeatedly. I asked the psychiatrist and the nurses why and they said, psych patients go up, and then they go down, and then they are re-hospitalized, and that is just what happens to them. I thought that if somebody didn't know how to do something, they would always do the same thing over again. If they didn't know how to manage life on life's terms, they would always end up with the same results. This is a principle from Alcoholics Anonymous.

In working with the individuals who were on my unit, I would try to teach them some of the life skills necessary for managing life on life's terms when they left the hospital, hoping that it would help them experience success.

Clients would come back, though, and I would ask them if what I taught them in their previous hospitalization was helpful, and some would say it was. But it occurred to me a lot of these folks really had no goal. Not only did they not know what they needed to do in order to do something different, but they really did not know why they should be doing something different.

I began working with patients to help them establish goals—goal setting. I would teach my clients that a goal is concrete. It is clear, specific, attainable, it has a reasonable timeframe, and that it is beneficial—all elements of goal setting. I also helped them to future pace and put themselves in a place where they could see themselves having accomplished their goals.

To a large extent, this is what the Well-formed Outcomes Pattern in NLP is all about. In NLP, it is interesting that we often start at the end: What would I like things to be like? Later, as I learned about Solution-Focused Brief Therapy, I learned about the miracle question. And the miracle question in Solution-Focused Brief Therapy is this, "If you were to go to sleep tonight and a miracle were to happen, and you were to wake up in the morning, and all of those things that have been distressing to you had been removed, resolved, ended, had been banished, how would you know that things had changed?" This miracle question is a question that helps us identify what outcome the client would desire.

In NLP, we start at the end because there is a metaphysical reality, and that reality is that anything that exists today had to be an idea first. And so, we want to start at the end because we want our clients to know in concrete terms where they are going to be. They cannot be anywhere unless they have a Well-formed Outcome from the processes or the interventions we create.

- **Step 1** — The first step in this process is identifying a problem or something the client would like to change. It may be to stop doing drugs or stop drinking alcohol or stop pathological gambling or stop stealing.

- When I practice corporate coaching, it might be to stop procrastinating or to start being creative or manage stress or live more mindfully so they can maximize each moment. But the first step is to have the client identify the problem that they would like to change.

- **Step 2** — This step is really the miracle question. "How will you know if this problem were solved?" We ask that question because the description that we are going to get tells us what it is that our client would like to have as the outcome of the intervention.

- **Step 3** — Here, the process is to identify the desired outcome of the change in concrete terms using submodalities, visualization, self-talk, our auditory aspect, and even physical feelings with the kinesthetic part.

- **Step 4** — In this step, we want the client to describe in greater detail, - chunking down those submodalities to an even greater level.

- **Step 5** — In the next step, we want the client to contextualize the outcome. We want to ask questions like, When? Where? With whom? Before? or After? To some extent, contextualizing this outcome that our client is creating in their own mind is a form of future pacing.

- **Step 6** — We can get as detailed or as short as we would like, describing the sequence for moving from here to there. Ask the client the question, "Now that you've described with whom and where and when you would like this outcome to take place, what do you need to do to get there?"

- For some clients, it may be one or two broad or specific actions. For others, there may be a series of five or ten or fifteen steps. The objectives in goal setting need to be there.

- **Step 7** — Have the client commit to being at the Well-formed Outcome to make this a reality in their own life. The difference between a goal and a dream is that a dream is something that we aspire to, but a goal is something that we are actually aiming for. Step seven is about the commitment process. I always say that a goal is always written. Whenever I work with clients to help them goal set, I have them take out pencil and paper and write their goals down. The practice of writing goals is part of that commitment process. You could have your client draw a picture or write down goals or objectives that are a part of committing to this Well-formed Outcome.

- **Step 8** — And then, NLP always encourages that Ecology Check. "Now that you have committed to this Well-formed Outcome, is it going to be beneficial to you? Is it something that you want? Is it something that's attainable?" We can go through the Cartesian Coordinates here as well.

This is really a process that could take an entire session with a client.

Eight: Visual Squash

The Visual Squash Pattern from NLP is a great pattern, and it is a lot of fun.

I find that when I can involve my clients visually and kinesthetically at the same time, it produces tremendous change. When I can involve people in the therapeutic process, and I am not just talking to them or listening to them, but can actually do something with them, it can be a lot of fun, and it really can enhance the results.

Think back to when you were a kid, and you probably had a yellow blob of Play-Doh and a blue blob of Play-Doh. And as you squashed them together, something happened. That Play-Doh was no longer yellow or no longer blue. It was now a green blob of Play-Doh. That is what we are going to do.

We are going to take two visual imageries or two visual representations and squash them together, and the end result is going to be something entirely different. You may be interested in neuroscience, how brain chemistry works.

I know that a lot of people work in the treatment of porn addiction, and a common phrase we frequently hear is "Thoughts that fire together wire together." A lot of people come to me as they have sexual difficulties. They have sexual difficulties because they have wired together, or they have anchored, as we often call it in NLP, certain thoughts with certain actions, and so that is what turns them on.

This can occur in any number of areas of life, not just in porn addiction. It can deal with depression. It can deal with self-defeating behavior. It can deal with emotions like anger or anxiety, or anything else.

The Visual Squash Pattern is one way to rewire the neurons or the brain chemistry that we experience. It is an excellent way to either break these associations or, in some ways, create new associations, and that's part of the reason why the Visual Squash Pattern is so powerful.

When I do this with clients, I ask them to hold out their hands, and I have them use their hands or the palms of their hands as sort of a tiny movie screen—a mini-movie screen to go—where they can see the visual representations. Then I ask them to squash their hands together.

- **Step 1** — Have the client identify two competing desires or behaviors that they engage in. One of the big issues we have in life is that sometimes we have competing desires that are occurring at the same time. For example, we have a desire to be dependent, to be engaged with other people and to let other people take the lead and, at the same time, we have a desire, a competing principle to be narcissistic, to be self-absorbed, and to just go ahead and get things done without waiting for other people.

You can see that life is full of these competing principles back to the example of porn addiction, and they use this Visual Squash Pattern since pornography is often a very visual experience for people of the two competing behaviors. They have the desire to experience sexual highs and fantasy and the desire and the pleasure that comes from sexual exploration. The competing fantasy here is that they have a desire to create a healthy relationship with one person to whom they are committed without bringing external sexual representations into their relationship.

- **Step 2** — These are competing behaviors or desires that people engage in. The second step is to work with the client and identify the visual imagery of each of these parts. Now not necessarily identify the visual imager of pornography or the happy relationship or the dependency or narcissism but of the core aspects of what that represents.

  We really want to break down the visual imagery and then have them identify the positive intention of each part. Every unhealthy thing that we do in life has a purpose and has a meaning.

- **Step 3** — What we want to identify is the positive intention of each part, and then we want our client to be able to move the resources from one part to the other. Have them essentially imagine that those resources are changing places. This is the beginning of molding that Play-Doh together.

- **Step 4** — Next, we have our client create a third image, the third image of those legitimate aspects of those competing behaviors. We are asking them to create a third mental image where those are melted or molded together. I have my clients hold their palms in front of them and in the right hand create the first picture and in the left hand create the competing picture and then move the hands together and when they are ready to simply begin folding them up like that ball of Play-Doh, to hold them together, to squash them together and then to open their hands and realize and recognize a third visual image. This third visual image, the legitimate aspects of each of these behaviors, are molded together into a new behavior.

We can combine this with the previous lesson, Well-formed Outcomes. Outside of the porn example and in the context of our healthy committed relationships, we can use communication strategies that elicit participation with our partner in activities that bring us to the height of sexual pleasure.

In our narcissism and our dependency, we can mold those together and find that the autonomy of narcissism, combined with the loyalty of dependency, can sometimes create a beautiful antithesis picture where we respect the contributions of others while filling a leadership role. The outcome here can really be remarkably different than either of the original competing behaviors. It is neither blue nor yellow. It is now green.

Nine: Falling in Love Pattern

Love is something for everybody!

Let me explain to you something about NLP and its history. The idea that Bandler and Grinder had was to model excellence. Let's look at those who are doing it right and then try to figure out how we can replicate that and then consider whether we can teach it to others. Although Bandler and Grinder, in the early days of NLP, did not deal with this Falling in Love Pattern, or the ideas that I am going to share with you, current research into neurochemistry, as well as communication, gives us some great resources for falling in love.

This pattern is not about seduction. There is an entire community that tries to use the language patterns of Milton Erickson and the idea of rapid or instant seduction, but that is not the focus of this pattern.

What is interesting to me is that research tells us that in the first ninety seconds when we meet somebody new, fifty-five percent of what attracts us to somebody else is actually non-verbal; it is body language. Thirty-eight percent is the tonality and the vocal qualities of the voice. In other words, the speed, the rate, the tone of the voice, and only seven percent of communication is the actual words that are used which produce an attraction response.

It is interesting that the seduction community is always trying to come up with the perfect words to snag that love prey. The reality is ninety-three percent of what is most important has zero to do with language patterns or the words used.

The paradox here is that the way to fall in love is to change yourself. That is really the most important step. As a family counselor, so many people came into my office, and what they were trying to do was change their partner to be the way that they want their partner to be. Or people called me up and asked me to help them experience love. What they try to do is they try to figure out how to change people. They often think that if they can get this person to do that and this person to do this, they will fall in love with them.

The easiest way to help people fall in love with you is to change yourself. Be an excellent person.

Here is a strategy for changing yourself. You will probably never find this in any other NLP book, but you will find it in books about mindfulness-based stress reduction or books devoted to personal improvement. I will share with you a meditation technique that is a loving-kindness meditation.

It is interesting there are researchers at universities who spend their entire careers studying the science of love. What these researchers have discovered is that love is a combination of really three things.

First, there are physical and chemical reactions in our brain. We have serotonin and dopamine receptors. We have hormones and neurochemistry, and love is, to some extent, determined by our brain chemistry. The second element of love, according to researchers, are our thoughts and our intentions. It is a lot easier for me to change my own thoughts and my own intentions than change somebody else's thoughts and intentions. By doing that, the research tells us it produces a loving response.

The third element of love is a metaphysical connection, a shared connection. We have two deep needs—security and significance. If I meet somebody, and there is a security, and there is a significance that has developed between us, loving occurs.

We often think of love in terms of romance as boyfriend/boyfriend, girlfriend/girlfriend, or boyfriend/boyfriend, or whatever the combination is. But the reality is love occurs in many other relationships as well. Like between a father and son, for example, or friends that you deeply care about.

And, there is another kind of love. C.S. Lewis wrote about storge love. That is an infinity toward other people simply because they are other people.

This combination of brain chemistry coupled with thoughts and intentions coupled with a metaphysical connection, which often does come about by talking to people, results in three stages.

The first, when we talk about romance, is lust. Then attraction, which is about linking shared experiences. We become attracted to people not just because of physical beauty or chemical attraction but because of a shared experience when we link with somebody. For example, if I meet somebody new and discover they are from the same hometown as I am, we suddenly have that shared experience. Then we go into the third phase, where love is sort of anchored, and that is the attachment phase, which researchers call the cuddle phase.

Here is what the research tells us the pattern for falling in love really is. We can call this the "Falling in Love in Thirty-Four Minutes Pattern." Some interesting experiments were done about love and about people who engaged in this process. One experiment was to take that knowledge that I just shared with you and come up with a process and replicate it to see if it works to produce love. In this particular case, romance. That is what NLP is all about. Looking at an event, trying to determine a process from it, and then seeing if we can replicate it. The pattern the researchers developed was a thirty-four-minute pathway to love.

The first step of the process or the pattern is to meet somebody new. A lot of times, people tell me they can't find somebody who will love them. In response, I will ask if they are out meeting new people. They tell me no, they aren't. The very first thing that I am going to do when I am working with lonely people is to help them meet new people, talk to those new people, share intimate details, as the researchers instruct for only thirty minutes with a back-and-forth exchange.

If you are interested in levels of communication, look for the Awareness Wheel. It's an invaluable tool developed in the early 1970s by Drs. Sherod Miller, Phyllis Miller, Elam W. Nunnally, and Daniel B. Wackman. Get into that search talk, as outlined in a previous chapter on the Awareness Wheel, with somebody for thirty minutes.

The researchers found out that eye contact is an essential component of nonverbal communication. Search talk for thirty minutes, staring into somebody's eyes for a four-minute period, resulted in feelings of romance and love from the experiment group. You might be asking if love lasted because it was an experiment group. Two of those couples in the experiment group got married.

That is the Falling in Love Pattern. Find somebody new, share intimate details with that person at a search talk level. We have been talking about search talk with submodalities and different aspects of questioning people throughout this book. Then make eye contact with the person, staring at them in the eyes for four minutes. It is amazing that when put to the test, that was the formula for falling in love.

Beyond falling in love, we want to go into a process where we can teach our clients to love themselves and love others. Not because of what they are getting but because simply being a loving person is a lot easier than being a mean person.

Here are the steps to my loving-kindness meditation:

- **Step 1** — Close your eyes and focus on your breath. Breathe in and breathe out and set aside any worry about the past or anxiety about the future. Simply attend to the present in the chair where you are sitting. This practice always begins with developing a loving acceptance of yourself, and sometimes resistance simply indicates feelings of unworthiness that may be present. But you do not have to worry about that because this means that there's work to be done, and the practice is designed to help you overcome any feelings of self-doubt or negativity.

  The idea here is not to sleep or even about relaxation. It is just breathing in and breathing out and being fully in the present.

- **Step 2** — Now, think about and identify a person who is respected by you or a beloved person that you are aware of. Maybe they are a teacher or a mentor, or a spiritual guide who has been important to you. Or it may even be somebody who, although you do not know them personally, maybe they are on the world's stage, or a famous author or somebody who you find carries the traits of a beloved and respected person and has been influential and important to you. The reason we start with this person is that it is easy for us to feel a sense of love and kindness to those who have contributed so much to the world and to us as well.

- **Step 3** — Now that you've identified that person, allow yourself to enter a resource state of feeling a sense of loving-kindness toward that person. You can, even as you sit in the chair, envision giving a sense of love and compassion toward that person, feeling kind toward that person who taught you, or mentored you, or supported you.

Notice how easy it is to feel a state of love and kindness toward that person, especially if they have given much back to our world.

As you breathe in and breathe out, allow yourself to sense loving kindness directed toward that person. That is an easy and natural thing to do. Most people have no difficulty with that. After all, it is a person known to us, a family member, or a friend who has deeply impacted us and who we deeply love.

- **Step 4** — Think of a third person, a neutral person, just somebody in the world who you know, but you have never really thought about having any special feelings toward. Maybe it is a shopkeeper or somebody in your office or school. Or even somebody you see walking their dog in the neighborhood or just on a regular basis in the places where you go.

  It is amazing how as you identify this person, you can actually allow yourself to feel a sense of loving-kindness toward this person, even though up until this moment, you've never described any special status to that person. Continue to feel loving-kindness toward this person as you breathe in and breathe out.

- **Step 5** — That brings us to the fourth person, a hostile person or at least a person in your world with whom you have had difficulties. A person with whom the ideas of loving or even feeling kindness toward has been difficult. Once you identify this person, at this moment, breathe in and breathe out, having practiced the sense of loving-kindness, extend that feeling of love and kindness from the three individuals we have already identified to this fourth person, a person toward whom you felt hostility or difficulty. It is amazing to know that as you breathe in and breathe out breathing in love and exhaling kindness, we extend the same feelings you easily give to others toward this fourth person as well.

- **Step 6** — Think of yourself and extend that compassion and kindness that you have extended to others in this time of meditation to yourself, loving and being kind to yourself, being nonjudgmental and fully embracing your strengths and resources, allowing yourself right now to feel a sense of loving-kindness and acceptance toward yourself just as you were able to do with others.

- **Step 7** — Take in a breath now and let oxygen fill your lungs. Let that oxygen rejuvenate every cell of the body and in a moment open your eyes and when you do, open your eyes feeling fantastic, recognizing that not only have you learned the basic process for creating a resource state of loving-kindness, but you've learned to help problem-solve and become more forgiving not only of others but yourself as well, despite any previous difficulties.

- **Step 8** — With the next breath, stretch out your muscles that need to be stretched. Sit up straight in your chair. Fill those lungs with oxygen. Let the oxygen energize every cell of the body and open your eyes, feeling fantastic from that experience.

Ten: As-If Pattern

You've probably heard the expression before, "Fake it till you make it." We hear it in all different areas in life. Sometimes in the context of personal training or sports training, it is an encouragement to continue. The coach believes in us and knows that even though it is difficult for us to continue, we will be able to step into that successful outcome in our sports performance. It is something we often hear with regard to emotions as well. You can take a crisis event or situation, maybe even a tragedy, and what is remarkable about tragedy is that the clock does not stop during periods of difficulties. Often there are essential tasks that must be completed.

The reality is that "Fake it till you make it" is an expression that, at its heart, is directly related to NLP. We know that any state in NLP that we would like to access, create, or experience is something that we have the capacity and the ability to create in our minds at some level or another. Even if we do not feel, for example, happy or confident or even if we do not feel encouraged, or whatever resource state it is, we can associate into that state even though it is not genuine now.

By associating into it, it fuses with us—it becomes who we are. And we do, in fact, step fully into that resource state. At some level, this pattern is very similar to creating a resource state, but it is a different process for really achieving, to some extent, the same outcome.

You have probably also heard the expression before, "You create your own reality." On a metaphysical level, I believe that is true. We create our own reality. But even beyond emotional expression, we have the ability—physically, spirituality, psychologically, even socially—to create our own reality. The As If Pattern is a great tool for manipulating reality into what we hope that it could become to help us achieve our greatest level of potential.

Often people ask me how they can increase their peak performance. They want to know how to rise to their greatest level of potential. The answer is creating your own reality. To some extent, I did this back in 1994 when I had been working for a couple of years as a substance abuse counselor in an in-patient psychiatric unit, contracted with the state of Texas to provide services to adolescents who had been in trouble with the law but had been sent to a treatment facility rather than the juvenile prison.

I really enjoyed working with the clients. I did not enjoy the bureaucracy and saw that systems could be improved, and better services could be provided to people, but I needed to be in a different position.

I went to the company's CEO, and I said to her, "Hey, I would like to be a CEO of a treatment center like this. Maybe even this one!" And she smiled, and she replied, "Richard, you are great, and I can see you easily rising to the CEO position. Why do you want to do that?" I said, "Well, because I am pretty good at seeing how decisions and bureaucracy impact the clients that we're supposed to care for, and I think that I can help both to efficiently manage the business, and the system side, while benefitting clients. I don't think that making money by contracting with the state is mutually exclusive to being able to provide good treatment." She said, "Well, I don't either. You're definitely on the right track." She continued, "I think that I could move you into a different management position, but at the upper end of lower management, and you could probably take some M.B.A. courses, and you could probably do that for the next five or ten years. Then you could move up to an executive position and, probably within twenty or twenty-five years, you too could be a Chief Executive Officer."

I was about twenty-nine at the time, so the idea of becoming a CEO at give or take fifty-five years of age was now on the table. I went home that night, and the next morning, I went into her office and handed in my keys, and said, "I quit." She said, "Why are you quitting? I thought you wanted to be the CEO." And I replied, "I do want to be the CEO, and I am the CEO. In fact, I am the CEO of a company called Peachtree Professional Education." She said, "What's that?" I said, "It's the company I just started."

She was fully supportive, even though she was certainly surprised. I started a continuing education company that allowed me to do two things: affect the systems within the mental health professions and teach people solutions and strategies that increase their effectiveness with a wide variety of different clients. How did that work out for me? In 1994, I started the company, and I continue to be the Chief Executive Officer at Peachtree Professional Education, which is one of the largest providers of continuing education, indeed in the state of Texas and in the state of Florida as well as many other states.

If we do not like where we are, we put ourselves there. I became the CEO in 1994 of that company even though I had no clients. I had no revenue. I had no business. In fact, I am not even sure if I had a concrete plan then for what I was going to develop. I told my family members that this was something that I decided to do. They looked at me like I was crazy, but I was completely at peace with my decision to create my own reality.

I always encourage people that if you do not like where you are, put yourself where you want to be. And do not wait to put yourself there until things are right. Put yourself there now, and things will become right. That is really the heart of the As-If Pattern. We can apply business, emotional, and practical applications to the As-If Pattern.

As we create the As-If Pattern with our clients, we need to recognize that some clients might not be able to fully associate into or step into an as-if state of their own. The reason why is they have never experienced it before. I had never been a CEO before, and I remember in the early days of starting this company, I really did not know what to do. I remember, in the early days, to some extent, modeling Michelle, who was the CEO of that hospital. She was a supportive person, who was a wonderful friend at the time, and remained my friend after I left, and I used her as an exemplar. I tried to conduct myself interacting with other individuals and creating ideas in the same way that she created those ideas.

We need to recognize that if our client has something holding them back from fully associating into their own as-if state, it is perfectly okay to help them fully associate into an as-if state they adopted from an exemplar, a model, or from an external resource.

One of my favorite sayings comes from Charles Haanel. He was a teacher in the early 1900s. Some people know who Charles Haanel is because most of the original ideas in the Law of Attraction movement came from his writings.

Charles Haanel was a metaphysician, an industrialist, and a businessman. He was the founder of the St. Louie Post-Dispatch, and he wrote some excellent books. He wrote a book called *Mental Chemistry* and another book called *The Master Key System*. Charles Haanel was the one who said, "For anything to exist, it must be an idea first." The As-If Pattern takes that idea and turns it into a reality on a metaphysical, practical, business, and emotional level.

There are many ways to apply the As-If Pattern. Here are the steps:

- **Step 1** — Have the client describe the desired state, the desired resource, the desired experience, the desired position, or even the desired value. This is a great way to help people adapt values. If you are familiar with Acceptance and Commitment Therapy (ACT), we try to help people select a valued path.

  The NLP As-If Pattern is one way to have them select that valued path. We can look at resource states, events, experiences, positions, and even values. We have our client identify that.

- **Step 2** — Next, have the client give themself permission to fully step into recreating, revivifying, or adapting from an external resource or some exemplar of this experience. When the client gives themself permission to step into this resource state, etc., determine if it is at some other level—Ecology Check. It is seeing whether it fits. "Does it feel good?" "Did you give yourself permission to do that?" "Are you comfortable with that permission you've given yourself?" This is important because we are often very hard on ourselves. And one of the ways to become less self-critical is to give ourselves permission.

- **Step 3** — Next step is to build an as-if frame. Try and incorporate as many sensorial experiences as possible to help the client amplify—kind of like stepping into a resource state—that experience, that state, that position, that value.

- **Step 4** — From that first perceptual position from within the frame of what they identified in the first step, we have our clients evaluate through a process of questioning inside of that experience, really filling it out, if you will.

You can put on a T-shirt, but you must fill it out to make it comfortable and get it to fit right and look good. That is really what we are doing here in step four. We are processing this position from an inside vantage point after we have fully associated into it from a first perceptual position.

- **Step 5** — The next step is to future pace. The line that I use with most of my clients in hypnosis is this, "Imagine yourself three days from now, three weeks from now, three years from now, even three decades from now fully experiencing what it is you've created here, today."

I do this with almost all my cigarette smokers—future pace. A lot of people come to me, and they have quit smoking for one year, and then they relapsed, or they quit smoking for three months, and they relapsed. Or they have quit smoking for ten years, and they relapsed. Now, they have been smoking again, for some period, they cannot quit on their own. They schedule an appointment with me. When I have clients, who have had that experience, I love it because they already know they can quit smoking.

What they do not know is that they can stay quit. With all my smokers, I always future pace their success beyond the level of success that they have experienced before. With my smokers, I sort of assess how long they are going to live. The vast majority of my clients for smoking cessation are not twenty-five and trying to quit smoking because cigarettes cost too much. They're fifty-five or sixty-five or older. I future pace out twenty or thirty years with them because I want them to adopt the idea that this is going to be far beyond the success they've had in the past. I always validate them and offer something they are going to be able to take with them to any point in the future.

- **Step 6** — The final stage in the As-If Pattern is back to an Ecology Check. "Was that valuable to you?" "Was it useful?" "Are you comfortable with that?" "Are you glad that we did this?" "Is there any part of you holding you back, either known or unknown, from success?" This As-If Pattern has become one of those patterns I use in coaching, NLP, clinical hypnosis, and counseling on a regular basis to help people experience success in many different aspects of life.

Eleven: Paradoxical Pleasure Pattern

This pattern is one that I do not actually use very often, but when I do use it, it is extremely valuable. It might seem strange to want to reduce pleasure; after all, is pleasure not awesome? However, pleasure can sometimes cause us difficulty.

I love pleasure as much as the next person loves pleasure, but the reality is sometimes our fusion to pleasure, our obsession with pleasure or our fixation on pleasure can distract us from accomplishing what it is that we genuinely want to accomplish. For example, have you ever procrastinated because doing what you needed to do was less pleasurable than what you had the opportunity to do? When you experience pleasure by procrastinating and doing something else, it felt awesome at that moment, but when you came back to what it was that you needed to do, you felt less than satisfied.

We are dealing with pleasure and scaling it into perspective. Our goal in the Paradoxical Pleasure Pattern is not to remove pleasure, but it is to scale pleasure into perspective, so it is one of our drives, one of our motivations, but it is not something that we obsess about or something that we become cognitively fused with.

What types of clients do I use the Paradoxical Pleasure Pattern with?

I have people who come to see me for weight loss, for example. When they come to see me for weight loss, I begin to talk to them about different issues that have contributed to their weight gain and their inability to lose weight. One of those chief things is that the pleasure surrounding the types of food and this pleasure is something that they recognize causes them difficulties. Clients say they want to be hypnotized and want to lose weight but don't want to stop eating chocolate Easter bunnies. They say I can hypnotize them to do anything, except give up chocolate Easter bunnies, because that's the pleasure in life that they refuse to give up. Of course, if you eat chocolate Easter bunnies each day, especially when they are fifty percent off after Easter, it becomes difficult to lose weight. So that tells me that this is the type of client where a Paradoxical Pleasure Pattern might be useful.

In my work with drug and alcohol clients, I have also found that the Paradoxical Pleasure Pattern is a useful tool. I have clients who report to me that the pleasure of cocaine, the pleasure of marijuana, the pleasure of alcohol, the pleasure of whatever drug of abuse is that they are ingesting into their body is paramount to being able to accomplish anything else.

They recognize that this is not even good for them. We know that on a neurochemical level, those substances affect the pleasure centers of the brain, particularly cocaine, and we know that nicotine has a similar effect.

They say when smoking a cigarette or cocaine that within eight seconds, that chemical transcends pleasure centers of the brain, and that rush of pleasure becomes something they pursue. I am convinced that cocaine addicts are always in pursuit of that first high one more time. It is that level of fusion to pleasure that continues to cause problems directly related to addiction.

This is similar to the compulsive gambler, who drives that pleasure from the reward pleasure center of the brain through the compulsive behavior of pathological gambling or any obsessive or compulsive behavior.

The idea is not to remove pleasure from life, remove pleasure from having a beer, or remove pleasure from taking an evening out spending forty bucks of entertainment money at the casino. The idea is not to remove pleasure, but the idea is to decrease the intensity of pleasure so that we can scale it into perspective, to defuse the obsession of pleasure, and that is important.

Here is the process.

- **Step 1** — The very first thing is to have the client identify their inflated pleasure. What is their inflated pleasure? What is the behavior, and what does the pleasure feel like? It is not enough just to say, "Well, I like pathological gambling." What is it about the pleasure? "When the bonus screen is red, and it gives me an extra spin, it's at that moment that I feel a lightness in my chest." I really want them to identify their inflated pleasure from the sensorial experiential perspective.

- **Step 2** — This step is to evaluate the meaning of this pleasure. Is it legitimate? I have always found that every unhealthy behavior always has legitimate needs attached to it.

- **Step 3** — In this step, we ask awareness state questions. Neuro-linguistic programming uses different languages. It asks awareness state questions and meta-state questions. These are questions like, "Why this way to gain pleasure?" "Why is this pleasure important to you?" "What does the pleasure feel like?" "How long does the pleasure last?" These questions are an effort to help a person identify the aspects of this inflated pleasure that is useful to them.

- **Step 4** — Next, I have my clients summarize in one word, one adjective that describes that pleasure. We reduce that feeling, that content, that experience into one word.

- **Step 5** — In this step, I engage in a process that I borrow from Acceptance and Commitment Therapy, which is Cognitive and Infusion Therapy.

The idea is to separate an experience from the word. If you are familiar with Acceptance and Commitment Therapy, you will be familiar with cognitive diffusion. The idea here is to defuse somebody from their thoughts. There is a thirty-second exercise where a person repeats a word that is attached to an experience over and over and over. By saying that word repeatedly, what happens is that the word just becomes sound, and it becomes less fused with the relational frames that we have attached to that word. It just becomes a word.

It is kind of a fun exercise to do. It fits neatly into an exercise related to NLP.

- **Step 6** — After we have gone through a cognitive diffusion exercise with that word associated with the client's pleasure, we do an Ecology Check. "Say the word. What is your response to it?" "Is the level of pleasure decreased?" "Is the way you relate to it different?" "Do you see it from a different vantage point?" And this is the Paradoxical Pleasure Pattern that I think is so useful.

You may download free resources for this book, and the actual forms I use with clients at:

SubliminalScience.com/NLPbook

To earn your certification as a Profession NLP Practitioner and as a Professional Life Coach visit:

SubliminalScience.com

Made in the USA
Coppell, TX
09 July 2021

58760975R00219